Qualitative Voices in Educational Research

Social Research and Educational Studies Series

Series Editor
Robert G. Burgess,
Professor of Sociology,
University of Warwick

1 Strategies of Educational Research: Qualitative Methods
  Edited by Robert G. Burgess
2 Research and Policy: The Uses of Qualitative Methods in Social and
  Educational Research
  Janet Finch
3 Systematic Classroom Observation: A Guide for Researchers and Teachers
  Paul Croll
4 Investigating Classroom Talk
  A.D. Edwards and David Westgate
5 Getting to know Schools in a Democracy: The Politics and Process of Evaluation
  Helen Simons
6 Doing Sociology of Education
  Edited by Geoffrey Walford
7 Collaborative Action Research: A Developmental Approach
  Sharon Nodie Oja and Lisa Smulyan
8 The Ethics of Educational Research
  Edited by Robert G. Burgess
9 Qualitative Voices in Educational Research
  Edited by Michael Schratz

Qualitative Voices in Educational Research

Edited by

Michael Schratz

The Falmer Press

(A member of the Taylor & Francis Group)
London • Washington DC

UK   The Falmer Press, 4 John St., London, WC1N 2ET
USA   The Falmer Press, Taylor & Francis Inc., 1900 Frost Road, 101, Bristol, PA
19007

First published 1993
Reprinted 1994

Library of Congress Cataloging-in-Publication data are available on request

A catalogue record for this book is available from the British Library

ISBN 0 75070 082 3 cased
ISBN 0 75070 083 1 paperback

Set in 9.5/11.5 pt Bembo
Graphicraft Typesetters Ltd., Hong Kong

Printed in Great Britain by Burgess Science Press, Basingstoke on paper which has a specified pH value on final paper manufacture of not less than 7.5 and is therefore 'acid free'.

Cover design by Caroline Archer

Contents

Series Editor's Preface vii

Voices in Educational Research: An Introduction 1
Michael Schratz

Part One: Giving Personal Voices a Chance in Social Organizations

1 The Theatre of Daylight: Qualitative Research and School Profile
  Studies 8
  Jean Rudduck

2 Event Analysis and the Study of Headship 23
  Robert G. Burgess

3 The Concept of Quality in Action Research: Giving Practitioners
  a Voice in Educational Research 40
  Herbert Altrichter

4 From Cooperative Action to Collective Self-reflection:
  A Sociodynamic Approach to Educational Research 56
  Michael Schratz

Part Two: Listening to the Silent Voice Behind the Talk

5 Finding a Silent Voice for the Researcher: Using Photographs in
  Evaluation and Research 72
  Rob Walker

6 Why I Like to Look: On the Use of Videotape as an Instrument
  in Educational Research 93
  Hugh Mehan

7 Crosscultural, Comparative, Reflective Interviewing in
  Schönhausen and Roseville 106
  George and Louise Spindler

Contents

Part Three: Keeping Authentic Voices Alive and Well

8 Understanding the Incomprehensible: Redundancy Analysis as an
   Attempt to Decipher Biographic Interviews   126
   Dietmar Larcher

9 Voices of Beginning Teachers: Computer-assisted Listening to
   Their Common Experiences   139
   Günter L. Huber and Carlos Marcelo García

10 Empty Explanations for Empty Wombs: An Illustration of a
   Secondary Analysis of Qualitative Data   157
   Shulamit Reinharz

   An Epilogue: Putting Voices Together   179
   Michael Schratz

Notes on Contributors   185

Index   188

Series Editor's Preface

The purpose of the *Social Research and Educational Studies* series is to provide authoritative guides to key issues in educational research. The series includes overviews of fields, guidance on good practice and discussions of the practical implications of social and educational research. In particular, the series deals with a variety of approaches to conducting social and educational research. Contributors to this series review recent work, raise critical concerns that are particular to the field of education, and reflect on the implications of research for educational policy and practice.

Each volume in the series draws on material that will be relevant for an international audience. The contributors to this series all have wide experience of teaching, conducting and using educational research. The volumes are written so that they will appeal to a wide audience of students, teachers and researchers. Altogether, the volumes in the *Social Research and Educational Studies* series provide a comprehensive guide for anyone concerned with contemporary educational research.

The series will include individually authored books and edited volumes on a range of themes in education including: qualitative research, survey research, the interpretation of data, self-evaluation, research and social policy, analyzing data, action research, the politics and ethics of research.

This collection of essays from a group of international researchers in education focusses on the ways in which those engaged in qualitative research use a range of voices to analyse and understand educational settings. Altogether these essays illustrate different ways of examining research questions and analysing data within the framework of qualitative methodology. This book provides a rich source of material for students and researchers who engage in the analysis of qualitative data.

Robert G Burgess
University of Warwick

Voices in Educational Research: An Introduction

Michael Schratz

The word 'voice' in the title of these collected articles has been chosen to throw light on aspects which are often faded out. Educational research based on quantitative measurement, variables, experimentation and operationalization usually transfers the original 'voices' of its research subjects into statistical data, mathematical relations or other abstract parameters. Therefore very little is left of the social context in which educational practices occur. What is left over represents the 'noise' in the transmission of data and is reduced to its minimal disturbance in the research process. Thus the original voices from the field become the 'disembodied' voices in the discourse of quantitative research presented through reports, articles and books.

In recent years many researchers have become increasingly disenchanted with the academic process of 'noise reduction' by suppressing the more disturbing aspects representing the individuality of human cognition in the domain of educational practices. As a consequence different voices of researchers have been heard within the scientific community suggesting more or less scientifically grounded ways to understand and improve educational practices. By paying more attention to the original *voices* of the actors in everyday life they tried to make room for a broader view of the social reality in their research. This has led researchers to break with some of the established conventions of objectivity, reliability and validity. In order to get beneath the surface of everyday activites and institutional structures new approaches in educational research developed ranging from ethnographic studies, naturalistic inquiry or case studies to more recent enterprises such as action research, biographical analyses and profile studies.

All these approaches aim at changing the nature of pedagogical knowledge by allowing the emotive and often more disturbing qualities of individuals in their culture to penetrate the research process. Therefore researchers direct their studies with a minimum of interference with the authentic situation of their field of study. To achieve this the research instruments have to be tuned to enable the study of educational practices as closely as possible without destroying the authentic meaning for the people involved. This research perspective adopts new methods of dealing with the everyday world of education, which will be presented in three sections.

Giving Personal Voices a Chance in Social Organizations

The chapters in the first part of this volume deal with the tension between the complexity of a research environment and the personal and professional understanding of the individuals within it. In recent years educational institutions as a whole have become more and more the focus of public accountability. Evaluating the performance of a complex learning institution such as a school has often been understood as a matter of merely measuring its academic output, for example student performance. Seen from a systemic perspective, however, this product-oriented view is very limited, since it neglects all the processes that account for the shared understanding of institutional culture:

> As a result, 'academic', 'pastoral' and other structures of roles ('subject departments', 'houses', etc.) in schools and colleges are all too often taken at face value, and the tensions involved in the dynamic relationship between different dimensions of the institutional structure, and between the formal role positions and the unique individuals who fill them, are ignored. To explore these tensions it is necessary for the researcher to delve into the meanings which teachers attach to the roles, structures and practices which constitute different aspects of the educational provision of particular institutions. However, it is easier to recognize this as necessary for an adequate analysis of the life of a school or college, than it is to say precisely how it is to be done. (Ribbins *et al.* 1988, p. 157)

In the first section different attempts are made to show possible approaches to this issue. What they have all in common is that voice which should be given to individual perspectives within the context of the micropolitics of a shared educational environment. In the first chapter Jean Rudduck presents school profile studies as a means of bringing together a variety of perspectives on a particular practical dimension. They represent a form of focussed, school-based enquiry in which researchers are commissioned by a school to investigate an issue that is important to the school. Observations and interviews with a range of people conducted by an experienced field researcher are used to construct a profile on the issue which is then offered back to the school as a basis for discussion. This feedback process, which turns out to be the most problematic aspect of school profile studies, is most important for the school. Issues of feedback for the participants themselves and utilization for outside audiences are usually given little attention in qualitative research reports. Here Jean Rudduck respects the original voices of the people involved and lets them speak for themselves by using the rich density of meaning of the direct quotation. Yet she uses this powerful tool of qualitative research in a careful manner and reflects on the risks of bringing into communal hearing voices that are often ignored or have become silent in the micropolitical realities of institutional life.

Robert Burgess' chapter focusses on the very centre of micropolitical activities in a school, the leadership issue. Headteachers are regarded as 'change agents' in institutional development and therefore the quality of leadership becomes a critical feature of school life. For Burgess the question arises how the study of headship can be used to examine fundamental social processes associated with the structure and organization of a secondary school. Studying these processes he links data collected through observation and interviews and a form of anthropological analysis based on the use of 'critical incidents' or 'event analysis'. Thus his chapter demonstrates ways in which such methods can assist in understanding a headship and in turn schools as social organizations.

Quality issues are also the starting point for the following chapter by Herbert Altrichter. He propagates an action research approach to give practitioners a voice in educational research by making them reflect on their professional action. By means of interview data he shows the tension between pragmatical, epistemological and ethical aspects which have to be clarified in the concrete research activity. As a result he exemplifies and discusses the value of quality criteria and thus tries to provide a framework of justification and orientation for professionals who want to innovate their practice within the social context of educational development.

Reflection on practice is also discussed by Michael Schratz, whose chapter focusses on collective memory within a research group. By presenting collective self-reflection as a qualitative voice in educational research, he describes an approach which renders more weight to these processes and thus plead for a greater emphasis on considering the epistemological origin of research results. In his chapter he introduces different kinds of approaches which aim at professional development, educational change and organizational development. He feels it is not so much the scientific design that determines the research findings but the interactions among the people involved. Thus he tries to throw some light on the dynamic force of the inter-group processes within collaborative research that keep the research process going and steer it in a particular direction.

Listening to the Silent Voice Behind the Talk

The chapters in part two are dedicated to those methods which help making silent voices of the subjects heard. The application of audio-visual media in field work has contributed to an extension of conventional ethnographic methods. Through the use of video recorders, tape recorders and cameras researchers were able to retain authentic images of scenes which could be used again and again for analysis.

Rob Walker describes the use of photographs with a view to find ways of capturing those aspects of educational life that cannot be caught by means of language. He uses pictures as a silent voice for deciphering complex social settings, like schools and classrooms. For him the picture becomes a window to an array of meanings, opening up new perspectives when related to other qualitative data gathered by interviewing, observation, discussions and so on. Although the use of photographs in educational research may vary depending on the circumstances they are used in, Walker emphasizes their application as a 'mainstream' rather than an 'add-on' device. Thus approaching critical issues visually rather than verbally gives access to an understanding of educational problems at a profound level of subtlety and complexity.

Similarly, Hugh Mehan uses audio-visual support in his research to get beyond the surface structure of observational experience. In his chapter he describes how video-recordings enabled him to trace the subtle patterns of students' interactions and uncover the powerful impact of 'situated cognition'. The use of the videotape as a tool to hear students' voices became the witness of socialization into the culture of classrooms around the world. For Mehan, analyzing the micro-world of classroom discourse enables the researcher to examine more critically the factors that explain school performance, such as social class, heredity, ethnicity on the macro level of society. Thus the video recording becomes a political tool in disclosing injustice of educational practice.

In the final chapter of the second section of the book George and Louise Spindler examine cross-cultural experiences in the use of audio-visual recordings which were taken at different locations. They presented evocative stimuli in the form of films taken in comparable areas in Germany and the United States and elicited voices of their 'native' informants in the opposite school environment, which again were recorded. Their chapter demonstrates and discusses this particular kind of research technique and the text that it produces, the crosscultural, comparative, reflective interview. Thus the voices of the natives become the dominant feature in the Spindlers' research, since they experience in a sense what ethnographers usually experience, whereas the voices of the researchers are muted. This shift in perspective enables the research 'subjects' to do their own cultural analysis by engaging in discourse about the self and other and the others thus making the ethnographer almost a bystander.

Keeping Authentic Voices Alive and Well

The chapters in part three include researchers' experiences in dealing with qualitative voices from the field in the phase of data analysis. 'Data handling' seems to be a crucial issue in the research process, because loads of authentic findings, usually in form of interview material, have to be reduced to a manageable size. Therefore it is not surprising that a great deal has been written about data collection in qualitative research, whereas less information is available providing useful help in the stage of analysis. When faced with all the collected material researchers often feel emptiness, powerlessness or even pain, as Woods (1985) describes:

> Pain is an indispensable accompaniment of the process. How often do we hear somebody admitting they 'sweated blood' in writing a certain piece; or the view that they know a certain stage in the research is near, and must be faced, but that they are 'dreading' and 'hating it'? This aspect of the research is best conceived as a 'rite de passage', a ritual, that is as much a test of self as anything else, that has to be gone through if the research project is to reach full maturity. If we do not feel pain at this point, there is almost certainly something wrong. Perhaps we are not progressing, and simply marking time on the spot, being satisfied with analysis at an elementary level which plays safe and avoids the risk of burning in the ring of fire, as well as the burden of hard work. But while such reports may not be entirely without value, they may not be making the best use of their material. Researchers must be masochists. We must confront the pain barrier till it hurts. (p. 87)

What the three chapters in this section have in common is that they do not offer an easy way out of the dilemma of paying due attention to the personal voices from the field and at the same time analyzing them from an external perspective. They show, however, that there are methods that help in the process of systemizing the findings. In his chapter Dietmar Larcher experiments with a method called redundancy analysis, which he uses to understand the incomprehensible, unconscious voice. Taking sociolinguistic theories as a starting point, he systematically analyzes the social context of utterances and explores the different shades of their social meaning. He applies this method to investigate socialization patterns of bilingual people and provides an empirical base for theory formation in intercultural education.

Günter Huber and Carlos Marcelo García take a different approach in their chapter. They use computer assistance when listening to the voices behind the conversation of probationary teachers who were interviewed about their classroom experiences after their pre-service training. By demonstrating the practical application of a software package for the analysis of qualitative data, they outline basic features of computer assistance to qualitative research and to show how such a program can help in identifying the voices behind the noise of a multitude of utterances.

The final chapter by Shulamit Reinharz illustrates an example of secondary analysis of qualitative data which have already been collected by another researcher. This situation may occur in the training of students when they are taught how to analyze data. In recent years, however, secondary analyses have become more popular when survey research or large-scale projects asked for a greater number of researchers to analyze the data load. Reinharz introduces the possibilities and drawbacks of secondary analysis before she illustrates its application in a study of miscarriage. Initially this might not be regarded as an educational use of such a method, although many people in the field of counselling and even teaching are confronted with this phenomenon. Moreover, feminist approaches to educational research demand qualitative work on issues related to the life and work of women in our society. Introductory textbooks usually do not offer secondary analysis as a qualitative method in educational research, therefore I regard the thematic orientation of Reinharz' chapter as appropriate to conclude this section.

The researchers' voices collected in this volume do not represent a certain scientific community within the qualitative movement, but draw their social identity from different academic 'tribes' with their own value systems. Therefore their work and educational research in general always has to be evaluated in the light of the broader theory and meta-theory of pedagogy. Through giving examples of concrete experience they not only provide information and ideas on different research methodology (in the sense of the methods used) but also invite the reader to share their overall concepts of educational theory and social practice (methodology in its broader sense). When designing their chapters the authors were asked to draw their attention to certain aspects in order to make their underlying principles more explicit. They can serve the reader as a frame of reference when comparing and contrasting the different approaches. At the end of the book I have added the questions in an epilogue, where I have also put together the different kinds of analytic procedures presented by the authors and given a general outlook.

References

RIBBINS, P.M., JARVIS, C.B., BEST, R.E. and ODDY, D.M. (1988) 'Meanings and contexts: The problem of interpretation in the study of a school' in WESTOBY, A.

(Ed.) *Culture and Power in Educational Organizations*, Milton Keynes, Open University Press, pp. 157–66.

WOODS, P. (1985) 'New songs played skilfully: Creativity and technique in writing up qualitative research' in BURGESS, R.G. (Ed.) *Issues in Educational Research*, London, Falmer Press, pp. 86–106.

Part 1

Giving Personal Voices a Chance in Social Organizations

Chapter 1

The Theatre of Daylight: Qualitative Research and School Profile Studies

Jean Rudduck

Voices

The word 'voices' suggests something different from the word 'dialogue'. Dialogue is part of a social convention where rules underwrite the possibility of speaking and being heard: turn-taking offers some promise of equality. Voices are more emotive, more disembodied, more disturbing. At one level they can 'represent' individuals or groups who have been denied the right to contribute or who have simply not been heard. Such voices speak to our conscience. At another level, voices remind us of the individuality that lies beneath the surface of institutional structures whose routine nature pushes us to work to 'sameness' rather than to respond to difference.

Translated into the context of qualitative research, the word 'voices' signals two things. First, it suggests the need for researchers, when they set out to help outsiders and insiders understand what goes on in schools, to give weight to the groups that seem, on past experience, more likely to be passed over: for instance, part-time female employees, black teachers, pupils. Second, it suggests the need to check out the extent to which the institution's stories about itself allow for and reflect authentic and important differences of perspective and experience.

In this chapter, the qualitative methodology that provides the frame for thinking about 'voices' is the school profile study — a label that we use to denote a form of focussed, school-based enquiry in which researchers are commissioned by a school to investigate an issue that is important to the school and which involves the use of condensed fieldwork (see Walker, 1974). In the setting of a school profile study, the word 'voices' points to a tension that makes all case study work interesting: it challenges the researcher both to keep trust with individual perspectives while, at the same time, building some kind of composite picture that both individuals and the school staff as a whole can recognize.

Background

'Whole school curriculum planning' is one of the most exciting and potentially powerful ideas to emerge in the 1980s. However, in the present climate, where schools are obliged to compete with one another and where school work is increasingly described in 'the language of the city pages and business news' (Lawn, 1990, p. 388), there is a danger that the educational task of understanding and thereby strengthening the 'whole school' way of working will give way to the technical task of measuring whole-school performance. Public accountability is currently holding the spotlight on whole-school *outcomes*, but if attention is not given to the *process* of building a whole-school ethos and way of working, we may find that models of institutional performance and student achievement are being constructed on very shaky foundations.

The move towards a 'whole-school' focus requires considerable thought about such things as power structures and patterns of participation; the relationship between personal and professional values; the nature and importance of shared understanding; and the means of achieving some level of overall institutional self-knowledge. In this chapter I suggest that one way of trying to build a firm foundation of institutional self-knowledge is to use what I and my colleague, Jon Nixon, are calling 'school profile studies', using condensed field work methods and democratic feedback techniques.

The title of the paper, 'The Theatre of Daylight' is taken from the Introduction to Tony Harrison's text (1990) of *The Trackers of Oxyrhynchus*. Harrison contrasts the theatre of darkness, in which people habitually sit, unseen, and watch actors on a lighted stage, with the theatre of daylight, in which Greek actors and audience took their places in full view of each other. The idea of a mutuality of awareness, responsiveness and respect among the totality of participants in the theatre seemed to engage with some of my concerns about whole school issues in schools, in particular about the development of collegial understanding and communal self-knowledge. 'The shared light', says Tony Harrison, 'begs a common language . . . a common wholeness, a common illumination, a common commitment . . .' (pp. x and xxi).

The Individual Teacher: Professional Self-knowledge in Context

I have argued elsewhere (Rudduck, 1988, pp. 210–1) of the usefulness of the biographical approach in helping individual teachers, particularly in a context of rapid educational change, re-examine their professional purposes and direction so that they can feel that they have some control over the agenda for change — or are at least clear about their own values and stance in relation to the changes that others require them to be part of. Biographical interviews offer teachers support in undertaking a personal enquiry into the nature of their own professional commitment, and a way of seeing that is different from 'the almost unconscious lenses' they normally employ (see Apple, 1975). As Nias (1984) reminds us, 'many of the profession seem to receive little significant assistance in the working out of their own professional values' (p. 14). It is difficult to get an analytic grip on the familiar context in which we work day in and day out and which we have probably been so effortlessly socialized into that its frameworks are no longer visible to us. Moreover, as Grumet (1981) says, we not only become part of that context but we are also responsible for it through our daily, albeit unconscious, reconstruction of it. If teachers are, in the main, so tightly meshed into institutional routines and regularities, it is not surprising that radical change is both unnerving for them to contemplate and difficult to accomplish. In order to release themselves from the complex and constraining webs of habit, they need some structure for standing outside their own work place in order to see how its values have been shaped and whether their own professional values are being expressed or are becoming muted. The biographical interview can go some way towards helping teachers construct a different perspective.

In much the same way did Frank Meadow-Sutcliffe, the Victorian photographer of Whitby in North Yorkshire, try to enable local people to 'see' familiar places with different eyes. His strategy was to photograph his subject 'at every hour of the day, on fine days and at intervals on dull days, (to) photograph it after it has been rained on for weeks, and after it has been sun-dried for months' (1912). By waiting and watching for unusual effects of fog, sunshine or cloud it is generally possible, he said, 'to get an original rendering of any place' (1914). In this way he offered the inhabitants of Whitby a fresh and surprising vision of the world they thought they knew and that familiarity had reduced to a predictable and unexciting outline.

The School Staff: Institutional Self-knowledge

If it is difficult for the individual to see beyond routine and re-engage personal and professional values, how much more difficult it is for a collection of individuals — for this is what a school staff often is — to re-view the structures and purposes of their work. Here the problem of socialization into conventional ways of seeing and behaving is compounded by various sub-group affiliations and mythologies that structure social encounters and perceptions in institutional life.

A recent study by Gillborn (1990) reveals something of the intricacies of building a whole-school commitment that confronts and is capable of working through personal and ideological differences. The school he worked in is known for its commitment to developing a democratic approach to policy-making. The inside story shows that it has not been easy. There has been some connivance in papering over the cracks, and a shift in the balance of power from the staff to parents and governors, effected by the Education Reform Act of 1988, has exposed the fragility of the consensus. For example, a head of department interviewed by Gillborn acknowledges his ambivalence towards the group of colleagues who, three years ago, successfully put the case for an integrated curriculum: 'The people who were getting involved in the change . . . are generally very articulate people', he begins. (Does he *mean* that innovative people are by nature articulate, or something slightly different — that such people talk about their ideas with a more persuasive excitement than is usual?) He goes on: 'to challenge them is very difficult'. In this case, of course, it was the innovators, as a group, who had the floor and it is often difficult for individuals to question the position taken by a united group — whether a radical group, as was the case in this school, or a conservative group. As a result, says the head of department, 'people tended to keep quiet rather than say (the) things, you know, that they felt in their hearts'. Thus, instead of learning to manage differences of opinion in debate within their institutional 'community' and to negotiate policy, the teachers accepted a false public consensus. But the 'support' that is offered in the public forum is not always sustained in private conversation, and criticism that should have been offered constructively in open dialogue can easily become sour and vindictive when expressed out of earshot of the rightful partners in the debate.

The picture that emerges from Gillborn's study underlines the complexities of communicating even in settings — such as the school he worked in — where considerable effort had been made by the headteacher to support the possibility of open decision-making. A swing in the external politics of curriculum construction enabled some actors to question the curriculum changes that had been introduced, thereby revealing that the consensus that had kept the school moving forward was, for them, merely a mask. Another teacher looks back and describes the micropolitics of in-school dialogue and decision-making:

> ... it depended on which group of the staff you were talking to as to how much of your real feeling you gave away, because it seemed to me there were sometimes fairly dishonest meetings where people were backed into a corner, defending something that, having spoken to them at other times, I knew they actually didn't really mean. But they weren't going to ... they weren't able to say ... They would have been in danger of denying the last two years' work if they said certain things. (Gillborn, 1990, ms p. 13)

Gillborn's study reminds us how ill-prepared schools generally are to manage their internal educational debate and achieve some depth of understanding, some genuine negotiation, and some integrity of whole-staff commitment. Without such a capacity it is exceptionally difficult for a school staff to begin to confront highly sensitive issues, such as issues of social justice.

The 'whole-school' concept does not only relate to policy-making; it also relates to shared understanding and the building of common knowledge about practice. Schools have got better at this but most still have a long way to go. The old caricature, drawn in words by Anderson and Snyder, presented a 'colleague' as someone who teaches on the other side of the wall. Writing in 1982, the authors could still fairly confidently say that 'education is among the last vocations within which it is still legitimate to work by yourself in a space that is secure against invaders' (p. 2). Things have changed but we found, only a few years ago (see Cowie and Rudduck, 1988), at a time when there was, nationally, a growing interest in cooperative approaches to learning, that members of school staffs tended not to know which departments and which individual colleagues were developing interesting approaches to group work. Instead, myths persisted: 'It's probably the English department — the drama teacher I should think'. This lack of knowledge of the school's own internal resources meant that teachers who wanted to develop new teaching strategies did not know that there was anyone to turn to for advice and support among their own colleagues.

What strategies are available to help schools realize a 'whole-school' way of working? School Profile Studies could, we think, make some contribution. They involve a partnership between experienced school case study workers and individual schools or clusters of schools. Experienced school case study workers tend to be found in universities or in other higher education institutions (in the UK, poly-technics and colleges), and in the present climate this can present a problem, for the nature of the relationship between schools and universities is being rapidly redrawn and made more problematic. Some critics of government policy (for example, Hargreaves and Reynolds, 1989) have suggested that the intention of central policy makers is to try to protect schools from the more radical challenges that many university courses offer. The one-year secondment programmes leading to the award of the MA and run by universities for practising teachers were a major route to the renewal of professional understanding and commitment but these have, as a result of new financial constraints, been severely cut back. Instead, money is available through programmes of categorical funding for specific government-approved initiatives which may or may not bring university staff into direct contact with teachers. Schools will also have their own in-service budgets but the money available for staff development is often absurdly low.

As a result schools are tending to turn to fellow teachers for practical guidance in staff development programmes or, if they do not have a specific expertise and if the myth of the university ivory tower is still strong in their consciousness, they may instead turn to the new breed of expert consultants — often ex-senior teachers — who are springing up in the educational market place. Thus, the circumstances under which schools and university-based researchers might enter into a contract to produce a Profile Study of a particular aspect of a school's work are undoubtedly problematic. The production and discussion of a School Profile Study takes time — and time, in the present climate, means money. In order to legitimize the expenditure, schools have got to be sure that greater self-knowledge is a crucial step in their development plan.

School Profile Studies

School Profile Studies are primarily developmental, serving the needs of the school or schools involved, but they also have some research potential. Briefly, they involve an experienced field worker spending two or three days in a school conducting interviews with a range of staff and managing some observation, as appropriate to the topic. (Depending on the focus of the study, interviews might also be undertaken with pupils or with parents/members of the local community.) The focus must be one that the school (by 'school' we mean its decision-making representatives) is currently interested in knowing more about. The interviews are recorded and partially transcribed. On the basis of field notes and passages of transcript, the researcher constructs a profile which is then offered back to the school as a basis for discussion.

There are various aspects of this seemingly simple and straightforward process that need to be unpacked, including the genealogy of the approach — for it does have one! The strongest methodological link is to 'condensed fieldwork'.

Condensed Fieldwork

> One has the feeling that nobody knows what goes on in schools, not even those who work in them . . . It needs the outside observer: it needs the anthropologist visiting the savage tribe.

Ottaway (1960) wrote that thirty years ago (p. 195; quoted in Burgess, 1983, p. 2). We know more now about what happens in schools and the image of the unknown culture of the savage tribe seems hardly relevant today. A distinctive feature of ethnographic study is, of course, the need for long periods of observation in the field in order to unravel the strange world of the study. The two best known studies of individual schools published in the UK in the last decade (Ball, 1981, Burgess, 1983) relied on sustained contact by the researcher:

> During the first year of the fieldwork I was *in* school for three days each week, during the second year four days a week, but in the third year my visits were occasional. (Ball, 1981, p. xix)

> During (a) sixteen months period I took a part time teacher role in the school. I took . . . (one) group on a regular basis for four periods each week and also took many substitution lessons in other departments in the school. As a part-time teacher I was a member of a house and department. I could therefore do participant observation, conduct unstructured interviews with teachers and pupils and collect documentary evidence. (Burgess, 1983, p. 4)

Walker (1974) paved the way for a different kind of study which does not involve 'the immersion of the researcher in the field for relatively long periods of time' (p. 30). Walker and MacDonald were involved at that time in a project looking at innovation and change in schools, and Simons (one of the team of fieldworkers) recollects that their interest in 'short time scales set boundaries for the case workers. In precise terms that meant that each of us was restricted to seven days in the field generating data . . .' (Simons, 1987, p. 91). Walker (1974) recognizes the need for 'long-term study' in order to determine 'areas of significance and to check the reliability and consistency of data', but he opens up the possibility of there being other contexts for study in which the 'area of significance' might be identified in advance (although the significant influences on that area of study will only be known through the fieldwork itself). Walker also recognizes the increasing pressure on researchers from 'simultaneous commitments to study in depth *and* to rapid reporting' (*ibid*, p. 31). This pressure has most certainly increased during the 80s. Walker proposes a way out of the dilemma which he calls 'condensed fieldwork'. The approach, as he first conceived it, involves 'a shift away from the notion of the researcher as prime interpreter' (*ibid*, p. 32) to one in which the reader takes more responsibility for dealing with the meanings of the data. In the case of school profile studies, this task becomes the responsibility of the school staff who are at the same time sponsors of the research, subject of the research, and audience for the research. The closest analogy might be with the commissioned self-portrait — although the motivations should be different!

Some of the main problems of case study research are these:

- problems of the researcher becoming involved in the issues, events or situations under study;
- problems over confidentiality of data;
- problems stemming from competition from different interest groups for access to, and control over, the data;
- problems concerning publication, such as the need to preserve anonymity of subjects;
- problems arising from the audience being unable to distinguish data from the researcher's interpretation of the data. (*ibid*, p. 35)

At some level these problems also apply to condensed fieldwork and to the development of school profile studies.

Walker goes on to suggest that condensed fieldwork has certain features in common with MacDonald's (1974, p. 15) conceptualization of 'democratic evaluation'. He cites the following passage:

> The democratic evaluator recognises value pluralism and seeks to represent a range of interests in his (or her) issue formulation. The basic value is an informed citizenry and the evalutor acts as broker in exchange of information between groups who want knowledge of each other. His (or her) techniques of data gathering and presentation must be accessible to non-specialist audiences. His (or her) main activity is the collection of definitions of, and reactions to . . . (the subject of the study) . . . The key justificatory concept is 'the right to know.' (parentheses added)

This sounds remarkably appropriate to the situation in which we are exploring the use of school profile studies. As MacDonald has pointed out, evaluators are frequently hired 'by those with power, to study those who are powerless' (quoted in Walker, 1974, p. 36), but in school profile studies the school teachers are in charge — although the power which the researcher can achieve through knowledge should not be overlooked. Walker goes on to say that studies within such a democratic mode 'will have a commitment to feeding back information quickly to participants in the situation under study . . . it is less important to generalize than it is to report accurately' (*ibid*, p. 39).

Thus, borrowing from Walker's summary, condensed fieldwork was an attempt to find ways of collecting and presenting data with some speed; what is retained from more extended case study work is the attempt 'to be objective, impartial and well-informed' (*ibid*, p. 43). Thus, the researcher, far from behaving as an anthropologist might need to do when 'visiting the savage tribe', is able instead to do what Blythe (1969, quoted in Walker, 1974, p. 47) describes as making 'a strange journey in a familiar land' — strange in that every school one goes to is at some level unknown.

Condensed field work can sound like ethnography on the dole — and school profile studies can sound like the pauper's version of condensed field work! But we have to see school profile studies as developing a conduct and purpose that is different from that of the ethnographic case study. Whereas in an ethnography, the researcher's aspiration is in most cases to become virtually invisible, or to become another inhabitant of the setting studied ('fly on the wall', 'part of the wallpaper', 'going native' — these are all indicative images), in profile studies the researcher's presence is strongly defined: the data gathering is scheduled, not opportunistic, and the researcher is, ideally, a welcome participant in a series of dialogues. And where an ethnography is many-layered and tries to capture the wholeness of a particular culture, a school study profile is narrow focussed — but the data are contextualized. Although the primary audience is the school staff, contextualization is important in that participants may need to see which aspects of the context are influential in relation to the topic under study.

What we have to be on guard against is that school profile studies are not taken up as a cut-price form of school-based research by lecturers who are pressurised by competitive university research ratings into 'being seen to be doing some research' and 'producing a written report'. School profile studies are not easy to do well: they have to be carefully negotiated and planned, and the topic has to be one that the school is concerned about and one that lends itself to exploration through this particular methodology. And above all the report has to be written with judgment and sensitivity and the feedback handled by researchers who understand what is at stake. Would-be researchers might well be cautioned by McCutcheon's recent account (1990) of how research contracts with schools can go wrong.

The Clinical Supervision Model

The other — more distant — influence on school profile studies is Goldhammer's 'clinical supervision model' which has been modified and renamed 'partnership supervision' (see Rudduck, 1987). In partnership supervision an outsider works in a one-to-one relationship with a teacher. The teacher identifies an issue in the classroom that he/she wants to know more about and the outsider gathers evidence through observation which will illuminate the issue. Such evidence is normally not accessible to the teacher, both because of the difficulty of managing reflection-in-action and because the teacher may have become socialized into not seeing certain facets of classroom interaction. The features that link partnership supervision with school profile studies are first, the sequencing of activities and second, the requirement that the outsider accepts the discipline of working to a focus defined by those who are the subject of study (in this way, the potential power of the outsider is contained). Major differences are, first, partnership supervision is usually concerned with brief episodes of activity (such as a single lesson or series of lessons) and, second, that it depends on observation rather than interview. I set out below the terms of the contract used in partnership supervision and, alongside it, a modified version which could provide ground rules for school profile studies.

Table 1.1

The terms of the partnership supervision contract:	The terms as adapted for school profile studies:
(i) The partner whose teaching will be observed proposes a focus for observation that he/she would like feedback on. The focus is discussed and clarified until both partners feel that they have arrived at a shared understanding.	(i) The school proposes a focus for study by nominating a topic that staff would like to have feedback on. The focus is discussed and clarified until the school's representative(s) and the researcher feel that they have arrived at a shared understanding (the school's representative(s) will probably — but not necessarily — be members of the senior management team).
(ii) The partners consider what kind of evidence would illuminate the agreed focus and, given the constraints of the situation, how best the evidence might be gathered.	(ii) The researcher and the school's representative(s) consider what range of people should be called on to talk with the researcher about their experience and perspective. Together they plan, taking into account the constraints of the situation, how best the series of interviews might be scheduled.

Table 1.1 (cont.)

The terms of the partnership supervision contract:	The terms as adapted for school profile studies:
(iii) The observing partner agrees to shape his/her observation to the agreed focus.	(iii) The researcher agrees to shape his/her interview questions and the content of his/her feedback to the agreed focus.
(iv) He/she agrees to discipline the content of the post-observation feedback by accepting a strict principle of relevance as defined by the focus.	(iv) The researcher discusses with the school's representative(s) the form of the feedback session and raises some of the issues that are at stake in using feedback constructively.
(v) The observing partner and the teacher agree to meet to discuss the evidence collected as soon after the event as possible. (See Rudduck, 1987)	(v) A short report is prepared and the timing of its presentation — either before or after the feedback session — is discussed and agreed.

Developing School Profile Studies — Some Examples

I first experimented with the approach in circumstances where I was seeking data about the ways in which schools used cooperative group work. A headteacher (i.e., school principal) who was keen to develop new teaching and learning strategies invited me to come to his school. I accepted the invitation. I made one preliminary visit at which I interviewed the headteacher and some senior colleagues, one of whom was appointed liaison person for the study. The head agreed to identify a range of teachers for me to interview, including teachers with different levels of experience and seniority, different subject areas, different attitudes towards teaching and learning, and both men and women. The headteacher's concern to develop new ways of working enabled him to offer me the range of perspectives and experiences that I had requested; he had nothing to gain from protecting me from certain attitudes that he may well have known existed; indeed, it was probably to his advantage to have some of these feelings expressed in a public document where other views can be set alongside. All staff were informed about the purpose of the interviews and of the approach to be adopted and the liaison teacher organized an interview schedule over two days. Staff were interviewed, in the main, in a free period (I agreed to take up no more than half the period so that they did not feel a total sense of loss) although many, once talking, said they would have been happy to give more time. Cover was found for those teachers whom I was to talk with who did not have a free period on those days. The interviews were partially transcribed and I put together a report which was sent first to the headteacher and was then made available in its original form to all staff to read a few days before I arrived at the school for the feedback session (which had been arranged at the end of afternoon school for all staff).

What did the report offer that the staff as a whole did not know already? Quite a lot. First, there was information. It was a relatively easy task to discover which teachers in which departments were doing interesting work. I found out, for instance, that one teacher, unbeknown to her colleagues, had been systematically tape recording small group discussions and analyzing the data over a period of time — she was doing the work as part of a higher degree course but there was no habit in the school of sharing insight about teaching and learning and so her experience was not known about. Second, I discovered that teachers on the staff were supporting two quite different views of group work: one, that it was only appropriate for low achieving pupils (this view was premised on a perception of group work as being essentially about social relationships); another, that it was only the high achieving, academically-oriented pupils who were capable of managing group work (this view was premised on the assumption that group work was about the development of independent thought and made powerful intellectual demands on young people). Some interesting perceptions of children lay behind these responses: a view of children as being intrinsically 'naughty' and therefore not to be trusted in settings where the teacher's presence was not close and constant; a view of young people as empty vessels to be filled; and a view that it was teachers and the conventional structures of schooling that were the break on pupils' capacity for progress in thinking. Various other issues emerged that the school could productively work on — for example, the reality of the constraints mentioned by teachers in the school as a way of explaining why they had not explored the potential of group work (which was, at the time, being given some national prominence):

'Group work? Colleagues might think the lesson is getting out of hand.'

'Unless you stand over them the kids in this school won't work.'

'They're quite happy to sit there like little jugs and let you pour it in.'

'You can't have cooperation at "A" level.'

'You see, you've got kids who say, "Mr Jones makes us work. We do real work in his lessons. We're writing it all down".'

'The rooms that we have by and large don't lend themselves to group work.'

'We've got 30-odd in the class for a session that's only 35 minutes. It's rather difficult to do anything other than the traditional (i.e., transmission) style.'

Finally, calls for help were coming through. Many teachers felt that neither their initial training nor subsequent in-service experience had offered them support in the development of non-traditional teaching and learning strategies. Moreover, the school's relatively isolated position made it difficult for teachers to travel to visit other schools to seek advice, even if they knew where to go for guidance and inspiration. There was a clear need for more opportunities within school for teachers to share their experiences of teaching and learning.

In the school profile study some contextualization was attempted. For example, it seemed important to remind the school staff about the historical dimension. This was 'a grammar school turned comprehensive' and many existing staff had taught at the old grammar school and were remarkably open in acknowledging the problems they faced in learning to 'cope with' pupils whom they expected to be less well-motivated academically than those they were used to. Staff were also aware that the other comprehensive school in the area — which had no roots in the grammar school tradition — seemed to find it easier to present a 'modern image' that, in times of low local employment opportunities, the community seemed to be favouring. Thus, the school needed to confront the implications of history, and understand what was at stake in developing new approaches to teaching and learning.

It took me three to four days, after the transcripts were typed to work through the data and to prepare the report — which had to be accessible, lively and clear without being too long (I produced just over twenty well-spaced A4 pages) and without being overtly judgmental.

My next experience of this kind of study was again the result of my being involved in a research project. This time there was a national concern about discipline and the government had set up a Committee of Enquiry (chaired by Lord Elton) which took evidence from a range of people within the education system and also made some day visits to schools. I and my colleagues were asked to conduct a school survey (under John Gray's overall direction) and also a series of short interview-based studies of inner city comprehensive schools (under my overall direction). Access was no problem. Schools were interested in the topic and anxious that teachers should have a voice in the national report. I worked with David Gillborn and Jon Nixon and we used the 'school profile' approach. The only difference was that this time, because of the nature of the contract with the Committee of Enquiry, oral rather than written feedback was presented.

We are now about to embark on a third stage in the development of school profile studies. We have been commissioned by a local education authority (i.e., a School Board) to assist a team of local curriculum coordinators and headteachers with the task of identifying and understanding progress and achievement in local schools. The coordinators and heads will identify topics that they and their schools want to know more about and I and my colleagues will undertake a series of school profile studies. The first commission from three schools that are part of a local curriculum consortium is to investigate reasons why boys do less well than girls in course work and examinations in the fourth and fifth years of secondary schooling (ages 14 to 16 years) (see Harris *et al.*, 1991).

Managing the Feedback Process

The most problematic aspect of school profile studies — and for the school the most important — is the feedback process.

In the burgeoning literature on school case studies there has been little sustained discussion of the way that case studies actually work to extend educational knowledge and understanding — whether for the participants themselves (feedback) or for outside audiences (utilization). Interestingly, some authors of school studies have presented worthwhile discussions of the origins of their study and of their methodology, either accompanying the publication (see, for example, Lightfoot, 1983, pp. 3–26) and/or retrospectively (see, for example, Lacey, 1976, pp. 63–88), but issues of feedback and utilization are given relatively little attention by the authors. It appears, to judge from the evidence of both published school studies and explanatory papers, that most authors see fellow researchers, policy makers or other practitioners as their main audience rather than the people whose work was the subject of the study. However, some authors of school studies which culminated in publication have written briefly about feedback, which they seem to regard either as a courtesy phase in the overall process or as a 'respondent validation technique' (Ball, 1984, p. 83). The question of what the school learns about itself is not much explored. Ball does, however, describe his attempts to present draft chapters to the teachers in voluntary 'seminars'; he comments: 'There was little or no discussion of the general issues I was trying to raise or the overall arguments of the chapter'; instead, teachers mainly wanted to comment on the presentation and wording of any passages that referred directly to themselves or to their department. We know, however, from discussion at research conferences, that the presentation and feedback stage of case studies can be particularly sensitive and the researcher may have to deal with serious objections raised by the school as to the authenticity of the facts of the case, the representativeness of the evidence, and the acceptability of the interpretation.

The Report: Letting the Voices Speak for Themselves?

I choose to tape-record interviews and to have sections transcribed. I do so because I want to be able to quote passages from the interviews. I respect the power of the direct quotation to capture succinctly and vividly what could only be expressed dully and less economically in the researcher's own words. Some statements carry a remarkably rich density of meaning in a few words. For example, in a study of teaching strategies and student autonomy in UK schools (Rudduck and Hopkins, 1984) I recollect quite clearly the insight communicated in a comment made by one 17-year-old senior student in the school — in what has traditionally been called, in the UK, 'the sixth form'. She said: 'Being in the sixth form is like being let loose on a slightly longer lead'. Quotations are powerful when they offer startling and memorable images — as this did — which our own experience immediately endorses as presenting a reality that we had not seen so clearly before.

I also feel that it is important to signal respect for teachers and students by allowing others — even their everyday colleagues — to hear their voices in print. As Apple (1990, p. 378) has said, the education system suffers already from the marginalization of certain voices (non-promoted women teachers, black teachers and students) and case-study research is one way of redressing the imbalance. I was struck, for instance, by the strength of the feeling expressed in the passages of interview quoted by Michele Foster in her presentation (1990) of the recollections of African-American teachers in newly desegregated schools in the 1960s. These are voices that need to be heard. On the other hand I am also aware that what is said is sometimes not easy to hear because it makes us uncomfortable. For instance, this is what Foster chooses to quote from her interview with Ella Jones:

> I couldn't use the bathroom with the teachers and everything. I would use the bathroom with the students. I didn't eat with them. You know, they just kind of treated me like dirt. We brought our black students. The teachers, the white teachers, would put the black kids, this is the

truth, on one side and white ones on the other so they wouldn't touch, and so they wouldn't mingle, and that's the truth. (ms p. 13)

The researcher needs to exercise judgment. If such comment were a testament to *contemporary* behaviours in the school in which the speaker is now teaching, and was presented raw, as direct quotation, in a school profile that was being made available to all members of the staff of that school, then the report might unleash such defensive reactions that its purpose in opening up the debate about issues of equality of treatment would be undermined. What such comments reveal, as Foster (*ibid*) points out, is the extent of the 'institutional racism and structural conditions that combine to limit the professional lives of African-American teachers and strangle educational possibilities for African-American pupils'. And although the speaker does not hold her white fellow teachers responsible — 'I mean, for God's sake, they're victims of their own society' — nevertheless if they did not already sense that things are as she depicts them and share with her some desire to confront them, then the power of the majority, who can claim simply that she is wrong, could set back the possibility of change still further.

So, direct quotation is a powerful tool but it must be carefully used. There is another reason for urging caution. When a report is built up from the evidence offered by members of a working community, the personal cadences or familiar angle of a particular quotation can leave the speaker open to identification even though other more obvious markers, such as subject and status, are not disclosed. And in School Profile Studies there is no time for the researcher to clear with individuals which passages of the interview they gave may be quoted in the text of the report. The researcher is always trying to thread his/her way between under-exposure of the controversial issues — an error which would result in the school not being able to move forward — and risky overstatement — an error which could lead the school to reject the report. The 'right to know' (see earlier) must take account of the right to privacy.

Conclusion

School Profile Studies are a symptom of the timeles. In a context of 'whole-school' thinking, the approach rests on the assumption that schools need to 'know themselves' in order to plan effectively. The approach takes into account the problems of achieving and sustaining a reasonable degree of institutional self-knowledge. Two things in particular make this difficult.

First, there is a centrally orchestrated attempt to change both what goes on in schools and the nature of schools' obligations to society. What David Hargreaves said in 1982 about the search for individual identity can be applied, in the 1990s, to institutional identity:

Today we are born into possibilities and our biography can become a migration through several successive worlds in which we take on different identities. (p. 97)

Given the strong tradition of individualism among teaching members of a school staff, the development of a capacity for communal negotiation and of a commitment that is founded in shared values will not be easy to achieve. The culture of individualism has bred 'a suspicion of collective action' (*ibid*, p. 227). There are no traditional strategies for building institutional self-knowledge and in the present climate the frenzied busyness of teachers and senior management teams in organizing frameworks for change does not leave space for genuinely collective views to be built up.

School profile studies have a modest aim. They enable the bringing together of a variety of perspectives on an issue or a dimension of practice. At one level, they prevent teachers from distancing themselves, as a staff group, from the micropolitical realities of institutional life for they bring into communal hearing voices that are often ignored or that have become silent through the frustration of knowing that they will not be listened to with respect.

The immediacy and therefore the quick timescale for the production of school profile studies can make them somewhat crude but they are, after all, constructed for insiders who are already familiar with the broad outlines of institutional structures and action. They do not aspire to the fullness and fineness of Lightfoot's case studies in which she sought to capture 'the culture of these schools, their essential features, their generic character, the values that define their curricular goals and institutional structures, and their individual styles and rituals' (1983, p. 6). School profile studies are partial and they are rapidly sketched — unlike Lightfoot's pictures which emerge 'slowly and deliberately' (*ibid*). But their limitations are also, at some level, their strengths, for they leave more space for the insiders themselves to work on; they require completion by a curious and responsive audience. They are a means of helping schools to take their place in the theatre of daylight.

References

ANDERSON, R. and SNYDER, K. (1982) 'Why such an interest in clinical supervision?' *Wingspan*, **1**, 13, pp. 1–10.

APPLE, W.M. (1975) 'Scientific interests and the nature of educational institutions' in PINAR, W. (Ed.) *Curriculum Theorizing: The Reconceptualists*, Berkeley, CA, McCutchan, pp. 120–130.

APPLE, W.M. (1990) 'The politics of official knowledge in the United States', *Journal of Curriculum Studies*, **22**, 4, pp. 377–400.

BALL, S.J. (1981) *Beachside Comprehensive: A Case-Study of Secondary Schools*, Cambridge, Cambridge University Press.

BALL, S.J. (1984) 'Beachside reconsidered: Reflections on a methodological apprenticeship' in BURGESS, R.G. (Ed.) *The Research Process in Ten Educational Settings*, Lewes, Falmer Press, pp. 69–96.

BLYTHE, R. (1969) *Akenfield*, Harmondsworth, Penguin.

BRUNER, J. (1986) *Actual Minds, Possible Worlds*, New York, Harvard University Press.

BURGESS, R.G. (1983) *A Study of Bishop McGregor School: Experiencing Comprehensive Education*, London, Methuen.

COWIE, H. and RUDDUCK, J. (1988) *School and Classroom Studies, Volume 2 of Learning Together — Working Together*, London, BP Educational Service.

ELTON REPORT (1989) *Discipline in Schools*, London, HMSO.

FOSTER, M. (1990) 'The politics of race: through African-American teachers' eyes', paper presented at the annual meeting of the American Educational Research Association, Boston, April.

GILLBORN, D. (1990) 'Crisis management: The effects of national reform on a progressive school', paper presented at the St Hilda's Conference, September.

GRUMET, M. (1981) 'Restitution and reconstruction of educational experience: An autobiographical method for curriculum theory' in LAWN, M. and BARTON, L. (Eds) *Rethinking Curriculum Studies*, London, Croom Helm, pp. 115–30.

HARGREAVES, A. and REYNOLDS, D. (Eds) (1989) *Education Policies: Controversies and Critiques*, Lewes, Falmer Press.

HARGREAVES, D. (1982) *The Challenge for the Comprehensive School*, London, Routledge & Kegan Paul.

HARRIS, S., NIXON, J. and RUDDUCK, J. (1991) *Equalising Opportunities: A Study in Three Schools*, a profile study prepared for Derbyshire LEA, Sheffield, QQSE publication.

HARRISON, T. (1990) *The Trackers of Oxyrhynchus*, London, Faber & Faber.

LACEY, C. (1976) *Hightown Grammar: The School as a Social System*, Manchester, Manchester University Press.

LAWN, M. (1990) 'From responsibility to competency: A new context for curriculum studies in England and Wales', *Journal of Curriculum Studies*, **22**, 4, pp. 388–92.

LIGHTFOOT, S.L. (1983) *The Good High School: Portraits of Character and Culture*, New York, Basic Books.

McCUTCHEON, G. (1990) 'Conflict about conflict: between a rock and a hard place', paper presented at the annual meeting of the American Educational Research Association, Boston, April.

MacDONALD, B. (1974) 'Evaluation and the control of education', *SAFARI: Some Interim Papers*, University of East Anglia, Norwich, CARE Publications, pp. 8–20.

NIAS, J. (1984) 'Learning and acting the roles: In-school support for primary teachers', *Educational Review*, **36**, 1, pp. 3–16.

OTTAWAY, A.K.C. (1960) 'The aims and scope of educational sociology', *Educational Review*, **12**, 3, pp. 190–9.

RUDDUCK, J. (1987) 'Partnership supervision as a basis for the professional development of new and experienced teachers' in WIDEEN, M. and ANDREWS, I. (Eds) *Staff Development for School Improvement*, Lewes, Falmer Press, pp. 129–41.

RUDDUCK, J. (1988) 'The ownership of change as a basis for teachers' professional learning' in CALDERHEAD, J. (Ed.) *Teachers' Professional Learning*, Lewes, Falmer Press, pp. 205–22.

RUDDUCK, J. and HOPKINS, D. (1984) *The Sixth Form and Libraries: Problems of Access to Knowledge*, Library and Information Research Report 24, Boston Spa, British Library.

SIMONS, H. (1987) *Getting to Know Schools in a Democracy: The Politics and Process of Tradition*, Lewes, Falmer Press.

SUTCLIFFE, F.M. (1912 and 1914) 'Photography notes', *Yorkshire Weekly Post*, 9 March and 3 October (quoted in HILEY, M. (1979) *Frank Meadow-Sutcliffe*, New York, Aperture Inc., p. 8.)

WALKER, R. (1974) 'The conduct of educational case studies: Ethics, theory and procedures' reprinted in DOCKERELL, E.B. and HAMILTON, D. (Eds) *Rethinking Educational Research* (1980), Sevenoaks, Hodder & Stoughton, pp. 30–62.

Chapter 2

Event Analysis and the Study of Headship

Robert G. Burgess

Voices

In all ethnographic studies there are many voices: participants and researchers in the field during the period of data collection and the researcher during data analysis and writing. In this chapter the focus is upon event analysis — a strategy used by anthropologists to understand the implicit and explicit meanings within a social situation. Here, the raw material consists of observational and interview data together with documentary evidence. Each type of data gives a voice to the participants and in turn the researcher. The unit of study is headship and many voices and many tones of voice are used to construct an understanding of headship in an English secondary school taking events and the commentaries that surround them as the 'critical case' or unit of analysis.

Introduction

Headship is a topic that looms large in many educational reports on schools. In the HMI report *Ten Good Schools* (1977), the quality of headship was seen as the critical feature of all the schools as the inspectorate remarked:

> without exception, the most important single factor in the success of these schools is the quality of leadership. (p. 35)

Indeed, they point out that the quality of a school relies on effective leadership. Yet despite such interest in headteachers, we find that they have been omitted from view in sociological studies in general and ethnographic studies in particular. However, Stephen Ball (1987) has devoted a considerable portion of his analysis of school organization to leadership and headship, as he argues that the headteacher is at the centre of micropolitical activity in a school. The question that confronts the ethnographer in this context is: how can the study of a headteacher be used to examine fundamental social processes associated with the structure and organization of a secondary school? This was a problem that confronted me in conducting a study and a restudy of an urban coeducational Roman Catholic comprehensive school (Burgess, 1983 and 1987). In both studies I engaged in an analysis of headship to shed light on the way in which the social organization of the school operated. Here, links were made between the data that were collected through observation and interview and a form of anthropological analysis based on the use of 'critical incidents' or 'event analysis' that would assist in studying processes associated with headship. This chapter, therefore, focusses on the use of event analysis to demonstrate ways in which such an analytic framework can assist our understanding of headship and in turn schools as social organizations.

Starting Points

When I began my study of Bishop McGregor School in 1972 I focussed on headship, as Geoff Goddard the headteacher was a critical reality definer who led, managed and defined school activities (Burgess, 1983 and 1984). The head was, therefore, central to an understanding of school organization. At that stage Goddard saw the headteacher as a manager whose main task was crisis management as he argued:

> My job is not to manage today's crisis, but to manage the crisis of four months time. The settlement of today's crisis is by principles established four months before. If it isn't, something has gone wrong with forward planning.

This statement was followed up with a set of principles that outlined the way in which crises or critical situations such as fires, crashes and explosions might be handled. In my first study I focussed upon three critical situations that the head had to handle: a bomb scare, a mass walk out of pupils and a crisis at the end of a summer term (Burgess, 1983). Yet this overlooked many critical situations that occur on a day-by-day basis and involve interpersonal relations between teachers and teachers and the headteacher that can assist in advancing our understanding of school organization.

When I returned to Bishop McGregor school in the mid-1980s (Burgess, 1987), I found that the head and his senior management team were having to handle a number of critical situations that occurred regularly in the annual, termly, weekly and daily cycle of the school year. These situations included: falling rolls, the redeployment of teachers and the national teachers' dispute between management and the teacher unions. While each of these phenomena were accompanied by established procedures that the management team in any school within the local authority was expected to follow, it was nevertheless difficult for plans to be laid down for handling day-to-day practice. In this respect, the head defined many of the activities that accompanied the teachers' dispute as placing McGregor School in a crisis. Indeed, he asked that I should not write anything about these critical incidents until after he retired.

Studying Crises

Studies of crises have been produced by the anthropologist Victor Turner (1957) who argues that a suitable unit of analysis in ethnographic study may be a situation, event or crisis that he terms a social drama. In using this conceptual framework Turner argues that the aim is:

Not to present a reputedly objective recital of a series of events; it is concerned, rather, with the different interpretations put upon these events, and the way in which they express nuanced shifts or switches in the balances of power or ventilate divergent interests within common concerns. (p. 352)

The social drama is therefore a mechanism that may be used to examine the social processes involved in a social situation. It is this framework that was used to examine an aspect of the teachers' dispute in Bishop McGregor School in the 1985 autumn term.

Stephen Ball (1987) has reminded us that industrial action in schools raises many issues for teachers and for schools as he remarks:

The notion of 'dispute' must be recognised in two senses: first the formal dispute between the teachers unions and their employers; second the concomitant disputes which have arisen between teachers themselves as a result of the action. Conflicts can emerge in the interpersonal relations of teachers in one school, in the relations between members of different teacher unions, between teachers and their management, particularly the head, and between teachers and the LEA. (p. 270)

Certainly, within Bishop McGregor several of these features were present; especially interpersonal relations between teachers and between teachers and the management team which invariably involved the head. It is, therefore, the purpose of this chapter to focus on an aspect of the teachers' dispute in Bishop McGregor School to examine how the head handled crisis management in the 1980s and to demonstrate how the analysis of a critical incident relies upon different kinds of observational and interview data that can be used alongside documentary data. In short, illustrative material will be used to outline the way in which the analysis is linked to the data that are collected.

The framework that I used to focus on different dimensions of the crisis is Turner's notion of a social drama that provides a 'limited area of transparency on the otherwise opaque surface of regular uneventful social life' (Turner, 1957, p. 93). Within Turner's work, four phases of a social drama have been identified. They are:

(i)   A *breach* of norm-governed relations between persons in the same system of social relations.

(ii) A *mounting crisis* where the breach may widen and become coterminus with a dominant division in the wider pattern of social relations to which all the parties belong.

(iii) *Redressive mechanisms* of a formal and informal kind that may be used by members of the social group to limit the spread of the crisis.

(iv) *Reintegration* of the social group and legitimation of the schism between the parties.

Each of these features can be identified in the teachers' dispute, but one critical incident will be examined to see how it can assist in our understanding of headship, teacher-management relations and headteacher-management relations.

The Context of the Social Drama

By November 1985, the teachers' dispute had run for ten months in Bishop McGregor School. The head and two of his deputies, together with some senior teachers who were not union members, were seen by staff to be attempting to break the unions, and to keep as many 'normal' routines as possible operating throughout the lunch hour. The result was that the head detected a change in his staff as he remarked in an interview that I conducted with him:

> (In the past) the staff with all its faults spoke its mind and was fairly open, fairly cheerful, now it is not as open and it is not as cheerful and does not speak its mind. It meets in small groups. My two deputies now if they greet someone, about 50 per cent of the cases they're greeting will be returned and 50 per cent of the cases the person who's greeted will walk straight past.

Many teachers regarded these two deputies (Phil Barlow and Gill Davies) as 'anti-union' and 'right-wing' as Phil Barlow no longer belonged to a union and Gill Davies was an AMMA (Assistant Masters and Mistresses Association) member who it was claimed did not attend school-based union meetings nor follow union instructions. Similarly, the head, who had been Secretary of the local branch of the NUT (National Union of Teachers) no longer participated in the union, did not attend meetings and did not withdraw from school as requested by the union.

Such actions were interpreted by teachers as an 'anti-union' stance of their management with the consequence that it strengthened the resolve of many teachers; especially the union representatives to keep up the action. Indeed, by November 1985 the head commented:

> The action is biting and the action is getting more desperate and the effect of the action is obvious at surface level: more kids going home, you know, no meetings — it's ten months since we had our last meeting.

However, his perception of the unions and the management were summarized as follows:

> There are huge tensions within the NUT membership and two have resigned last week I understand, and there are others who are, who say they've had enough, but are not you know. There's huge tensions between the conscience of the NAS/UWT rep and what he sees he has to say and he is torn, there's no doubt. There's tensions, considerable tensions and bitterness between those who are hard for the action, and determined to go to the bitter end, and management. Management is seen as anybody who doesn't take the hard line. It's been a bitter half term and an angry one, and a sad one. Now those are the things that characterise it, and there isn't a huge amount of joy and delight anywhere in the world.

Similarly, the head had a more pessimistic view of headship. In the 1970s, he had told me of the freedom he enjoyed (Burgess, 1984), but by 1985 he was commenting on constraints that operated on headteachers and the extent to which the head was isolated from teachers and from other members of the senior management team — a situation that many teachers at McGregor considered had developed during the teachers' action. Goddard summed up the situation by commenting:

> No, it (headship) is lonely. You've . . . most heads perhaps have been successful deputy heads or heads of departments, it's, within the normal route, it's head of department, pastoral head, deputy head, head . . . to be successful they've been gregarious, they've been social, they've organized things, and you get into headship and suddenly you find it is different and the way people approach you is different. You're on the other side of the desk. There's no doubt whatsoever. Secondly, the style and the manner of a school depends substantially on the head and the head can't play favours. You may have your favourites, but you can't play favours. Thirdly, your loyalty as an assistant teacher is to your fellow assistants. Your loyalty as a head must be to the children first and almost secondly to yourself. Now one of the things that we're crossing is that you leave your friends behind you and that's lonely and I would say myself that my previous deputy could move backwards and forwards and could comfort me and could strengthen me. One house head does it from time to time. Gill Davies (a deputy head) is very loyal but her loyalties are not just to me, they are to a team and she's very loyal to Phil Barlow (another deputy) and she's very loyal to me. She works in well together (laugh), but ultimately when it comes down to it, you're on your own and you're answerable to everything. Command is lonely. A ship's captain is quiet, by design, eats separately, and has his own cabin and his own servant, and ultimately is held responsible for everything that goes on on his vessel, whether he's commanding a frigate or whether he's commanding an aircraft carrier, and I don't think it's too strong to say that under English education heads have got not identical, but they've got similar strength of . . . they've got similar freedom which is getting less.

In these circumstances, there was a situation in which the head felt relatively isolated and where divisions occurred between management and unions — a situation that widened in the autumn term. It was, therefore, these data that provided a context in which the subsequent collection and analysis of data could be located using the phases that Turner had identified.

Breach

In the first half of the 1985 autumn term, the NUT representative, Sally Jackson, had challenged the way in which pay slips were distributed in the school by Gill Davies. The result was a ballot, which was organized by the head to see if a new system could be devised that would satisfy all teachers. However, this was a minor irritation compared with a complaint made by the NUT representative in the second half of the autumn term.

In the middle of October, the head was out of school and his deputies had to take responsibility for organizing the school. This included operationalizing the local Accommodation Agreement between the unions and the local authority which included instructions on supply cover, curriculum initiatives, timetabling and cover for absent colleagues. Here, union members in the NAS/UWT and the NUT received the following instructions from their unions:

(i) No member of the NAS/UWT or NUT shall cover classes of absent colleagues except where no other member of staff is able to provide cover by virtue of having a timetabled non-contact period available.

(ii) Should members of the NAS/UWT or NUT be required to cover, then those members providing such cover shall receive a restoration of their non-contact time by the sending home of pupils timetabled to be taught by them. A period of two weeks shall be allowed for such restorations to take place.

(iii) School reps shall be provided with records of cover provided by all members of staff on a weekly basis. (Extracts from Local Authority Accommodation Agreement)

This Agreement required careful checks to be kept by the management in each school of absent colleagues, the number of classes to be sent home, and the restoration of non-contact time. Any account of these activities had to be regularly given to the union representatives who in turn checked all the figures. At McGregor, it was Sally Jackson who checked all the figures as the NAS/UWT representative relied on her to do it. Often in the autumn term she had queried the figures and complained about the non-arrival of the record of cover. However, this all reached a climax when the head was out of school in mid-November. Sally Jackson explained what had happened:

SJ: It all came to a head really when the headmaster was out of school for three days, starting on Tuesday 12 November, for three days I was dealing then with the deputies and there were a number of fairly urgent matters which I wanted an answer on. On one of them I got no reply at all, and on another I got a reply which didn't satisfy me and then there was a certain amount of . . .

RB: Can you say what those were?

SJ: Well, just briefly they . . . one of them was the exclusion of the DES group, and having that counted as four classes whereas in fact there are only nineteen children involved, I think that was wrong. Because they're taught by you know, in all four teachers on a Friday afternoon and did not follow the normal pattern of exclusion — that was one of the problems. The other one was teachers being forced . . . teachers being expected to teach unregistered classes. The NAS as you know would go out for an hour and the class was told to come in. I took this up with my union and they instructed me to seek an indemnity from management saying that if in the event of any emergency such as a fire that they would take responsibility for the fact that no register was available, to check who was supposed to be present and who wasn't, and I was instructed by the union to ask for that. Well, I received no reply from management on that. This was at the time when the St Ives case was being reported in the paper and one of the things that the teacher in charge was accused of was not having a list of pupils available. Anyhow, it seemed to me a fairly important point as I don't think that . . . that action is going to end overnight. It's something which had to be cleared up. There were two or three matters like that and by the time Friday morning came, I felt upset and rather angry because I hadn't been able to have a dialogue, the deputies had refused to discuss.

As a consequence, Sally Jackson decided to write to the head on 15 November (the day he returned to school). She explained:

I was angry about the way the union had been treated and when I came into the school on 15 November I took out a little record card — 4 inches by 2 inches — and wrote down:

Dear Mr Goddard,

'Due to the intransigence and incompetence of one of your deputies' (I think I said your deputy cause I wasn't really thinking clearly) 'the Accommodation Agreement is now in jeopardy at Bishop McGregor School and I will be discussing the matter with my union secretary' and I left it at that.

It had not been Sally's intention to get a formal response, but to get the head to come and talk about the problems. Instead, she received a letter that read:

Mrs S Jackson

Dear Mrs Jackson,

Thank you for your card which I read at 8.35 this morning. In accordance with the instructions that I have, I have communicated the contents of your message to the office. I have been told that the office will ring me at 1.30 this afternoon. I understand that the situation now is that you are requesting Mr Ball (the NUT secretary) to arrange a withdrawal of the Accommodation Agreement at McGregor, that he will take this up with the office and that some form of meeting will take place, at which the issues between members of the NUT and the management of this school will be explored together.

The NAS/UWT has been in to see Mr Barlow (the deputy head) and myself this morning and says that during next week, while the NAS/ UWT are withdrawing their labour periods 5 and 6 each day and periods

1 and 2 Monday to Friday, the Accommodation Agreement should in fact not operate for staff absences but that the debts be calculated the following week.

He tells me that you have already agreed to this, but I would be grateful for confirmation of your agreement.

Yours sincerely,

G. Goddard

It was these activities that marked a deep division between the management and the union at Bishop McGregor School. However, the crisis was to deepen and data could be collected on the subsequent phase of this social drama.

The Crisis

Having received the card, Goddard had also shown it to Phil Barlow, his first deputy who considered that he and Gill Davies had had to take many decisions about union action even when the head was in school. However, he considered that his misinterpretation of the way in which classes were to be sent home in the early autumn resulted in the NUT representative challenging whatever he did as he explained:

> I found that from there on at every opportunity, I might be wrong, I don't think I am, at every opportunity from then that particular union, the NUT, whether they got on to the boss when he was in school or not I don't know, but they certainly took the opportunity of when he was out of school, buying something, and it got to the stage where I was sending a reply two or three times a day to another request from the same union rep saying to her, look I'm sorry the office say this isn't right, you know, what you're requesting isn't right, or I'm sorry the office say definitely 'no'. I think every decision that I took all the way along that autumn term was challenged.

However, he considered that the critical incident in his relationship with the NUT and with the union representative came when he was asked for a written indemnity for those teachers in the NUT against teaching a class that was not required in school until mid-morning. He commented:

> I had to give a written indemnity to the NUT teachers, that I would take full responsibility for those children because they shouldn't have been on site. I think that's where things really blew up because I refused to give that written indemnity. It wasn't my place to actually, I mean, if the boss is out then obviously the thing comes down to me, I'm in charge but I wasn't going to take over a legal responsibility other than the one I really have. I rang the office who rang me at home late one night and said under no circumstances whatsoever must you do that because you

set a precedence if you do for a start and it's not your place to take on the responsibility. Fine, so I didn't give that and that then started the ball rolling, there were accusations made against me in writing to the boss and I thought well, I'm not standing for this . . . At that point it was very hurtful and I did get the feeling that that person was attempting, in the allegations she was making, to kind of exacerbate that problem, you know, that I had a personal thing, I felt deeply hurt and she was trying to stick the knife in. I think she succeeded. So I immediately . . . well one of my god parents is a solicitor and this thing came in on the Friday and the boss arrived back on the Friday after being off all week, showed the thing to me and I said 'I'm not letting her get away with that', and he said something like you know, 'fine, I shouldn't or something like that, but don't go off half cock, go and set some advice'.

After Phil Barlow returned to school after the weekend he explained that he had sought legal advice — a situation that was quickly interpreted by union representatives that it was now all in 'the hands of a solicitor'. The result was a venomous situation among all parties that the head had to attempt to resolve. Observational and interview data together with documentary evidence therefore allowed me to construct an account of the way in which the head handled the third phase of this social drama.

Redressive Mechanisms

On the Wednesday following the week when the card had been sent, the head set up a meeting for the union secretary, the NUT representative and Phil Barlow, the deputy. However, the latter could not attend the meeting but it still went ahead. Goddard made a set of notes on the meeting that were subsequently agreed by the NUT in which the union secretary commented on the poor relationship between management and the union representative at McGregor. Indeed, Goddard's note contains a verbatim quotation where David Ball comments on Phil Barlow's action by saying:

He was 'staggered that anyone feels it helpful to approach the governors, let alone seek a legal opinion on such an issue. I cannot believe it was a sensible or sensitive approach to a problem . . . I am shocked and this could be interpreted as intimidation to NUT rep . . . I am anxious to give SJ my full support . . . It is symptomatic of a management attitude . . . I know of few NUT reps who would not have hit the roof . . . It is a major breach of the normal procedures . . . Do you not agree?'

However, the notes indicate that the head did not agree, nor did he comment on or reply to any of the observations made by the union secretary.

It seemed that no solution was possible at this stage. However, the head was seeking advice from the LEA officers at this stage as he told me that he considered a written response was required to Mrs Jackson's letter. His letter went through five drafts with him writing it, an officer correcting it and two further drafts before a final draft was produced with a senior officer. The file records the following letter being sent:

Dear Mrs Jackson,   26 November 1985

Following the discussion I had with you and Mr Ball (the union secretary) last week I undertook to consult the LEA on certain issues. It has now been suggested to me that I seek formal answers on certain points, that I ask two further questions and put a suggestion to you.

Firstly, you use the phrase 'your deputy'. Technically we have three deputies. Will you please confirm the identity of 'your deputy'. Secondly, I need in writing the evidence you put to me verbally of the 'incompetence and intransigence' you mention in your letter.

Next, I do ask whether you think this manner of letter is helpful. In view of the implications it makes and the impact it could have on a colleague's professional reputation, you should have brought it to my attention without sending a copy to that colleague.

Finally, it has been suggested to me that I give you a formal opportunity to withdraw your criticisms without reservation. I would welcome your replies and observations to these points by Monday 2 December.

I am sending a copy of this letter to Mr Ball. In the meantime though, having prepared answers to the outstanding questions I am advised I should wait for your reply before I attempt to reply to you and Mr Ball.

Yours sincerely,

G. Goddard
Headteacher

The letter was described to me by Goddard as 'a very short and to my mind a very curt and abrupt letter'. However, he explained:

Since at this time I hadn't known whether I was on my head or my heels, I needed the Authority. I needed to be sure the Authority was going to stay in its corner with me. I wasn't enrapt and so I took almost word for word from what the representative of the Authority put down.

Certainly this was the case as a copy of the letter in another style of writing was lodged on the teacher action file in the school. The result was a meeting between Sally Jackson and Geoff Goddard that they recalled in slightly different terms. Sally was surprised to receive this letter having previously been told by Goddard that her letter was not at issue. She remarked:

It seemed nonsense to me. I went straight back to Geoff Goddard and said, what do you mean by this? I have substantiated my grievance formally in your presence and in the presence of the union secretary, and I asked him if he remembered what I'd said, if it was true that he'd taken it down to which he answered 'yes', and my final question was 'Am I on solid ground with Geoff Goddard?' and I didn't get an answer to that so I left.

Meanwhile, Geoff Goddard explained that his letter resulted in a chain of events that culminated in a meeting at the office. He commented that the letter brought about:

a blistering six minute interview in which Mrs Jackson came in and told me exactly what she thought of me and using a tactic that over the years I've found fruitful at preventing having to apologise and so forth I simply said 'I know what you say, I know what you say'. 'Is that all you can say?' she said. The fact that it's a very infuriating tactic hasn't escaped me. It's done . . . it's done more to protect me than to irritate the person I'm talking to, it means that I have no answers that I'm prepared to articulate at the present time. I needed time to think after that bust up and then there was two sessions with David Ball that withdrew the offending letter, without any apology of it. That caused another bust up with Phil Barlow and Gill Davies and then there was the famous Wednesday morning session in the office.

During this period Goddard had worked both formally and informally to resolve the dispute. He had talked informally with the NUT representative and with the NAS/UWT rep. He had also sent the formal letter which publicly he claimed to dislike but which he had sent to his deputies with a note in which he stated that:

This approach puts pressure on SJ (the NUT rep) and DB (the union secretary) instead of putting us up front.

It also continued by saying that the officer claimed:

The most damaging thing to any member of staff is to acquire a reputation as quickly 'litigious'. We must be seen to come to this slowly with considerable reluctance and compelled only as a last resort.

In these terms, the attempt to gain a solution included a management strategy to ally with the deputies and to 'spoil' the union representative's identity before union members and colleagues.

The result as Goddard indicated was a letter from the union secretary withdrawing the initial letter. However, the union secretary also expressed surprise at the events that had occurred which he recorded as follows:

I am surprised at your decision to write to our representative concerning her letter of 15 November. I met you informally concerning her letter of 15 November and offered to withdraw the letter. I understand that following this conversation you met Sally the next day and stated that the letter was no longer central to the dispute. When I met you formally the next day with Sally, my impression that the letter was no longer relevant to the dispute was confirmed by the fact that you made little reference to it during the discussion.

The letter also commented on relationships in McGregor as David Ball remarked:

It is my view that relationships between the union and the management of the school have deteriorated further than in any other secondary school in the division.

Copies of this letter were sent to the church representative on the LEA and to an officer which in turn resulted in a further meeting. Meanwhile, Goddard summed up the impact this had upon his school in a note written on the day he received Ball's letter. The note provides a summary of the situation and is a personal statement placed on file in which Goddard records the pressures on himself and his management team in the following terms:

2 Pressures

There always are pressures but one seeks to balance these and to devise systems for coping with inequalities. During the last ten months the pressures have grown steadily until September. Through September and October the pace of increase was stepped up and the place of impact of that pressure narrowed until it concentrated itself on two of my deputies and one head of year at McGregor. I am told by my NAS/UWT rep 'There's nothing personal in this'. My NUT rep by the letter now withdrawn to me drove a wedge between my deputies and myself.

However, he also reflected on the 'cost' to the school when he commented:

3 A Caring School

Since McGregor began I/we have set out to create a caring institution. Until this summer this was still true but tragically the care that was the hallmark of McGregor is also under attack. Adults are putting themselves first. Children come a long way second. The glue that held us together is more brittle than it ever was. The spirit that infused us is dying and I am unsure whether it can be revived. McGregor is no longer the interesting, exciting loving place it was. It is a place of deliberately created conflict with wounds that will take months to heal and the scars of which will mark us all. They are not honourable scars. They say civil war is more damaging than general war. History teaches us that religious wars are more ferociously fought than wars of conquest. But for the damage they do to the inner man family battles outdo all other feuds in their ferociousness. And families are slow to forgive.

On this basis, it was evident to Goddard that a strategy was required to bring about reconciliation among staff. Indeed, this was also a view held by Sally Jackson who also followed a path of reconciliation with the deputy. It is to these reconciliation strategies that we now turn as the final phase of the social drama.

Reconciliation

In my first study of Bishop McGregor School (Burgess, 1983) I identified the strategies that Goddard had used to bring a crisis situation to a conclusion among his staff. In the second study in the 1980s I found that he relied on a similar approach as the mechanism for reintegration and reconciliation was put into operation before a weekend break — a strategy that in the past had helped to 'cool out' situations. In turn, he also used the Catholic character of the school to try and redefine the situation and to remind teachers of the norms and values to which they all subscribed.

However, the teachers' dispute had resulted in bitter conflicts that the head had identified. The result was that he took, what some teachers regarded as the extreme action of sending a photocopied letter that was individually signed to all staff. The letter began by outlining meetings that had been held to 'bring about discussion and reconciliation' between some 'parts of our staff' and went on to indicate that an agreement had been reached with the unions not to intensify industrial action before the Christmas holidays. It then continued to remind teachers of the central value system in the school when he stated:

> We are in a situation that not only divides us one from another because of our principles and our consciences. It also tears many if not all of us, apart because of the conflict between our love of (most of) our children and the way in which central government treats the profession. We, more clearly than anyone else, see the effects upon a growing number of youngsters of the actions we feel compelled to take. We watch almost with unbelief the lack of any sense of urgency on the part of our political masters to search for an acceptable settlement.
>
> We must not fail in the same way. We must recognize urgency for peace among us. We must recognise the still greater damage our failure to find peace will bring to all of us at McGregor. I wish I could write with clarity and precision about how exactly we are to move forward. The truth, my dear friends, is I do not know. We must begin with some visible signs of our desire for reconciliation. We can begin with cheerful greetings each day. We can help each other. We can talk to each other. We can accept that even when we disagree with what someone else is doing, they are doing it from conviction and not from malice. (I disagree with what you are saying but I will defend to the death your right to say it.) We can leave on one side any wounding words, in private and in public, which might hurt another.
>
> We must then move inwards to explore further the details of our disagreement and try gently and with clarity to understand each other. We must try and ease from our joint path anything that has been a stumbling block in the past. We must listen to each other. We must care for each other.
>
> But all this will be hollow unless each and everyone of us searches our souls to discover and strengthen our will to peace.
>
> We all recognize that this will place great demands upon all here at McGregor. It will need a huge willingness to try and understand each other more fully and if we are to be successful, it will call for a commitment to caring for each other that has been so powerful a characteristic of this staff through all our sixteen years.

Here, the symbol of the Catholic school as a caring school was brought to teachers' attention. In addition, he also continued by portraying himself as a head who cared for his staff and the situation in which they were placed, while at the same time explaining why he had taken no part in the action when he stated:

> A word or two about Geoff Goddard and the salary dispute. I understand the long growth of disappointment and almost despair amongst many teachers as they watch their standard of living fall. I have enormous sympathy especially with those on the lower scales as many find it more and more difficult to manage on what should be, but is not, a professional salary. I believe the unions represent the real anger of their members over the apparent contempt with which politicians and others speak of so many of us. I believe that the actions taken by the leaders of the unions have for many months sought to bring pressure to bear upon those who reach decisions about teachers' salaries.
>
> My own position as head of the school and in my last full year of teaching, is that I am asked not to take part in ballots and exempted from taking industrial action myself. I realize that this may seem to colleagues mealy-mouthed and timid. If such it be, I regret it, but I also am aware that under the law of England, the ultimate responsibility for the welfare of everyone on this site lies at my door. As head of the school I am genuinely mindful of the care I must take to walk this very delicate line between my responsibilities to the pupils and my responsibilities to all members of this staff.

Finally, the letter ended with a call for consensus, commitment to the values of the school and for prayer.

In contrast to previous crisis situations I had witnessed at McGregor, this attempt at reintegration did not succeed. Indeed, some senior staff considered it as an act of betrayal with the head attempting to align himself with the NUT. Indeed, there were accusations that he was supporting the union against the management team.

In these circumstances, Phil Barlow considered that he should also write a letter to the staff to explain his interpretation of the activities surrounding union action. He explained that the draft of his letter outlined the situation that had arisen and was critical of himself and the way in which he had handled the events in the autumn term. However, on showing the letter to the NAS/UWT representative he was persuaded not to send it. Meanwhile, he discussed his feelings about the situation with two teachers who had come to tell him what was being said in NUT meetings as he explained:

> They (the two teachers) were very concerned at the way the NUT meetings had been going. Some of the things that had been said are not right. Not Christian to be saying some of the things that were being said and they wanted to see the other side of the story so I just produced it all for them.

Further discussions also took place between Phil Barlow and a teacher governor. Phil had approached the teacher governor to give his account of the situation and in turn this teacher approached Sally Jackson. She explained:

Phil Barlow approached our teacher governor on Monday and said to him that he was still very upset about my original note and he said that it hadn't been withdrawn. Then the teacher governor came to me and asked me to make a further formal withdrawal which I said I wouldn't do and showed him that letter (from the union) and I told him that Phil had a copy of that letter. The following day I came in Wednesday and Phil was coming into school at the same time, and although he does speak to me now, I looked at him closely because we were within a few feet of one another, and he looked absolutely white, he looked deathly white and all screwed up, if you'll pardon the expression, and I saw the teacher governor in the day and told that person what my feelings were. I was then told 'Phil is absolutely devastated by the idea that somebody has charged him with incompetence and he still feels that this cloud is hanging over his head'. That was Wednesday and I said 'Well, I have tried to meet with him and I'm still trying and the headmaster has promised to try to bring us together and he's promised to do that before Christmas and I don't feel like making any move. I don't feel inclined to make any move because quite frankly the union is in a very strong position and I don't see why we should give away all that we fought for, at all'. However, Wednesday went on and I began to feel more and more that Phil was in a difficult position, an impossible position. He apparently admitted to the teacher governor that he had been intransigent and deliberately awkward but it was the word 'incompetent' which he was worried about. Why he was worried I don't know, because it was rashness on my part, it was an ill-judged word and I did withdraw it. However, I went to Geoff Goddard on Thursday and I asked him was it true that Phil still felt this charge was being held against him and after a bit of waffle he said 'yes, it is' so I said 'Can you get him down here now?' and he picked up the phone and asked Phil to come down and told him I was there, so Phil came down and I just said to him that I understood he was still not clear about whether my letter was on record, and I assured him that it had been fully withdrawn in the union secretary's letter and it was no longer on record on our part. It was no longer an issue on our part and then I assured him personally that I withdrew it and that I withdrew the words, both of the words I had used and I also told him that I was sorry for any offence that it had caused him and he thanked me for that and I shook his hand and said, 'Can we go forward from there?' and he said 'Yes, thank you very much' and I left thinking we left it at that, and he apparently was quite happy with that. He was prepared to accept that and let it go and I received a letter later in the day from Geoff Goddard thanking me for doing that and saying he felt personally touched by the gesture so I think the union lost nothing by it.

By this time, it was one day before the end of term. From the beginning of the crisis on 15 November to 19 December many events had occurred that revealed some of the fundamental processes at work among staff at Bishop McGregor School. My involvement in the school during this period allowed me to collect data that could contribute to the analysis of a social drama — a critical incident that assisted my understanding of the way the head operated and the ways in which the school worked.

Concluding Discussion

This account of a critical incident that occurred during the teachers' dispute highlights some of the formal and informal processes that took place between the head, the Church and the LEA, the head and his deputies, the head and a union representative and the head and his staff. In this section of the chapter I turn briefly to each of these sets of relations in turn to indicate the way in which this analysis could be linked so as to advance my understanding of aspects of school organization:

(a) *the Head, the church, the LEA*: As Hall, Mackay and Morgan (1986) have indicated, the teachers' dispute highlights the relationship between the headteacher and his/her employers. In this case, the head involved church representatives in critical meetings with the union and the LEA and in turn used the local authority for legal advice in handling the situation. However, even in this church school it was the LEA that had defined the terms in which the union and the union representative should be handled.

(b) *the head and his deputies*: Goddard had up to the point of this incident organized the management end of union action with two of his deputies. However, with this incident, questions were raised about:

   (i)   who controlled whom? For some staff this event illustrated the deputies had been in control and it was Goddard's intention to regain control by publicly using the church, the LEA and a teacher union to bring one of the deputies back under his control;

   (ii) loyalties. For the head, there was the question of loyalty to his pupils, their parents, his staff or his deputies. While for the deputies questions were raised about the head's loyalty to them or to his union.

(c) *the head and the union representative*: Goddard had been an active member of the NUT branch in the Authority before union action become widespread in the mid-1980s. Given his position, and his loyalty (that he saw was first and foremost to his pupils), it meant that he attempted to manage the school which resulted in continual challenge from the unions and the union representative. However, his actions raise questions about the public and private faces of management.

Publicly he was attempting to bring about consensus with the unions but privately he was also involved in discussion and debate with the LEA which would attempt to isolate the union representative as a 'quickly litigious' individual.

Here, the ambiguities of headship in the mid-1980s were clearly demonstrated to the extent that the head became physically ill during the course of this incident and considered advancing his retirement by one year from that which he had planned.

(d) *the head and the staff*: headteachers are isolated from their staff (Weindling and Earley, 1987) and Goddard was no exception when it came to the teachers' dispute. However, this was a marked change from earlier years. It was during this time that Goddard began to appreciate the way in which the teachers' dispute was dividing staff and creating conflict. Here, attempts were made to create consensus and to remind teachers of the dominant value system of the caring Catholic community supported through prayer, salvation and reconciliation (cf. Lesko, 1988).

In short, this incident not only highlighted some of the processes associated with the different groups and individuals with whom the head worked but also illustrated the stresses, ambiguities and dilemmas of headship in the mid-1980s.

Acknowledgment

I am grateful to the teachers and to the headteacher at Bishop McGregor School for granting me access to this material and discussing it with me. I am also grateful to the Nuffield Foundation and the University of Warwick Research and Innovations Fund Committee who provided grants to support my fieldwork. An earlier version of this chapter was read to the 'Histories and Ethnographies of Teachers' Work' conference held at St Hilda's College Oxford.

Note

1 For similar accounts on headteachers and management teams during the teachers' dispute see Hall, Mackay and Morgan (1986).

References

BALL, S.J. (1987) *The Micro-Politics of the School*, London, Methuen.

BURGESS, R.G. (1983) *Experiencing Comprehensive Education: A Study of Bishop McGregor School*, London, Methuen.

BURGESS, R.G. (1984) 'Headship: Freedom or constraint?' in BALL, S.J. (Ed.) *Comprehensive Schooling: A Reader*, Lewes, Falmer Press, pp. 201–26.

BURGESS, R.G. (1987) 'Studying and restudying Bishop McGregor School' in WALFORD, G. (Ed.) *Doing Sociology of Education*, Lewes, Falmer Press, pp. 67–94.

HALL, V., MACKAY, H. and MORGAN, C. (1986) *Headteachers at Work*, Milton Keynes, Open University Press.

HMI (1977) *Ten Good Schools*, London, HMSO.

LESKO, N. (1988) *Symbolising Society: Stories, Rites and Structure in a Catholic High School*, Lewes, Falmer Press.

TURNER, V.W. (1957) *Schism and Continuity in an African Society: A Study of Ndembu Village Life*, Manchester, Manchester University Press.

TURNER, V.W. (1971) 'An anthropological approach to the Icelandic saga' in BEIDELMAN, T.O. (Ed.) *The Translation of Culture: Essays to E.E. Evans Pritchard*, London, Tavistock, pp. 349–74.

WEINDLING, D. and EARLEY, P. (1987) *Secondary Headship: The First Years*, Windsor, NFER-Nelson.

Chapter 3

The Concept of Quality in Action Research: Giving Practitioners a Voice in Educational Research

Herbert Altrichter

Action research is 'the study of a social situation with a view to improving the quality of action within it' (Elliott 1981, p. 1). Action research is not a method of data analysis. Neither it is characterized by specific methods, but rather by integrating various methods in a methodologically consistent strategy. This strategy aims to help those people directly concerned with a situation under research (and that is in educational settings, teachers and students in the first place) to articulate, validate and develop their views and to design action in order to improve the situation they live in.

Thus, a chapter on action research might seem misplaced in the context of a book on data analysis if it is not taken as a challenge to consider the relationship of strategic and tactical questions within a broader research endeavour which always comprises a series of important decisions *before* and *after* data collection and analysis that, eventually, will shape the research results and their relevance for the social field under investigation. Strategic consideration should prevent us from becoming too deeply immersed in the technical aspects of specific research tactics (as profound tactical deliberation should help us to reconsider how to translate more general long-term ideas into specific actions which can be considered concrete interactional expressions of these more general ideas).

Consequently, I want to concentrate on a truely strategic issue for the development of action research which hopefully will pose relevant questions for other qualitative research strategies (and analysis tactics employed within their context): *'What are the quality features of action research and how can they be communicated in an understandable way to practitioners?'* During the last years we have been concerned with answering this question which is, at the same time, a theoretical attempt of explicating a possible methodological foundation and a practical necessity for a research approach which is currently thriving both in Austria and in English speaking countries. To begin with I want to sketch briefly the theoretical basis of our quality criteria. These criteria are presented in the following section. Finally, fields of application and critical issues of the approach are discussed.

The Theoretical Background

What Kind of Methodology are We Aiming for?

Action researchers, like many other 'alternative' researchers, usually feel that the traditional-empirical, vaguely falsificationist methodology is not adequate to their work. Very often they react by claiming that their research is profoundly different to traditional-empirical research and by formulating 'alternative' methodological criteria. However, empirical research *practice* is in many respects quite different from a number of popular items of the canon of traditional-empirical research *methodology*, too. On the other hand, many of the everyday activities and decisions within an action research project are not so profoundly different from those in projects based on the traditional-empirical rationale. Thus, my hunch is that it might be sensible to critically examine the well-foundedness and appropriateness of some claims of traditional-empirical methodology before devising an alternative methodology for action research and, thereby implicitly accepting, the rightfulness of traditional-empirical methodological criteria at least for specific areas of research.

New developments in substantive natural scientific research as well as in philosophy of science may be interpreted as paving the way for a reincorporation of alternative research traditions' into a 'unified methodology' (which, this time, is not a tool of hegemony of traditional mainstream research but is possible in a way which does justice to 'alternative research approaches').[1] I agree with Weingart (1984) that what we see nowadays is a profound crisis of a philosphy of science conceived as a 'science of order', as a 'board of censors of research', as an 'institutionalized ideal method'. The way out, I would suggest, cannot be found by quickly devising some new norms and rules to replace the obsolete ones. Rather, we have to reframe our thinking what a methodology is for and what it should look like. Ironically, Feyerabend (1976) who is usually considered as a funny, but destructive guy seems to provide the most inspiring ideas for this task. Drawing on Feyerabendian thought, I want to sketch the main features of such an 'alternative methodology'.

Avoiding general rules for research
The methodology does not include a limited set of general rules by the help of which we can distinguish scientific from unscientific research, no firm foundation by the appeal to which we can secure the decency of our research even from the outset. The main intention of a methodology is, on the contrary, defensive. It attempts to keep the space of research and insight open since it is aware of the fact that useful procedures and methods may be developed we cannot foresee, and that the procedures which we know to be problematic on a general level may be of limited worth in specific settings.

Inserting research experience into an inventory of rules
Feyerabend (1977) is not against all rules nor is his cardinal rule 'anything goes': 'I neither want to replace rules, nor do I want to show their worthlessness; I rather want to increase the inventory of rules, and I want to suggest a different use for all of them' (p. 368). He denies the superiority of a specific methodological procedure in demonstrating the scientificality of research but suggests collecting

different procedures in an inventory of rules. These rules may prepare a researcher for his/her task since they provide historical examples of dealing with research problems and illustrate the complexity of the endeavour. However, they must be justified, criticized and developed within any project by the research anew.

Research into one's research

Invention, scrutiny and application of methodological rules and criteria is a right and duty of the researcher working within a concrete project rather than a pre-rogative of specialized methodologists. Research is not the application of pre-specified methods, but it is methodical in itself, is essentially a reflexive endeavour. Its methodical structure, the coherence of its elements, however, have to be argued within every specific research enterprise. These arguments provide a methodological justification for a hint sometimes given by action researchers: 'The methods we choose are (. . .) there to be tested as much as the substantive hypotheses' (Walker, 1985, p. 47). Doing research into research methods is a methodological necessity once the methods are not considered as fixed givens any more. Researchers must scrutinize their 'methods-in-use' to learn more about the potential and pitfalls of these methods in specific contexts and to prevent them from becoming petrified.

Situating the research in a democratic context

Who is to choose between alternative research programmes in the absence of firm methodological rules? Feyerabend's solution is as follows: give the power to select research programmes to lay committees of tax-payers concerned with the respective research. His concept of 'democratic research' is clearly moulded on the liberal democratic image of elective participation. I personally feel more comfortable with the model of democratic research which action research offers: Research aims to involve all those who are concerned with a practical problem in a collaborative effort to change situations according to shared aspirations.

For the practice of research and research facilitation it would be helpful to develop such an inventory of 'rules of thumb'. One way to arrive at such an inventory is to stimulate action researchers to monitor, collect and reflect their research experiences and insert them into such an inventory which is tested and developed within further research (we have experimented with such a practitioner-developed 'methodological inventory'; c.f., Altrichter 1990a, p. 230). On the other hand, it might be sensible to search for potential elements of such inventories in other fields. As a means of *'showing contrasting realities'* they might stimulate further development of practitioner-based rules. In a recent paper (Altrichter and Posch, 1989) we analyzed the 'grounded theory' approach which is attractive to many action researchers, however, we argued that it is incompatible with some important tenets of action research. With reference to Donald Schön's analysis of professional practice we concluded:

> . . . it is not necessary for teacher research to rely on imported methodological criteria from other fields of research, but it should concentrate on further developing reflective features of professional action which in the context of practice itself are responsible for enhancing the quality of action, . . . Quality in both professional research and professional teaching is achieved by tightly interlinking theoretical and empirical, inductive

and deductive aspects in the way Schön characterized as 'reflection-in-action' . . . Thus, we think: What's good for practice is good for research. (*ibid*, p. 29)

There are, indeed, at least two reasons which make theories of professional action and knowledge a promising source for the development of such a 'defensive methodology' of action research:

— Firstly, research activities and instruments are not profoundly different from but rather are derived from *everyday competencies* by which practitioners observe, interpret, make sense of and develop their practice. Action research attempts to give assistance to developing, differentiating, and systematizing these professional competencies rather than to replacing them. To know more about the specific features of everyday reflection might help to explicate and formulate 'rules of thumb' conducive to practitioner research.
— Secondly, since *professional practitioners* are seen as main agents of action research it might be helpful to clarify the specific features of professionality and their relationship to clients and the wider society.

What are the Features of Reflective Professional Action?

The traditional conception of professional practice is: 'professional activity consists in instrumental problem solving made rigorous by the application of scientific theory and technique' (Schön, 1983, p. 21). This view has been dubbed the *model of technical rationality*; it presupposes undoubted aims and stable institutional contexts. These demands may be met by simple and repetitive tasks; the majority and the most relevant situations of professional practice are on the contrary complex, uncertain, ambiguous and unique. Because of the complex situations (and not because of the repetitive ones) professional expertise is called for. Within situations of such a kind, professional action cannot be conceived as instrumental problem-solving, because the 'problem' is usually not unambiguously given. It has to be construed through the non-technical process of 'problem-definition' which creates the preconditions for the operation of technical expertise (*ibid*, pp. 39ff).

Donald Schön has analyzed case studies about professional work from different professions to formulate a more realistic *epistemology of practice*. To act constructively in complex situations typical of professional practice, practitioners must have the *ability to develop 'local knowledge'*, *the ability of reflection-in-action*.[2] Rather than applying general results other researchers have arrived at they themselves become 'researchers in the practice context' (*ibid*, p. 68).

Schön describes the concrete course of such reflection-in-action through the vivid metaphor *reflective conversation with the situation*: Reflection-in-action starts with the *experience of a discrepancy* between one's implicit or explicit expectations and reality; i.e., the problem cannot be solved by routine. It follows an attempt to define the problem by *naming and framing* drawing on a repertoire of analogies, examples, images, interpretations, and action strategies. The implementation of this initial problem definition is, at the same time, a *frame experiment* testing the usefulness of the problem definition and the action strategies. In a frame experiment the hypothetical problem definition is resolutely laid over the situation. At the same time, the practitioner must be open to the unintended consequences of his/her experiment. Thus, the competent practitioner must hold a kind of *double vision* while experimenting: 'At the same time that the inquirer tries to shape the situation to his frame, he must hold himself open to the situation's back talk' (*ibid*, p. 164). Since: 'Through the unintended effects of action, the situation talks back' (*ibid*, p. 135).

Schön's analysis is compatible with the related research concerning 'problem solving in complex situation'. Dörner (1982) summarizes his findings by sketching two main competencies individuals need for autonomous orientation in complex environments:

— the competency for 'self-reflexive transformation of one's own thinking' (through reflection on one's own problem solving actions, different strategies are compared and scrutinized for common elements; misleading stereotypes are eliminated).
— the 'competency to "import" knowledge from an area into a partly unknown area through inferences by analogy and through subsequent correction and extension of the thereby generated hypotheses' (*ibid*, p. 147).[3]

On the Relationship of Epistemological, Ethical and Pragmatical Criteria

To sum up the argument so far: Action researchers can enhance the quality of their research by *expressing reflective features of professional action (which in the context of practice itself are responsible for enhancing the quality of action) in their research and further developing it*. Quality in both professional research and professional teaching can be achieved by tightly interlinking reflection and action in the way Schön characterized as 'reflection-in-action'. The argument has been *epistemological* so far. However, there are two additional, equally important sources for quality in action research: ethics and pragmatics of research.

Research is an intervention in social situations; many research instruments are 'reactive' (i.e., they stimulate persons being researched to do things they would not have done otherwise); the research situation is a learning situation itself. Thus, teacher researchers take care that their research activities comply with *ethical quality criteria*. There are two interpretations to ethical quality:

— Action research should be *compatible with the educational aims of the situation under research*. It should be even *conducive to these aims* not only in the long term but also as much as possible through immediate research activities.
For example, data collection by performance tests based on individualistic competition will be incompatible with a classroom which aims to develop students' cooperation.
— Action research holds that profound and lasting development of practice will only occur in collaboration with other persons concerned with the situation under research and not against their will. Thus, the research strategy must *build on democratic and cooperative human relationships and contribute to their further development*.

Action researchers attempt to comply with these criteria by binding their work to *ethical codes* which have to be negotiated at the beginning of collaborative work and frequently renegotiated during its course as their meaning has to be clarified on occasion of concrete cases. The ethical principles 'negotiation' (see principle 1 below), 'control' (see 5) and 'confidentiality' (see 6) are of central importance within these codes.

Some researchers consider ethical considerations as nowadays highly necessary, others as unjustifiable hinderance of progress. Most of them, however, would view them as quite distinct from the strive for insight, i.e., from the epistemological side of research. It must be emphasized that the argument here proposed is different. At least for a type of research like action research which aims to integrate understanding and change in a consistent strategy *ethical considerations are also highly practical and conducive for the progress of insight.*

Let me explain this claim: Argyris and Schön (1974, pp. 68 and 87) have distinguished two typical 'behavioural worlds': Model I is characterized by an attitude of 'mystery and mastery'. Actors try to remain in control of the situation and withhold information from their partners 'as a precaution'. In model II, on the contrary, action and problem solving is seen as a shared task of all persons concerned which only can be achieved if all persons can influence the development of the situation and have access to all relevant information. Research itself is based on the accessibility of information and cannot flourish if important data are withheld or faked. If researchers themselves are playing the game of 'mystery and mastery' they will further a similar attitude of their partners and thereby undermine the very basis of research. In this sense, ethical claims are at the same time epistemological claims aiming to ensure that the epistemological basis for insight and understanding is not destroyed.

Pragmatic quality criteria, on the other hand, check whether the research strategy and the specific research instruments are pragmatically compatible with classrooms and teachers' work conditions (in the sense that they are usable for teachers without too much additional training, that they fit to the economics of time and resources). At the first view, these pragmatic criteria look rather misplaced in an epistemological and ethical discussion. At the second view, one becomes aware that pragmatical, epistemological and ethical criteria stand in specific and sometimes tensionful relationships within each research activity. For example, a data analysis technique which is pragmatically problematic because of its extensive demands on teachers' time is also epistemologically problematic: opportunities for insight, cross-checking and critique cannot be realized because of sheer lack of time. Additionally, it is ethically problematic: if other persons concerned cannot understand its results without extensive effort there will be a tendency to avoid negotiation.

The Quality Criteria

In the following sections I want to propose a formulation of the main quality features of action research derived from the concept of reflective professional practice. They are phrased in such a way that there are always pragmatical, epistemological and ethical aspects to them which sometimes might be in a tensionful relationship which has to be clarified within the concrete research activity. They are presented as potential parts of an 'inventory of rules' in need of being tested, developed and modified through professional reflection and research practice.

Let me quote a piece of data which is virtually 'archetypical' for the action research tradition:

The Humanities Curriculum Project (HCP) aimed to expose 14–16 year-old students to controversial topics from the humanities and social sciences (for example, war and peace, race relationships etc.). The basic teaching strategy of the project included two central ideas:

— the teacher was to be relieved from the task of providing information but rather was to concentrate on facilitating the students' discussions as a 'neutral chairman';
— short provocative pieces of information (excerpts from literature, newspapers, graphs etc.) were provided as hand-outs meant to illustrate different points of view and to stimulate students' discussions.

One day John Elliott, who was a member of the HCP-team, was asked to call on a school because of problems with the written material. Students would read the hand-outs but no discussion would start. The teacher assumed that students did not understand the information because it was too difficult. To alleviate this problem the teacher started to abandon the HCP-teaching strategy and to explain the content of the hand-out by mini-lectures.

When Elliott heard this story he suggested collecting some more information in order to improve the understanding of the situation. The teacher selected six students who had the following conversation with Elliott:

Interviewer (I): Well, what do you think of this new approach?
Student (S): I don't like it!
I: What don't you like about it?
S: We don't like these materials, these documents, we don't like them.
I: So, what don't you like about them? Are they too difficult to read?
S: Oh, no. — Oh, no, we can read them.
I: Can you all?
S: Of course, we can read them.
I: So, what's the problem?
S: The problem is we disagree with what they say.
I: Oh, good. You actually disagree with what they say?
S: Yes!
I: Well, then you can express your disagreement in the class.
S: Oh, no, you can't!
I: Why not?
S: The teacher would not like it.
I: Well, why wouldn't the teacher like it?
S: Because the teacher agrees with what these documents say.
I: How do you know that the teacher agrees with what these documents say?
S: (looking very surprised at the interviewer because of this stupid question): The teacher wouldn't give you these documents in the first place if he didn't agree with them, would he? (c.f., Elliott, 1986)

I am using the interview to discuss and exemplify the value of these quality criteria and also to indicate by what strategies action research aims to enhance quality of practitioner research.

1 Action Research is Characterized by Confronting Data from Different Perspectives

What can we learn from this little story? Firstly, that we as practitioners are theorizing anyway in problematic everyday situations. Confronted with a problem (with a discrepancy between expectations and reality), the teacher reacts with an 'explanation', with a 'theory': *The teaching strategy does not work because the hand-out is too difficult.* Secondly, this little story illustrates that practical theories which do not take into account the interpretations of all relevant social actors concerned in the situation are in danger of yielding misleading explanations which, in turn, will result in flawed 'problem-solving' actions. For example, the teacher's strategy *to give mini-lectures to explain the hand-outs* wrongly assumed that the students' perception of the situation was identical with his teaching intentions. Putting this action strategy into practice would most likely have reinforced the students' perception that *the teacher agrees with the hand-outs.* That would not only have failed to enhance student discussion but also made it more and more difficult for all parties to understand the situation.

Generally, action research acknowledges that social reality is constituted by the contributions of different actors who all hold — sometimes differing — interpretations about what is happening. When a practitioner formulates a practical theory about an issue of his/her practice it is — implicitly or explicitly — also a 'theory about theories', (i.e., a theory about the different actors' views about the same social situation).

Practically, action researchers tackle this problem by the following strategies:

* *Collect also other views than your own*: Interviewing the students in our example obviously makes the 'practical theory' more comprehensive and improves the chance that some reasonable action strategy might be derived from it. The views of all relevant parties directly concerned by the situation under research must be represented in the 'practical theory'. Who is actually 'directly concerned with the situation under research' is sometimes only found out through research itself.

* *Confront different perspectives on the same situation and use 'discrepancies' as a starting point for the development of your practical theory*: For example, the discrepancy between the students' and the teacher's perception asks for the development of some action to reconcile them — otherwise it would be impossible to successfully teach the HCP-strategy. Action research's emphasis on the confrontation of different perspectives is expressed, for example, in the procedure of *triangulation* which has come to be taken as typical for this type of research (Elliott, 1976, p. 22; for a practical example see Somekh, 1983). To confront different perspectives might also be interpreted as a practical way of helping researchers to uphold Schön's 'double vision'. Furthermore, it mirrors validation strategies in traditional-empirical research which are all based on the idea of 'laying a second research process on top of the original one and trying to reduce discrepancies' (c.f., Altrichter 1990b, p. 107).

* *Develop your research into a 'collaborative project':* If social reality is constituted by the contributions of different actors then constructive development of social reality must not by-pass (however benevolently) the participants' reasoning but must eventually be a 'collaborative task'. The confrontation of different epistemological perspectives and their integration with respect to specific issues is so important for action researchers that such a principle is included in the *ethical codes* which govern the conduct of action research. Action research is considered 'ethical' if research design, interpretation and practical development produced by it have been *negotiated* with all parties directly concerned with the situation under research. Even when we concede that teachers as professionals will have a leading role in initiating action research, involvement of students and other persons concerned will remain a long term aspiration as will making the project eventually a 'collaborative' one.

2 Action Research is Characterized by Closely and Iteratively Linking Reflection and Action

Unlike many other research and development approaches, action research does not want to replace the practitioners' thinking by expert knowledge but rather aims to build on it and to support it. Compare for example, the story from the HCP: 'outsiders' do not come in to tell the practitioner 'how it is done' (because they are simply not able to do so due to the lack of 'local knowledge' necessary to deal intelligently with fairly complex situations of practice). Rather they support the practitioners in their reflection on their own situation, for example, by helping them to get access to additional aspects of the situation (as the students' perception were). The students' perspectives were not any 'new information' brought to the situation from outside; rather they were — in principle — available *in* the situation (but access was difficult or too little attention was being paid).

A characteristic feature of traditional empirical research is its personal and institutional separation of reflection and action. The experimental setting is designed in the institutions of scholarly research; it has to be implemented by practitioners in the institutions of practice whose 'fidelity' is supervised by some emissaries of the world of social science. Data are collected by professional researchers and brought back to the research institutions to be analyzed.

Compared to everyday deliberation, the practice being researched and the reflection on it are strangely fragmented. This fragmentation brings some advantages:

— leaving the stage of practice dispenses from the pressures of subsequent action, and, thus, wins some time for analysis;
— the separation of the roles of acting and reflecting brings some detachment from the motivation and loyalities in the action system for the 'reflection specialists' which expands their room for manoeuvre.

However, those advantages do not come without potential disadvantages:

— leaving the stage of practice does not only dispense from the pressures of subsequent action, but also from the opportunity to have the results of reflection continuously tested: The practitioner is forced to act on the basis of his/her practical reflections and will feel their shortcomings as action problems;

— the separation of the roles of acting and reflecting may detach researchers from the motives and loyalities of the practice system, however, it does not detach them from all motives and loyalities. Rather, reflection specialists are governed by their own loyalities to the system of institutionalized research. Thus, there is some danger that 'science goes its own ways', the results of which sometimes seem to be very far off the needs of everyday practice. The necessities of professional action can provide some rationale which helps to focus one's research and from which to critique its results.

Action research opts against this methodological separation. If follows that it has to *build its strategy consistently on the advantages of the integration of action and reflection.* Practically, that means:

* *Closely interlink action and reflection*: Try to express the 'circle of action and reflection' (c.f., figure 3.1) in your research design. Looking back on one's practice one tries to develop an explanation for what had happened, that is a 'practical theory' (in our example *students don't discuss because the handouts are too difficult;* or later: *students don't discuss because they think the handouts reflect the teacher's opinion and they don't want to challenge the teacher*). From any practical theory one can also 'look forward' and develop ideas for subsequent action (for example, *teach information via mini-lectures;* or later: *work towards changing students' perception of the teaching strategy*).

Figure 3.1: *The 'circle of action and reflection'*

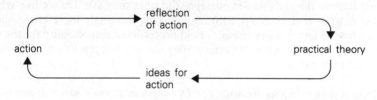

* *Emphasize 'iterativity' of research*: The circle of action and reflection does not stop with having developed 'new ideas for action'. Practitioners are under pressure to act and, thus, will have to put these ideas into practice. And they will directly experience the results of their action (which are — indirectly — also the results of their reflection, of their practical theory): This should be a good reason for continued reflection which will lead to further development of the 'practical theory'. Precisely the fact that the practitioners' reflection is rooted in their everyday practice allows them to put a practical theory to a series of tests, and to develop and refine it in several 'cycles of action research'. This characteristic repetition and progression of action and reflection in several cycles of research which we dub 'iterativity' is the main source of 'rigour' in action research.

3   Action Research Incorporates Reflection and Development of Educational Values

The HCP-teacher felt that his teaching strategy was not efficient. He tried to develop his 'practical theory' of the situation in a way that allowed him to derive a more *efficient* teaching strategy. However, this is only half of the job for a reflective practitioner. Even if he had been successful with his new teaching strategy he would have had to ask himself: What happened to my original *educational intentions* (which made me adopt the HCP-strategy)? Which educational values do I promote with my new teaching strategy? Am I happy with these values?

Action research holds that a teaching strategy is an attempt to realize an educational idea in a concrete interactional form. As educational ideas always incorporate educational values, it does not make sense to separate instrumental questions ('how can I promote learning?') from intentional ones ('what kind of learning am I promoting thereby?'). Thus, by researching an issue of our practice we *both* reflect on the effectiveness and the educational value of the teaching strategies employed.

4   Action Research is Characterized by Holistic, Inclusive Reflection

Unlike many experimental researchers, reflective practitioners cannot content themselves with checking whether their actions were instrumental in achieving the objectives they were aware of from the start. Rather, they also have to examine whether unexpected side-effects result from the action strategy or not. For example, if the HCP-teacher had gone ahead with giving mini-lectures, unwanted student perceptions could have been reinforced as an unintended side-effect: *the teacher is the one in possession of the truth which is not to be disputed.* This side-effect obviously runs counter to the intended main effect of the HCP-teaching strategy.

Reflective practitioners do not evaluate their practical experiments by asking 'Did we achieve the ends we set ourselves?'; rather they ask 'Do we like what we got?', as Argyris *et al.* (1985, p. 218) argued. This seemingly more vague question accounts for the fact that practitioners hold professional responsiblity for the whole situation and cannot ignore side-effects they did not happen to anticipate in their theoretical expectations.

5   Action Research Implies Research and Development of one's own Self-concept and Competency

In our HCP-story, the teacher finds out that he had misjudged the situation. Maybe, his new practical theory (*students understand the hand-outs but they don't want to dispute them*) calls for teaching strategies which he does not readily have available in his routine repertoire.

Unlike traditional researchers, action researchers do not research other persons' practice but their own. It follows that, by investigating a situation they themselves are deeply implicated in, they also scrutinize their own contribution to this situation and, consequently, their own competency and self-concept. This is what gives action research rigour and seriousness: Action researchers also research and develop themselves and they have to live with the effects of their theories and experiments. This is one reason for the fact that some action researchers undergo phases of anxiety, uneasiness and feelings of being 'deskilled' (c.f., Elliott, 1981, p. 23).

Practically, action research aims to counter these feelings by the following strategies:

* *Peer collaboration and consultation by 'critical friends'*: Action research projects or courses try to establish a supportive climate through 'group support' and 'facilitation through tutors/external consultants'. In group discussion researchers can explore if their concerns are shared by their peers and sometimes detect that what seemed to be personal inadequacies are widely shared problems. Sometimes 'external consultants' are called in as 'critical friends' who are supposed to give both sympathetic and constructively critical feedback to the practitioner's actions and reflections.

* *'Control of research' by the persons directly affected by the situation under research*: This ethical principle aims to ensure that action research is not 'highjacked' by external persons. Stenhouse (1985, p. 57) argued that responsibility for and control of the course of practice-oriented research should rest with those persons who are directly concerned with it and who have to live with its effects in their daily practice. The principle of 'control' commits external consultants (who often have more experience in research and are, therefore, quicker in offering research designs and theoretical explanations) to subject their work to the deliberations of those people directly concerned with the situation under research.

* *Start small and develop your research gradually*: One of the clever catchwords of the environmental movement is 'think globally, act locally' and it should also form part of every sound action research strategy. It is sensible to select a relevant, relatively feasible issue out of the endless sea of all the things which ought to be done. It is reasonable to start small; to 'think big' (in the sense of being aware of more complex connections and repercussions of one's selected issue) will help to gradually develop one's research.

This also holds true for the research methods employed: Experience shows (c.f., Elliott, 1978) that *peer* feedback is more threatening than *student* feedback which, in turn, is more threatening than feedback given by an *external person* without any anchoring in the hierarchy of the school system. It is pragmatically and epistemologically sensible to start with research designs which are potentially less threatening (for example, methods based on self-reflection, like diaries) and gradually introduce more challenging research settings (for example, student-interviews, peer discussion).

6 Action Research is Characterized by Inserting Individual Findings into a Critical Professional Discussion

Action and reflection gained a new quality in the initial HCP-example because the teacher was prepared to discuss his experience outside the walls of his classroom. Action research encourages practitioners to communicate not only with persons they directly interact with (c.f., section 1) but also to formulate their experiences and practical knowledge in order to share them with fellow professionals, clients and an interested public. There are three reasons for that:

* Participating in a professional discussion is a means of *validating and developing the insights of individuals*. By exposing my practice and my practical theories about it to a public discussion I have a better chance of becoming aware of shortcuts and flaws of my reflection. Chances are also better for linking my insights with other persons' findings and for getting feed-back and appreciation for my work.
* Sharing individual insights makes them accessible for other professionals and *broadens the knowledge base of the profession*.
* Finally, publication of accounts of reflective practice also expresses an important political idea: For the constructive development of the educational system it is necessary both

  — that *educational professionals get more say in the discussion about future developments of the educational system* (a precondition for that is that they increasingly make their views known and provide understandable and well-founded arguments and examples from their practice); and
  — that *educational professionals are responsive to the public* and are in the position to satisfactorily answer questions about their own and their institution's accountability. Reflective practitioners need reflective clients. They must be able and willing to communicate the knowledge base of their actions to clients and to negotiate mutually beneficial ways of practising their profession (c.f., Schön, 1983, p. 290).

Practically, we try to organize seminars in action research projects which give the opportunity to cross-read individual case studies, to critically discuss them, to relate their findings, and to examine them for overlaps and contradictions in order to establish the range and the conditions of their validity. Also, we try to provide for opportunities to publish practitioners' case studies (see for example, Altrichter *et al.*, 1989; ARGE Umwelterziehung, 1990) and to organize peer in-service training where action researchers share their experiences.

When research findings are published the ethical principle of '*confidentiality*' has to be observed: Data are 'owned' by the persons who have provided them. They must not be made accessible to third persons without authorization by their 'owners'. Research reports and case studies must not be published without having given the opportunity to comment to persons concerned with the situation under research. If persons are clearly identifiable in a research report the researcher must obtain their agreement to the publication. Anonymisation of data is usually not sufficient when concrete cases are investigated. While the researcher is formally protected, local people will not have any difficulty in recognizing the actors (Walker, 1985, p. 24). Doing otherwise will undermine the epistemological basis of research: other persons will not see any point in continuing collaboration with a person playing games of 'mystery and mastery'.

Contexts and Prospects

When I am now talking about '*areas of application*' of action research or, more specifically, of this set of quality criteria then 'application' is not meant in the technical-rational sense of using general knowledge to organize behaviour in specific cases. Rather it is meant in a Stenhousian (1975, p. 142) sense as providing — hopefully intelligent proposals — for experimentation and development. Our own research and development work at the University of Klagenfurt, Austria, has been stimulated and influenced by the English CARE/University of East Anglia tradition (Stenhouse and Elliott). In the meantime, we have been conducting action research projects in inservice training of teachers (Posch, 1986), in teacher education (Altrichter, 1988) and in the establishment of regional teachers' centres (Wallmann *et al.*, 1987). Most remarkable among these is the OECD/CERI project 'Environment and School Initiatives' which presently sees teachers and students from twenty-one nations working on a two-fold aim: to raise 'environmental awareness' and to develop 'dynamic qualities' of students (Posch, 1990; OECD/CERI, 1991).

Our own experience with action research is in the area of education (cf. Altrichter *et al.* forthcoming). However, action research seems appropriate for other social fields if only two major conditions are met: There is *an interest in development and change*, a social field where professionals want to collaborate with 'clients' in a mutually beneficial development of practice. And there is some readiness to have this development guided by a close, interlinked *relationship of reflected practice and practice-oriented reflection*. Consequently, action research is not indicated when mandated change has to be 'sold' to practitioners and clients, when reflection and change are only allowed within very narrow margins, or generally: whenever reflected professionalism is inhibited.

In my opinion, there are two major *strengths* to action research: Firstly, it is providing a framework of justification and orientation for professionals who want to innovate their practice in a socially responsible way. We find very often that teachers who had been innovative before are virtually waiting to insert their experiences into a consistent professional discussion. Secondly, by relating the 'context of use (application)' and the 'context of discovery and justification' in a more coherent image of the research process, action research offers a more realistic understanding of what 'rigour in research' can sensibly mean.

These strenghts are related to what I see as major *weaknesses and potential dangers* of action research: Its insistence on voluntary participation and its attraction to innovative, professional teachers repels, at the same time, less innovative, less professional teachers. Thus, action research is in constant danger of elitism and of being the hobby-horse of an 'avantgarde' who lose sight of the 'average people'. Secondly, its strong methodological claims and its reintegration of practice into the research process are very demanding; these demands are frequently incompatible with the existing working conditions of practitioners and with the culture they have to live in. Thereby, pressure on individuals is sometimes increased where working conditions for professionals are in need of being altered.

Action research is clearly situated in a *political context*: it is based on a concept of a socially responsible professionalism and wants to develop a social field through action and reflection of the persons concerned with this field. Thus, action research is biased towards decentralist decisions, local developments, open schools, flat networks of professionals and clients instead of hierarchies, responsible professionals negotiating qualitative accountability with clients instead of formal accountability. It does not come as a surprise that action research is presently attracting increased attention in Austria from groups who are interested in decentralization of the educational system and in professionalization of the teaching force, while in the UK it offers some kind of alternative culture and identification for professional teachers confronted with the quite different ideology of the Education Reform Act 1988 (CARE/UEA, 1989, p. 28).

There are some areas where *theoretical and practical development* of the rationale and the practice of action research seems both necessary and promising: testing, elaboration and development of the underlying theory of professional action should be pushed forward. It seems attractive to investigate in what form professional knowledge in conversations between teachers, between teachers and outsiders, or between supervising teachers and teacher-students is verbalized, received and developed. Through 'second order action research' (Elliott, 1985) facilitators could develop both their facilitation practice and a 'practical theory' about it. To investigate and develop practicable options for networking of locally produced teacher knowledge is a further pressing problem of the approach as is the linking of the levels of individual and institutional development.

Notes

1 This argument has been more extensively developed in Altrichter (1990a and 1990b).
2 As I have argued elsewhere (c.f., Altrichter 1990a, p. 206) I consider reflection-in-action as the core element of professional action. Full professional competency, however, calls for two additional elements: Tacit-knowing-in-action (or routine action; c.f., Schön 1983, p. 49; Bromme 1985) is the basis of professional action in smoothly flowing and unproblematic situations. Reflection-on-action (i.e., reflection distancing itself from and 'objectivating' the primary course of action) opens up a wealth of new possibilities of analyzing, reorganizing and communicating knowledge underlying action for example, to colleagues, clients, and persons to be initiated into the profession. Both action types cannot sensibly be excluded from the concept of professionality.
3 Quotations from German sources have been translated by the author.

References

ALTRICHTER, H. (1988) 'Enquiry-based learning in initial teacher education' in NIAS, J. and GROUNDWATER-SMITH, S. (Eds) *The Enquiring Teacher*, Lewes, Falmer Press, pp. 121–34.

ALTRICHTER, H. (1990a) *Ist das noch Wissenschaft? Darstellung und wissenschaftstheoretische Diskussion einer von Lehrern betriebenen Aktionsforschung*, Munich, Profil.

ALTRICHTER, H. (1990b) 'Do we need an alternative methodology for doing alternative research?' in ZUBER-SKERRITT, O. (Ed.) *Action Research for Change and Development*, Brisbane, CALT/Griffith University, pp. 103–18.

ALTRICHTER, H. and POSCH, P. (1989) 'Does the "grounded theory" approach offer a guiding paradigm for teacher research?', *Cambridge Journal of Education*, **19**, 1, pp. 21–31.

ALTRICHTER, H., POSCH, P. and SOMEKH, B. (forthcoming) *Teachers Investigate their work*, London, Routledge.

ALTRICHTER, H., WILHELMER, H., SORGER, H. and MOROCUTTI, I. (1989) (Eds) *Schule gestalten: Lehrer als Forscher, Fallstudien aus dem Projekt 'Forschendes Lernen in der Lehrerausbildung'*, Klagenfurt, Hermagoras.

ARGE UMWELTERZIEHUNG (Ed.) (1990) *Environment and School Initiatives*, Series of Case Studies, Vienna.

ARGYRIS, C., PUTNAM, R. and McLAIN SMITH, D. (1985) *Action Science, Concepts, Methods, and Skills for Research and Intervention*, San Francisco, CA, Jossey-Bass.

ARGYRIS, C. and SCHÖN, D.A. (1974) *Theory in Practice: Increasing Professional Effectiveness*, San Francisco, CA, Jossey-Bass.

BROMME, R. (1985) 'Was sind Routinen im Lehrerhandeln?', *Unterrichtswissenschaft*, **2**, pp. 182–92.

CARE/UEA (1989) *Coming to Terms with Research*, Norwich, University of East Anglia.

DÖRNER, D. (1982) 'Lernen des Wissens- und Kompetenzerwerbs', in TREIBER, B. and WEINERT, F.E. (Eds) *Lehr-Lern-Forschung*, Munich, Urban & Schwarzenberg, pp. 134–48.

ELLIOTT, J. (1976) *Developing Hypotheses about Classrooms from Teachers' Practical Constructs*, North Dakota Study Group on Evaluation-series, Grand Forks, ND, University of North Dakota.

ELLIOTT, J. (1978) 'The self-assessment of teacher performance', *CARN-Bulletin* **2**, pp. 18–20.

ELLIOTT, J. (1981) Action-research: A framework for self-evaluation in schools, TIQL-Working Paper No. 1, Mimeo, Cambridge.

ELLIOTT, J. (1984) 'Improving the quality of teaching through action research', *FORUM* **26**, 3, pp. 74–7.

ELLIOTT, J. (1985) 'Facilitating educational action-research: Some dilemmas' in BURGESS, R. (Ed.) *Field Methods in the Study of Education*, Lewes, Falmer Press, pp. 235–62.

ELLIOTT, J. (1986) 'Action research and in-service training of teachers', paper given at the University of Salzburg.

FEYERABEND, P.K. (1976) *Wider den Methodenzwang*, Frankfurt/M., Suhrkamp.

FEYERABEND, P.K. (1977) 'Changing patterns of reconstruction', *British Journal for Philosophy of Science*, **28**, pp. 351–82.

OECD/CERI (1991) *Environmental Society and Active Learning*, Paris, OECD/CERI.

POSCH, P. (1986) 'University support for independent learning: A new development in the in-service education of teachers', *Cambridge Journal of Education*, **16**, 1, pp. 46–57.

POSCH, P. (1990) 'Educational dimensions of environmental school initiatives', *Australian Journal of Environmental Education*, **6**, pp. 79–91

SCHÖN, D.A. (1983) *The Reflective Practitioner*, London, Temple Smith.

SOMEKH, B. (1983) 'Triangulation methods in action: A practical example', *Cambridge Journal of Education*, **13**, 2, pp. 31–7.

STENHOUSE, L. (1975) *An Introduction to Curriculum Research and Development*, London, Heinemann.

STENHOUSE, L. (1985) *Research as a Basis for Teaching*, (RUDDUCK, J. and HOPKINS, D. (Eds)) London, Heinemann.

WALKER, R. (1985) *Doing Research*, London, Methuen.

WALLMANN, H., SEILERBECK-TSCHIDA, W. and KAUFMANN, H. (1987) Pädagogisches Kommunikationszentrum St. Andrä — Langeck, Mimeo, PI Eisenstadt.

WEINGART, P. (1984) 'Anything goes — rien ne va plus', *Kursbuch*, **78**, pp. 61–75.

Chapter 4

From Cooperative Action to Collective Self-reflection: A Sociodynamic Approach to Educational Research

Michael Schratz

Doing Educational Research: An Interactive Process

Committing oneself to educational research activities which cover a certain time has consequences on different levels. For the researcher it means spending a lot of time planning, realizing and evaluating one's research programme so as to achieve desirable results. Afterwards a professional audience is needed for the findings to be implemented in educational practices or at least discussed among as many interested people in the scientific community as possible. Very often, however, research reports end up in a drawer or get dusty on a bookshelf without practical consequences.

Everybody who has been involved in a research project for a longer stretch of time knows that there is also another level of experience which is rarely mentioned in project reports. It consists of the multifold structure of relationships of human beings who are willing to venture into the experience of several months and years of project work, usually without knowing a lot about the inner dynamics of such an academic adventure. Although everybody who has taken part in collective research knows how intensely research activities can affect the members of a team, very little research has recently been done on how the interactions within the research group influence the research process itself and vice versa.

Most research in that area was done in the German speaking scientific communities of the seventies when *Handlungsforschung* became the spearhead in the revolt against mainstream empirical educational research at that time (c.f., Gstettner, 1973; Rathmayr and Wagner, 1976; Horn, 1979). However, after a century of committed work among teachers and researchers, school projects were stopped on a wide scale, which brought school reform into a severe crisis. This crisis is expressed in a crisis of confidence in the reformers who ask themselves whether the school reforms were good policy, whether and whom it helped, and if it had to take place at all. Indeed, there are hardly any actions which seem to have been thoroughly successful (c.f., Klemm, Rolff and Tillmann, 1985).

New impulses came from ethno-psychoanalytical studies, which revealed how scientific experience can be destroyed by the academic environment (c.f., Nadig and Erdheim, 1984). Nowadays literature pointing in that direction can be found most in the field of the more recent action research or reflective practitioner movements. 'Action research is simply a form of self-reflective enquiry under- taken by participants in social situations in order to improve the rationality and justice of their practices, their understanding of these practices, and the situations in which the practices are carried out' (Carr and Kemmis, 1986, p. 162). Action research concepts have mainly been employed in the context of classroom re- search (Altrichter and Posch, 1990; Gregory, 1988; Hustler, Cassidy and Cuff, 1986; McKernan, 1988; Oldroyd and Tiller, 1987), teacher training (Elliott, 1993; Goswami and Stillman, 1986) and higher education (Cross and Angelo, 1988; Schratz, 1990). Although action research 'is sweeping through faculties of educa- tion in universities across the world' (Elliott, 1989, p. 1), this concept has not yet been applied to the improvement of practices in doing educational research itself.

Kurt Lewin (1946 and 1952), one of the forefathers of action research, first stressed the importance of intergroup relations in the context of social research and proposed certain action steps in the sequel to planning, fact-finding, and execution based on the diagnosis of the respective situation. However, he focussed his action research on the group behaviour of what are traditionally called 'research subjects' (in his research, for example, minority groups). This chapter tries to throw some light on the dynamic force of the inter-group processes within collaborative research that keep the research process going and steer it into a particular direction. Whereas the goal of a particular research programme can be defined in advance, the inter-group relations among the individual researchers cannot be planned beforehand on a theoretical level. They only materialize in the fulfilment of practical steps during research. Through this process the aim of the research problem itself changes along the way, which itself undergoes a change (Berger, 1985, p. 33), influenced by both the researcher(s) and other people involved on a wider scale.

By presenting *collective self-reflection* as a qualitative 'voice' in educational research, I want to describe an approach which renders more weight to these processes and thus plead for a greater emphasis on considering the epistemological origin of research results. According to this sociodynamic approach to educational research it is not so much the scientific design that determines the research findings but the interactions among the people involved, as depicted in the following figure.

The results achieved in the research process always depend on the interactions among the people involved: the individual researcher(s) and the other members of the research group on the one hand and their individual and collective interactions with the other people involved in the research process on the other. The space for moving on to the original research goal is not only limited by the interactional framework but also by the here and now of the situation and the respective sociocultural context. Therefore, educational researchers have to readjust their individual steps of action according to the sociodynamics of the interactive process within the situational context. Thus, similarly to Schön's 'reflection in action' processes (1983), this readjustment of the original programme design leads to what could be called 'design in action'.[1]

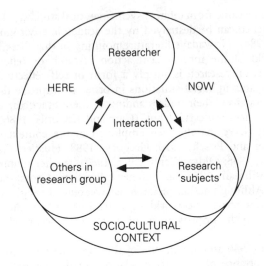

Figure 4.1: The sociodynamic pattern of the research process

Researching into Educational Affairs: A Means to What End?

As shown in figure 4.1, a research programme cannot develop outside the limits defined by the people involved and both the specific situation and the socio-cultural context. Since people involved in research are usually busy achieving their research results, they pay little attention to the interdependency of these aspects. Whereas there is little that can be done to change the sociocultural framework in which research takes place, the interactional pattern within the research group very much depends on the individual and collective behaviour of the people involved. Similar to what Popkewitz (1984) attributes to the intellectual who 'becomes the expert in legitimation, influencing moral conduct and direction of will by controlling the communications through which a society establishes purpose and describes and evaluates its institutional conditions' (p. 185), the researchers establish purpose through their own actions and interactions embedded in the situational context.

In order to deconstruct the idelogical impact of the group processes involved, the interactions among scientists doing educational research have to be studied from a distant perspective. According to Altrichter (1990) it is an expressive indicator for the consciousness of a research process how the people involved find the balance between distance from and involvement in the respective actions. Historical processes within a (research) group, regular occurrences in field work, structural conditions and the actions of particular individuals contribute to persistence and change in doing research. In a research process each chain of events has, as its consequence, a new formation that rejoins the events in such a way that there are new conditions and circumstances in action. This sociodynamic process and its complex conception of causality makes it difficult to inquire critically into the multitude of interdependent actions.

To engage in critical inquiry into the sociodynamic aspects of educational research it is necessary to analyze the research process from a meta-communicative point of view. Metacommunication is communication *about* how people interact among each other, how successfully communication takes place, how people behave in certain situations and so on. In the sociodynamic approach to educational research this metacommunication is achieved by means of phases of self-reflection, which offer a good way to:

— throw light on the (usually hidden) motives of the individual members of a research group;
— deconstruct the individual perception of the research process and to decipher the social construction of certain key situations involved;
— analyze the research process according to certain discursive patterns used in collaborative work;
— put research findings into a broader context of the wider educational community or even society at large;
— assess work on the micro-level of educational change for its transformational power on the macro-level of societal development.

According to these aims, the sociodynamic approach to educational research can be used in different areas of application when analyzing the design of research activities in action. They mainly differ in the respective time span covered in the particular phases of reflection. The three main areas of application are:

(i) Microanalysis through collective self-reflection aiming at professional development,
(ii) Medium-range collective self-reflection of group processes after decisive steps of action in a research programme in the management of educational change,
(iii) Macro-analysis, the *ex post facto* application of collective self-reflection after finishing a major part or even the whole research project with a view to organizational development in critical pedagogy.

Microanalysis Through Collective Self-reflection

In this area of application, self-reflection follows the action itself and is based on the concept of the reflective practitioner by Schön (1983). For him the current crisis in professional education lies 'in an underlying and largely unexamined epistemology of professional practice — a model of professional knowledge institutionally embedded in curriculum and arrangements for research and practice' (Schön, 1987, p. 8). He describes how in his practicum he uses reflection on reflection-in-action as a method of assessing a student's performance in practice. 'Hence, coach and student, when they do their jobs well, function not only as practitioners but also as on-line researchers, each inquiring more or less consciously into his own and the other's changing understandings' (*ibid*, 298).

If collective self-reflection is modelled along Schön's reflection processes in a research group, its members will not so much rely on a coach but on the sensitivity of everybody involved. In their respective inquiries into the research development, they depend on each other's awareness of his or her experience, ability to describe it, and willingness to make it discussable — conditions not easily met . . . At any given time, concurrent processes are underway, any one of which might cause a change in understanding. And some of the most important of learning are of the background variety . . . Often, therefore, it is impossible to distinguish strong signals from ambient noise or to attribute a clearly discernible change in behavior to the interventions that caused it. (*ibid*, pp. 298–9)

A practical application of short-term collective self-reflection can be found among teachers who have started an action research project and want to monitor their own development as teacher researchers. The individual group members who inquire into their own and the others' teaching, act as 'critical friends' in this research process. Since it is often very difficult to act critically as a fellow researcher (c.f., Kroath forthcoming), regular phases of collective self-reflection can help in establishing an atmosphere for such 'critical friendship'.

Medium-range Collective Self-reflection of Group Processes

In the medium-range model, collective self-reflection does not occur as a regular activity in the course of a research programme. It rather serves as an evaluative instrument at a decisive stage. This area of application of medium-range collective self-reflection has an impact on the practice and management of educational change and is geared towards the concept of the self-evaluating institution. After extensive evaluation work on an institutional level, Adelman and Alexander (1982), for example, report:

Standing now well back from the experiences and placing them as we have done in a broader analytical framework, we can perceive two sets of problems. Firstly, those relating to the organizational frameworks for evaluation: matters like human and material resources, the acute pressure of time, the restrictions on methodology, the challenge of achieving adequate dissemination and discussion and so on. Many of the problems in this category are avoidable. (p. 181)

Concluding their principles in the management of educational change, Adelman and Alexander would commend using questions of this sort in order to 'evaluate evaluations'. This step in second order research seems to be particularly necessary in educational practices where institutional changes depend on a continuing process of appraisal and modification. The 'product' view of the achievement of significant educational progress, since it is the very individuals and groups with different interests and perspectives that determine how progress can be achieved. If they do not have the room and time to collectively reflect on the development of their own activities, they might easily come to a dead end, with the *status quo* as the only resort left in order to survive institutionally. 'In this view the evaluation process itself is seen as having as significant a potential for supporting development as the evaluation finding or product, provided that the process is collective and open' (p. 183).

Very often institutional analyses end with a research report based on the findings of self-evaluation without paying attention to the sociodynamic forces steering the evaluative processes. Professional and institutional growth and development largely depend on the exchange of interpretations in a multitude of decision-making contexts. Collective self-reflection can help in achieving a better understanding of the shared truths about particular activities, which are often concealed beneath the formal report of the research findings.

Collective Self-reflection as a Long-term Strategy in Collaborative Action

Educational changes are often initiated by organizational development programmes. Because of their complexity, such concepts depend on individual as well as collective action on various levels of an educational institution which not only works on the structural level of organizational development but heavily relies on the support of the various personal interpretations of situations in organizations:

> Organizations are not things. They have no ontological reality, and there is no use studying them as though they did. They are an invented social reality of human creation. It is people who are responsible for organizations and people who change them. Organizations have reality only through human action, and it is that action (and the human will driving it) that we must come to understand. The alternative I am proposing rejects theory that explains human behaviour as though a depersonalized organization and its devalued, nonhuman environment *caused it.* The alternative theory grants a measure of free will to individuals, and so places a measure of responsibility upon them for their action. People do not exist in organizations. Organizations exist in and through individuals. The concept of organization should be understood as a moral order deeply embedded in each of us — an order that is arbitrary, nonnatural, and often backed by enormous power, even by violence. But that power may be redeemed by love, that is, by a dedication to better values. (Greenfield, 1988, pp. 132–3)

Although this view seems to overemphasize the possibly human in organizational work, it points to the important relationship between the subjective and objective factor in the dynamics of institutional development. Educational change is rarely based on an analysis of this inner structure of institutional design which heavily influences the actions taken in a research process. Moreover, managerialist views of organizational change often deal with their human potential in a technologized way that is inherent in a managerial philosophy based on decision-making, goal setting and authority. To counteract such tendencies,

> we must create learning communities able to act — empowered to act — and able to reflect openly on the consequences of their actions. By subjecting our experience to joint self-reflection, we may incorporate wider group understandings and create a shared language and a shared identity — an identity formed in co-operative action and cooperative self-reflection. (Kemmis, 1983, p. 25)

Recent developments in organizational development in educational affairs show that traditional managerial concepts can no longer satisfy the demands of global responsibility. Therefore a new philosophy of *transformational leadership* has emerged that attempts to deal with the complexity of educational change (Fischer and Schratz, 1990), which 'requires dedication to political action and a frame of mind that both *believes* and *critically reflects*. The school *leader* puts critical theory to work — through reflection, understanding, and education' (Foster, 1986, p. 201). Without going into further detail of particular applications here I want to describe in the following section some concrete experiences from this kind of collective self-reflection based on a cooperative action research project in adult education.

Reflection on Collaboration: Deconstructing Psychosocial Realities

The main aim of this action research project was an attempt to involve as many people as possible in an educational needs analysis within the community for the institutional development of a local adult education institution (c.f., Schratz, 1984). Together with the inhabitants of its neighbourhood, the researchers engaged in a number of activities. There was little time, however, to reflect on the underlying processes of planning, doing and evaluating cooperative action. It was when problems among the people involved arose that the research group had to deal with psychosocial aspects in the research process. The subsequent figure 4.2 (from Achleitner, Haring and Schratz, 1988) depicts a typical situation in collaborative research.

Figure 4.2

Because of the usual time constraints in an ongoing research process, the team members rarely pay attention to the worries of a particular person in the group, who, for example, feels neglected by the others. The following extract from a collective self-reflection phase in educational research at an Austrian adult education institution (c.f., *ibid*[2]) conveys this conventional attitude.

> O: We cannot afford such time-consuming . . . Well, how shall I put it, a working method which tries to integrate relationship . . . problems. We'd never be able to finish anything. We could quit our job. That's the reality. There are projects to be finished; there are dates to be

kept, and all this has to be accomplished in a set time. And above all, I feel that the atmosphere in a group and the mutual understanding through one's achievements, which always happen step by step, turn out to be much better than if one argues about this and that for some time . . . about things like I don't like your hair-style today . . . and, and . . . I suffer from gas pains, and I'm just not in the mood right now. I'm exaggerating a bit, but as I said before, in real life things look somewhat different . . .

Voices of this kind, which in the 'distinctive qualities of a character's discourse always strive for a certain social significance, a social breath' (Bakhtin, 1981, p. 333), stand for a view on how results can be achieved in collaborative work which is often found even in educational research. In such a view, the thematizing of aspects of relationship among the members of a research group has little or nothing to do with the actual work. Such a view, however, neglects that in setting concrete actions human beings are led and governed by hidden motives and driving forces, which they are not aware of but which nevertheless determine their social behaviour (Brody, 1983). An important function of collective self-reflection lies in throwing some light on the workings of such hidden motives and inner impulses. The following extracts from collective self-reflection phases may serve as examples:

M: We were not at all sure about which goals of education each of us supports . . . There is no clear definition, and each of us has a different definition of what educational goals are.

I: All those attempts to find a common mission for our team were not successful, because the other members of the group didn't agree with my views, which were more directed towards the organization.

F: From the beginning, it was not possible to explicitly clarify the interests of each individual in the project . . . It took at least about a year which left us in the belief that communication functioned in our team . . .

The following extract shows that only the collective self-reflection phase afterwards clarified some of the relationships between the people involved and the content of the research at hand.

H: Well, it is possible that looking back I've misunderstood that, you know. I've seen this, er . . . er, perhaps rather as an agent of the ministry, an agent of these regulations. May well be . . . I'm not sure myself today whether I really wanted it that way, or . . . whether, because I wanted it that way, I saw it that way. I definitely saw it more strictly and rigidly than you did. Well, this might have been a subjective view of mine, or it may even be that way.

Only by looking back from a distant point is it possible for the group member to interpret this behaviour as a misunderstanding. Even at present he is not sure yet, which indicates how difficult it is to deconstruct the history of project life and reconstruct it from a later perspective. This process also brought a problem to light which one member envisaged as a paradox.

> *M:* For me the paradox was that one should have thought about the relationship among the team members at the beginning, when there was neither time nor maturity to talk about a certain need for arguments and work on relationships. However, it would have been far more important to invest this energy directly into the project rather than into trench wars. — It was a great pity that we never struggled for a clear goal consensus at the beginning.

An important goal of the underlying project lay in the participatory approach of needs-oriented educational work, which ran through the project like a red thread. This turned out to be somewhat problematical and appeared frequently in the collective self-reflection phases, as can be seen for example in the following extract:

> *A:* Well, look at the outline of the project . . .
>
> *F:* Yes, I think there was a paragraph . . .
>
> *A:* . . . in the goal definition.
>
> *F:* And we struggled a lot about it, especially the part dealing with participant orientation and the . . . creation of a programme which was to be modelled along the needs of the people who live there.
>
> *A:* The people there don't have any particular needs. If only you understood, people don't have any needs.
>
> *I:* They do have needs, for example to somehow solve the problem with the dogs . . . it somehow bothers them . . .
>
> *A:* Right.
>
> *I:* . . . that there is such a problem.
>
> *A:* But such needs can never be satisfied by an adult education institution.
>
> *F:* Well, but part of it then. It can't solve the overall problem, but it can take over parts of it; that's for sure. Don't you think so?
>
> *A:* No.

This scene turned out to be typical of the situation that by general discussion the different points of view in the team could not be resolved on an abstract level. Above all at the beginning of the research project, when the individual viewpoints were not easily available, a lot of energy was invested into respective discussions without finding a way to move on to the concrete level. Therefore, the team members found it a relief to talk about their experiences in the group and their influence on the research work. The following excerpt from a collective self-reflection phase gives an insight into the powerful dynamics during research work:

> M: ... for us it has been very motivating to talk about this process that we found out certain aspects which we hadn't been aware of in the course of research but which had a heavy impact on the work itself. This has got to do with people ... and the motives of an individual person and such things, which were not available then. It is only now that we've found out that many things were responsible, contents-wise, ... for the way it worked out ...

From Action to Self-reflection: Reliving Collective Processes

The motivation for collectively reflecting on the process of a research project can be manifold. Usually it is a decisive cut or turning-point during the work, which confronts the people involved with the need to reconsider the programme. They are either caused by the inner dynamics of the group, for example, if one or more members of a team decide to withdraw, which normally has a decisive impact on the further development of the group situation. However, it can also be the case that influences from outside cause the research work to go into a different direction or to come to a complete halt. Such a process was recently initiated by Sanger (1990), when grant money was taken away from a university-based action research project. Under the expressive title 'Awakening a scream of consciousness', he analyzes the evolution of a different group identity from the original, grant-dependent group and its effect on their educational philosophy and practice.

In the adult education research work mentioned above the project had already been finished, and everybody was fed up and only wanted to produce the usual project report. When the remaining members sat together to put an end to the work involved, everybody felt liberated from, and relieved of, several years of intensive field work. When this pressure had gone from the group and everybody started talking freely about their personal experiences, we were surprised at how many aspects in the team members' behaviour and the resulting turns in the research work no obvious explanation could be found for. Suddenly new questions arose: Why did the project develop in that direction? How did everybody feel about it? How was everybody affected by the work?

Anybody who has ever climbed a mountain and looked back from the top knows this feeling. It is not a matter of looking back from an uninvolved position, but a retrospect which takes possession, which incorporates, which makes one aware of what one has gone through and what one has achieved, a participating perception. Walking along one only sees the few metres in front of oneself — stony, narrow and tiresome. The goal only exists in one's imagination; the outlook is usually blocked. One is fully occupied with the next step. This image of looking back signalled the starting point for the continuation of the research group's further steps.

In this phase a transformation of team identity took place. The original, action-oriented group changed to a self-reflective one. The individual team members wanted to find out and understand how everything in the project development really went. During this phase new questions occurred:

- Which were the important phases in the research process?
- Where were decisive turning points?
- Where were the periods of strained circumstances?
- When did members of the team diminish (or leave altogether)?
- Where did individual team members get 'blisters'?

As a consequence the research group had to find out collectively which steps and people could give such a view of the research process that a cross section of the work came to life and the history of the project became clear to everybody involved. The individual team members tried to find out more by looking at the following key aspects which in turn became the respective topics of a collective self-reflection session:

- Individual people's entrance into the project
- The relationship between the project and the national educational frame-work
- The group dynamics of the team formation in the preparatory phase
- The dropouts and their motives
- The view of the head of the local adult education institution
- The role of project management
- A team event with the people in the community
- The educational fair organized by the team

At each of the meetings which were organized for the individual collective self-reflection sessions about six people who had been involved in the project took part. Each lasted for about two to three hours; however, it was not thought necessary to set a time limit. This time frame proved to be the maximum per session to be mastered by everybody, since the intensive discussions made a high demand on everybody's concentration.

Every collective self-reflection session was taped by means of a cassette recorder and transcribed afterwards so that nobody was distracted by writing when freely associating about certain phases of the project. Moreover, it was helpful to have everything available in written form afterwards for the reconstruction work on the history of the project. This material made it far easier for the analytical work to follow. There was no formal discussion leader during the sessions, the discussion was more or less carried by the free flow of discourse. Only if the discussion came to a halt or if the original topic disappeared in the course of the talk, did somebody try to make this clear from a meta-communicative perspective.

Once the discussions had been transcribed, the texts were given to the team members to look through them closely, and then they were photocopied and handed out to everybody. The collected material gave a look into the inner world of the project life, which was only possible if one went through the dynamics of its history again. Another positive aspect was that through talking about situations from a distance, tensions between team members mitigated. It suddenly became exciting again for the team to continue the research into the group history on the basis of jointly lived-through experiences. The joint effort in sorting out previous team activities also helped in finding ways of implementing the experiences and results of the research project.

Looking Back: Towards an Ontology of Educational Knowledge

The experiences with collective self-reflection as a qualitative method of researching into the history of the life of an educational research group can be regarded as a challenging attempt to analyze educational research which demonstrates how the psychosocial context is essential to a proper understanding of pedagogical practice. Following the first steps of such analyses in the natural sciences (c.f., Knorr-Cetina and Mulkay, 1983; Knorr, 1981; Latour and Wolgar, 1979; Latour, 1987;), it represents a 'qualitative voice' investigating into the social reality of educational research in the making (c.f., Hug, 1990).

In this sense collective self-reflection serves as a method in ideological deconstruction. This has to happen as a collective process because, as Giroux (1983) states, 'ideology operates at the level of lived experience, at the level of representations embedded in cultural artifacts, and at the level of messages in material practices' of research actions (p. 145). The theory-practice relationship which underpins any research activity has a special meaning in educational research because of its pedagogical claim to democratize society. If educationalists do not look critically at the epistemology of the creation of their knowledge, they may easily miss this overall aim and adhere to a functionalist tradition.

According to our findings, collaborative decision-making processes in team research on the micro-level mirror practices in educational organizations on the macro-level. On the assumption of this structural similarity, collective self-reflection can contribute towards a necessary transformation:

* from a position where scientifically derived knowledge is deemed superior, to a circumstance in which artistic and intuitive knowledge may be equally appropriate;

* from an a priori instrumental view of knowledge, to one that reflects knowledge as being tentative and problematic;

* from a view which pre-supposes answers to complex social questions, to one that endorses the importance of problem posing and negotiated resolution. (Smyth, 1989, p. 195)

In order to make this political aspect more explicit I want to conclude this chapter with the following

Ten principles of collective self-reflection

1 Collective self-reflection is more than the collection of individual views on a certain action. It rather constitutes the collective 'consciousness' of numerous histories and traditions of individuals and institutions.

2   Educational research results are constructed by the sociocultural mediation among the people involved. Collective self-reflection represents a way for deconstructing its underlying processes.

3   The reconstructed history of research in action must not be seen as the true view of how things actually happened, since collective self-reflection processes construct new social realities. However, the reconstruction process supports a more reflective view of knowledge (rather than an instrumental one).

4   The potential for social change in educational practices depends greatly on the interactive capacities of the people involved in research activities.

5   Collective self-reflection is an educative process itself. By talking about collective experiences, the individual group members learn more about the others, themselves, and the workings of a group.

6   Reflecting about collective research action and the ends of the research actions are parts of an integrated process. The more immediate the reflection on the action, the more the underlying processes come to light.

7   Collective self-reflection becomes a transformative force which develops from mere action orientation to a person and group-oriented process, a process which negotiates underlying meaning in educational research.

8   Since educational research always takes place in the sociocultural context of institutional settings, collective self-reflection examines the power relationship among the people involved.

9   Reflecting on one's own experience in collective action helps educationalists to better understand the organizational culture of collaborative work and to act more effectively in joint activities.

10 Doing collective self-reflection challenges the dominant functionalist views of doing educational research and provides a new way of looking at educational practices from a more personal perspective.

Notes

1   I want to thank Herbert Altrichter, who has triggered off this idea and also given other valuable comments on the manuscript.

2   This and all subsequent translations from this report are mine.

References

ACHLEITNER, I., HARING, F. and SCHRATZ, M. (1988) *Erinnerungsarbeit als Forschungsmethode. Wiederbeleben von Teamerfahrungen bei der Organisationsentwicklung im Bildungsbereich*, Innsbruck, Department of Education.

ADELMAN, C. and ALEXANDER, R.J. (1982) *The Self-Evaluating Institution: Practice and Principles in the Management of Educational Change*. London, Methuen.

ALTRICHTER, H. (1990) *Ist das noch Wissenschaft? Darstellung und wissenschaftstheoretische Diskussion einer von Lehrern betriebenen Aktionsforschung*, München, Profil.

ALTRICHTER, H. and POSCH, P. (1990) *Lehrer erforschen ihren Unterricht. Eine Einführung in die Methoden der Aktionsforschung*, Bad Heilbrunn, Klinkhardt.

BAKHTIN, M.M. (1981) *The Dialogic Imagination*, Austin, Tx, University of Texas Press.

BERGER, W. (1985) 'Über die Rückkehr des Motivs in die Wissenschaft' in BERGER, W.

(Ed.) *Beiträge zur Wissenschaftsdidaktik*, Vienna, Hölder-Pichler-Tempsky, pp. 29–44.

BRODY, N. (1983) *Human Motivation: Commentary on Goal-directed Action*, New York, Academic Press.

CARR, W. and KEMMIS, S. (1986) *Becoming Critical*, Lewes, Falmer Press.

CROSS, K.P. and ANGELO, T.A. (1988) *Classroom Assessment Techniques. A Handbook for Faculty*, Michigan, NCRIPTAL.

ELLIOTT, J. (1989) 'Academics and action research: The training workshop as an exercise in ideological deconstruction' Paper presented to the annual meeting of the American Educational Research Association, San Francisco.

ELLIOTT, J. (1993) *Reconstructing Teacher Education*, Lewis, Falmer Press.

FISCHER, W. and SCHRATZ, M. (1990) 'Transformational Leadership: Impulse für eine neue Führungsphilosophie in pädagogischen Leitungsfunktionen', *Schulmanagement*, **21** pp. 34–41.

FOSTER, W. (1986) *Paradigms and Promises: New Approaches to Educational Administration*. Buffalo, NY, Prometheus Books.

GIROUX, H.A. (1983) *Theory and Resistance in Education: A Pedagogy for the Opposition*, South Hadley, MA, Bergin and Garvey.

GOSWAMI, P. and STILLMAN, P.R. (1986) *Reclaiming the Classroom. Teacher Research as an Agency for Change*, Portsmouth, NH, Boynton/Cook.

GREENFIELD, T.B. (1988) 'The decline and fall of science in educational administration' in WESTOBY, A. (Ed.) *Culture and Power in Educational Organizations*, Milton Keynes, Open University Press, pp. 115–41.

GREGORY, R. (1988) *Action Research in the Secondary School*, London, Routledge, Chapman and Hall.

GSTETTNER, P. (1973) 'Handlungsforschung unter dem Anspruch diskursiver Verständigung — Analyse einiger Kommunikationsprobleme', *Zeitschrift für Pädagogik*, **22**, pp. 321–33.

HORN, K. (Ed.) (1979) *Aktionsforschung: Balanceakt ohne Netz?* Frankfurt/M., Syndikat.

HUG, T. (Ed.) (1990) *Die soziale Wirklichkeit der Theorie. Beiträge zur Theorievermittlung und-aneignung in der Pädagogik*, München, Profil.

HUSTLER, E., CASSIDY, A. and CUFF, E.C. (Eds) (1986) *Action Research in Classrooms and Schools*, London, Allen and Unwin.

KEMMIS, S. (1983) 'Empowering people: A note on the politics of action research' in PITMAN, A. *et al.* (Eds) *Educational Enquiry: Approaches to Research*, Geelong, Deakin University, Quoted from SMYTH, W.J., *Leadership and Pedagogy*, Geelong, Deakin University Press, p. 9.

KLEMM, K., ROLFF, H.-G. and TILLMANN, K.-J. (1985) *Bildung für das Jahr 2000. Bilanz der Reform, Zukunft der Schule*, Reinbek, Rowohlt.

KNORR, K. (1981), *The Manufacture of Knowledge: An Essay on the Constructivist and Contextual Nature of Science*, Oxford, Pergamon Press.

KNORR-CETINA, K. and MULKAY, M. (Eds) (1983), *Science Observed. Perspectives on the Social Study of Science*, London, Sage.

KROATH, F. (forthcoming) 'The role of the critical friend in the development of teacher expertise'.

LATOUR, B. (1987) *Science in Action: How to Follow Scientists and Engineers Through Society*, Cambridge, MA, Harvard University Press.

LATOUR, B., and WOOLGAR, S. (1979), *Laboratory Life. The Social Construction of Scientific Facts*, Beverly Hills, CA, Sage.

LEWIN, K. (1946) 'Action research and minority problems', *Journal of Social Issues*, **2**, pp. 34–46 reprinted in KEMMIS, S. and MCTAGGART, R. (Eds) (1988) *The Action Research Reader*, Geelong, Deakin University, pp. 41–56.

LEWIN, K. (1952) 'Group decision and social change' in SWANSON, T.M, NEWCOMB, M.

and HARTLEY, E.L. (Eds) *Readings in Social Psychology*, New York, Henry Holt, pp. 459–73. reprinted in KEMMIS, S. and McTAGGART, R. (Eds) (1988) *The Action Research Reader*, Geelong, Deakin University, pp. 47–56.

McKERNAN, J. (1988) 'Teachers as researchers: Paradigm and praxis', *Contemporary Education*, **59**, pp. 154–8.

NADIG, M. and ERDHEIM, M. (1984) 'Die Zerstörung der wissenschaftlichen Erfahrung durch das akademische Milieu — Ethnopsychoanalytische Überlegungen zur Aggressivität in der Wissenschaft', *Psychosozial*, **23**, 7, pp. 11–27.

OLDROYD, T. and TILLER, T. (1987) 'Change from within: An account of school-based collaborative action research in an English secondary school', *Journal of Education for Teaching*, **13**, pp. 13–27.

POPKEWITZ, T.S. (1984) *Paradigm and Ideology in Educational Research: The Social Functions of the Intellectual.* Lewes, Falmer Press.

RATHMAYR, B. and WAGNER, I. (1976) *Wissenschaft als Innovationshilfe*, Wien, Jugend und Volk.

SANGER, J. (1990) 'Awakening a scream of consciousness: The critical group in action research', *Theory Into Practice*, **29**, 3, pp. 174–8.

SCHÖN, D.A. (1983) *The Reflective Practitioner*, New York, Basic Books.

SCHÖN, D.A. (1987) *Educating the Reflective Practitioner. Toward a New Design for Teaching and Learning in the Professions.* San Francisco, CA, Jossey-Bass.

SCHRATZ, M. (1984) ' "Auf den Hund gekommen". Oder: Wenn einem das Curriculum davonläuft' in EHALT, H. CH., KNITTLER-LUX, U. and KONRAD, H. (Eds) *Geschichtswerkstatt, Stadtteilarbeit, Aktionsforschung*, Wien, Verlag für Gesellschaftskritik, pp. 221–35.

SCHRATZ, M. (1990) 'Researching while teaching. A collaborative action research model to improve college teaching', *Journal on Excellence in College Teaching*, **1**, pp. 98–108.

SMYTH, J. (1989) 'A "pedagogical" and "educative" view of leadership, in SMYTH. J., (Ed.) *Critical Perspectives on Educational Leadership*, Lewes, Falmer Press, pp. 179–204.

Part 2

Listening to the Silent Voice Behind the Talk

Chapter 5

Finding a Silent Voice for the Researcher: Using Photographs in Evaluation and Research[1]

Rob Walker

You can't say more than you can see. (Thoreau, quoted by photographer Paul Strand, quoted by critic Susan Sontag)

Photographs do not in themselves narrate . . . they quote from appearances. (John Berger, painter, critic and writer)

Voices Without Words

Writing is a more central activity in research in the social sciences than it is in the sciences, providing us with an apparent escape from the tyranny of empiricism, yet I often feel that we are at a disadvantage in qualitative studies in being constrained by language itself. One of the reasons why I am intrigued by the use of photographs in educational research is that their use touches on the limitations of language, especially language used for descriptive purposes. In using photographs the potential exists, however elusive the achievement, to find ways of thinking about social life that escape the traps set by language. My aspiration, in using black and white photographs, is therefore to find a silent voice for the researcher. To write of such things is instantly to admit failure, but I have tried to preserve some tremor of ambiguity in doing so.

I believe that there is a significant tension in qualitative research in education which derives from the recent re-emergence of qualitative research in a context dominated by measurement. Because the recent history of research has been dominated by an empiricist view of science, many of us who are qualitative researchers have inherited a view of knowledge from the measurement tradition. While the surface appearance of our research is qualitative, in many instances our procedures and methodological concerns remain primarily with issues of reliability, validity and interpretation.

There are other researchers and other projects, generally more influenced by European social theory, whose concern is with directly confronting the issue of subjectivity: the subjectivity, of both the subject and the researcher. Here the notion of 'voice' is critical, because, while for researchers of the first kind, the issues are essentially those of objectifying the voices of their subjects, for those of us more interested in questions of the second kind, the notion of 'voice' involves both subject and researcher and, in doing so, precipitates the contradiction between individual experience and socially structured meaning.

A practical research issue which faces us all is the intrusive and imperial nature of the research voice, for as soon as we begin an interview, draft a questionnaire or engage others in conversation, the very language we use creates frames within which to realize knowledge. Whether we see this as an intrusion to be controlled through systematic research design, or as inextricably part of the research process, there is no doubt that our use of language determines to a large degree what we will learn. Inevitably, our research is always limited by what it takes for granted.

A question that intrigues me is how we might stand outside our own use of language, even if only for a moment during the process of research, to catch ourselves unawares. The fact that this is probably an impossible achievement does not diminish its attraction as an aspiration. How can we use language as a basis from which to develop a degree of reflexivity about our use of language? One possibility is to find forms of communication that offer the possibility of triangulation on the use of language itself. I believe that still photographs hold this promise.

The Use of Photographs in Evaluation and Research

In evaluating educational programs and in educational research, pictures are more often misused than well used. Photographs are commonly used for illustration and for publicity purposes in promoting books, projects, programs, exhibits and events, but in such cases the purpose is usually to break up slabs of text, to catch the attention of the casual reader or passer-by, or to promote personalities, events, agencies or organizations. Almost always, photographs are an after-thought, tacked on in the final phase of a project or program. There is rarely any attempt to use photographs to provide complex information, to stimulate discussion or sustain engagement or to play a part in encouraging participation or self-reflection.

Paradoxically these more complex functions are all things that photographs can do well, but more often than not we accept a non-educational definition of photography which sees photographs as simply recorded images and as less valid than print when serious issues are at stake. We are tuned to see photographs as illustration and we neglect the power of the photograph to engage thought, extend the imagination and to undermine the implicit authority of the written word.

Science as Pictures, not Words

It is a strange paradox that in its striving for status as 'science', educational research appears to have missed the fact that much of science research is visual. It is visual in the way it relates to the world (pictures of one kind or another are the stock in trade of particle physics, molecular biology, archeology and a host of other fields). It is visual also in that it uses visual imagination in its thinking, problem-solving and theorizing (perhaps nowhere more obviously than in the classic case of the 'double helix'). Those who doubt this is a generalisable feature of science should read Stephen Jay Gould on fossil reconstruction (in *Wonderful Life*), or Max Charlesworth and his colleagues on molecular biology (in *Life Among the Scientists*).

Despite the significant part played by visual imagination in the physical and biological sciences, in the social sciences generally, and in sociology particularly, we seem to have let ourselves become dominated by numbers and words to the point where we have lost touch with the visual. In the history of the subject this was not always the case (Stasz, 1979, reports that early editions of the *American Journal of Sociology*, frequently carried photographs and photographic essays) but in histories of sociology the retreat from the visual is usually treated as progress towards science. The textbook view of science as essentially concerned with numbers and theories is one that dominates sociology texts.

One of the consequences of the systematic exclusion of photography from the social sciences is that, when we do encounter photographs, we are at a loss with what to do with them. We lack what sociologist Robert Witkin called an 'intelligence of feeling' (Witkin, 1976). We tend to fall back on a view of photographs as behavioural records, and we miss the significance of published discussions of photography in literature and cultural studies (Sontag, 1979; Barthes, 1982; Berger, 1978 and 1980; Berger and Mohr, 1982).

Part of the difficulty I believe is that we assign roles to photographers that place them in technical roles that are both kept apart from our thinking and kept outside the frame of action. We take, view, edit and use photographs in ways that reinforce the alienation of the photographer and the production of the photograph from the event as a source of meaning. Nowhere is the relationship between the object and the audience more attenuated than in press photography, which is where most of us gain what visual literacy we have. In newspapers and magazines photographs are processed, cropped, edited and designed to fit with text by people who have virtually no contact with the photographer, the taking of the photograph, or the event being pictured. Less crassly, but just as effectively, social scientists have removed visual methods, and photography in particular, from critical discussion. The visual has become silent in the social sciences at the very point in history when it dominates both science and contemporary culture. Social science struggles to force ideas into words as the culture of which it is apart becomes increasingly visually oriented. Curious.

In this chapter I take the view that, in using photographs in evaluation and research, it is more important to question the assumptions about photographs and photography we carry with us than it is to concern ourselves with questions of technique. In research it is not just a question of adding photography to a grab bag of available techniques but of realising that in using visual media we tread the margins between social science and cultural study.

We need to find ways of talking about the use of photographs in research that are not restricted to questions of method and a good way to begin is with John Berger's distinction between the 'public' and 'private' uses of photographs.

'Public' and 'Private' Photographs

Consider the following photographs which are extracted from a study in which a teacher, curriculum developer and evaluator attempted to co-operate on the task

of observing what was happening in a classroom (Walker *et al.*, 1981). The class is working on a history program that attempts to get students working with documentary material rather than with secondary sources.

These photographs raise a number of issues about interpretation. Is what the outside observer sees, what the participants see? Can the photographs be said to have a 'voice'? What kind of evidence do the photographs provide? In what ways is a photograph of an event different from a description?

A common sense view of photographs, often adopted in research, is that still photographs provide a record that is necessarily selective but nevertheless objective. Christopher Isherwood (1945) went so far as to adopt this view as an aspiration for the writer:

> I am a camera with the shutter open, quite passive, recording, not think-ing . . . Some day all this will have to be developed, carefully printed, fixed. (p. 7)

Isherwood's metaphor captures neatly the dialectical nature of the two sides of documentary photography, or come to that of ethnography: data collection and analytic writing. However, once we start to rethink these oppositions, seeing recording as less passive and analysis as more problematic, then the nature of the expertise needed to carry through a project changes also.

John Berger, in several of his writings about photography, develops the idea that photographs are best thought of, not as records of reality, but in terms of their capacity to 'quote from appearances'. In a critical review of Susan Sontag's influential book, *On Photography*, he writes:

> Photographs in themselves do not narrate. Photographs preserve instant appearances. Habit now protects us against the shock involved in such

a preservation. Compare the exposure time for a film with the life of a print made, and let us assume that the print lasts only ten years; the ratio for an average modern photograph would be approximately 20,000,000,000 : 1. Perhaps that can serve as a reminder of the violence of the fission whereby appearances are separated by the camera from their function. (Berger, 1978, p. 51)

One consequence of the methodological violence that the photograph inflicts on its subjects is to create spaces between pictures and appearances, appearances and memory. Most of us, when faced with a photograph, or a set of photographs, have little difficulty in talking about the relation between the photograph and the event, especially if it was an event where we were present or where the people or places are familiar to us. There are different ways in which photographs can be read, but even the most naive viewer has no difficulty making a start. Unlike the written word, photographs carry little with them in the form of high cultural baggage, social class connotations or other pretensions. Berger would claim that

this is due to the fact that the photograph is close to human memory. Susan Sontag makes a similar point. For better and for worse, photographs are a part of the vernacular culture. Perhaps our easy ability, indeed our compulsion, to talk about photographs stems from a need to close the gaps between the photograph as an image and our memories or assumptions about people, places and events.

Complex social settings, like schools and classrooms, are particularly appropriate as sites for photographic research. They are appropriate because our experience of them (as Philip Jackson has argued) is closely associated with our memories of childhood, but also because the very violence that photographs inflict on appearances is isomorphic with the fragments of experience most of us have of schools and schooling. We have argued elsewhere (Walker and Adelman, 1975) that while photographs provide records of classroom events that are lacking in coherence, this incoherence is in itself characteristic of life in classrooms.

This social construction of meaning requires the researcher to enter the process by which individuals close the spaces between what is personal and what is social (and between what is agency and what is structure). 'All photographed events are

ambiguous', writes Berger elsewhere, 'except to those whose personal relation to the event is such that their own lives supply the missing continuity' (Berger and Mohr, 1982, p. 128). An important set of questions about photographs and the uses we make of them concern the relations between the photograph and human memory. When we talk about photographs, part of what we do is to construct or reconstruct shared memories. Voice, memory and biography are inextricably interrelated. The reading of a photograph is a cultural act and one that allows the observer some glimpse of ways in which individuals create meaning in their lives. The narration that Berger finds missing in the photographic record is supplied at the point of view.

This leads to an important distinction that needs to be made between two uses and intentions for photography. There is the public photograph which Berger says' . . . usually presents an event, a seized set of appearances, which has nothing to do with us, its readers, or with the original meaning of the event. It offers information, but information severed from all lived experience. If the public photograph contributes to a memory, it is to the memory of an unknowable and total stranger . . . It records an instant sight about which this stranger has shouted: Look!' (Berger, 1980, p. 51). The public photograph is familiar to us in the press and in art, and it is also the staple of advertising, illustration and publicity.

Quite different is the private photograph which, in contrast to the alienated object that is the public photograph, belongs within the realm of lived experience. 'The private photograph — the portrait of a mother, a picture of a daughter, a group photograph of one's own team — is appreciated and read in a context which is continuous with that from which the camera removed it . . . such a photograph remains surrounded by the meaning from which it was severed. A mechanical device, the camera has been used as an instrument to contribute to living memory. The photograph is a memento from a life being lived' (*ibid*, p. 52).

One of the themes of this chapter is that the distinction that Berger makes between 'public' and 'private' uses of photography parallels the distinction I made in the introduction between two ways of approaching qualitative research.[2] The 'public' photograph, I believe, is similar to the quote, ripped from its context and relocated in a text created by the author; a technique we conventionally use in qualitative research. The 'private' photograph cannot be understood without engaging subjectivities, for to do so is, by definition, to return to the realm of the 'public' . . .

Once we begin to look at photographs as keys to memory, rather than as illustrative of social facts, their potential role in research becomes clear. We can use the photograph in the context of memory-work, as an instrument for the recovery of meaning, in a way that we all recognise when we think of how we view collections of photographs in the drawer at home. What is important is not the image in itself so much as the relationship between the image and the ways we make sense of it and the ways in which we value it. (John Berger's collaborator-photographer, Jean Mohr writes perceptively about the ways we value some images rather than others (Berger and Mohr, 1982), and Susan Sontag makes a similar point in a film she made for the BBC about her book, *On Photography*).

The power of the photograph lies to some extent in its exactness and precision, which lend it an undeniability, despite its acknowledged capacity to select and distort. The ways in which the camera 'sees' are very different from the ways in which we see things, but in that difference lie important keys to understanding the intersection of what is personal and what is social.

Why the Distinction?

For evaluation and research the distinction between public and private uses for photographs has considerable importance. It provides the key to purposes that depend on developing uses for photographs that go beyond the positivist assertion that photographs provide a literal truth and it provides an alternative to viewing photographs as inert visual records. Part of the challenge for research I believe, despite what I said earlier about the use of visual material in science, lies in moving away from a conception of photographs as data. In using photographs in educational research, what is most often important is not the use of photographs in the process of producing data but the role of research in looking at their context of use. The questions are not about photographs as records so much as about the ways in which they are interpreted.

Similarly, photographs are often best used in evaluation as a way of engaging an audience in the process of evaluation. This form of engagement has long been an aspiration of evaluators, especially those who are concerned with what Barry MacDonald, (1974) has called 'democratic evaluation', but in practice the kind of participation required by participative models of democracy is very difficult to achieve.

As against print, photographs can be used to engage audiences in different ways, to disrupt the expectations that people may have about forms and channels of reporting, and to undercut the assumptions that they may hold about where power and authority lie in the relations between those involved. It is, for example, not uncommon for those in bureaucratic positions of power to be dismissive of photographs, for their use often touches on the investment that they have in the control of the word, especially the written word, as a way of maintaining, extending and reinforcing their position. Any uses of information that look likely to threaten this policing of language may be treated with suspicion. Most evaluators work primarily with numbers or with words and, whatever their intentions, these are both systems which tend to reinforce perceived hierarchies. In any text the reader and the writer are separated in ways that parallel the separation of teacher and student in a class. Numbers and words trigger responses of deference and demeanour effectively discriminating against the less well educated, the less articulate and the less numerate, especially when the context is public.

Of course photographs have the same potential to create the basis for manipulation, distortion and the exercise of authority, but for Berger's notion of the private photograph, which relocates ownership and authority in the process of interpretation, which confuses and complicates the relation between the subject and the object, which multiplies the sources of information brought to bear on interpretation and which threatens to mock any attempts that are made to impose singular views.

Practical Ideas

There are many ways in which photographs can be used depending on the circumstances. Most of them depend crucially on what John Collier, an American photographer and anthropologist, calls the 'can-opener effect', that is the capacity of photographs to open up conversations between people. For many years Collier trained anthropologists in the use of photography and one of his key themes is the way in which photographs can be used to speed up the process of establishing fieldwork relationships, of getting to know people and to develop a degree of trust between outsiders and insiders (Collier, 1967).

Building on Collier's work, ideas I, various colleagues and students have found effective include:

— *using photographs as a basis for interviewing*:
Try giving people large numbers of prints of an event and asking them to sort them, this will give you some insight into their categories rather than yours. Extract photographs that seem to be particularly puzzling, or elicit particular responses and show them to others. Get some sense of the diversity of response, for instance, in schools children often respond very differently to teachers and parents' responses are different again.

— *using photographs to get children to talk about life in classrooms and in schools*:
We have found that rapid sequences are particularly useful, that 'clearing up' time photographs at the end of the lesson are often very revealing and provide a natural opportunity for people to talk about their responses to the lesson as a whole.

— *using photographs to get people to write*:
Photographs are effective as a stimulus for writing. In assembling displays of photographs we have found that people are as interested in seeing what they

and their friends have said as they are in the pictures themselves. This is especially true of students, who often have very different perceptions of events.
— *using photographs as a means of exchange between people who have never met*: At Deakin University, we routinely get teachers in distance education courses to exchange photographs of themselves teaching in exchange for commentaries on the photographs written by someone else on the course. Howard Becker, an American sociologist and photography teacher, gets photography students to exchange exposed but unprocessed film with students on another course elsewhere, each student then has to process, print, select and display the work of someone else. This separation of the 'taking' of photographs from their presentation is superficially like the situation that exists in newspaper production but, as we use it, the emphasis is on exploring the ways in which meaning is constructed rather than on imposing one interpretation over another.
— *using polaroid photographs of people as the basis for making finger puppets*: An idea developed from play therapy, this is a good alternative to asking young children directly to recall what happened in an interview, as well as having a creative capacity in itself.

Planning an Evaluation

The points I have been emphasizing are that photographs are best used in evaluation and research as a 'mainstream' rather than as an 'add-on' device, and that it is important to relate photographs to interviewing, observation, displays and discussions. This in turn implies that a degree of planning and organization is necessary. It is not just a question of making sure that there is film in the camera, but of having some idea what it is you want the photographs to do in the context of the research or evaluation design.

There are different ways of going about this, one is to create space for an experienced photographer or photojournalist, to agree a set of themes and a way of working and to develop the study collaboratively. This was the strategy Janine Wiedel and I used in a study of a class of students in a London secondary school (Walker and Wiedel, 1985). The advantages of an open design of this kind include the capacity to be responsive and provide space for the photographer to exercise aesthetic judgment. It is a style of working derived directly from the participant observation tradition.

In contrast, a more organized approach has been developed by Pat Templin, who has used photographs on a number of occasions as a means of evaluating conferences. Here the evaluation problem, by its nature, imposes the need to attend carefully to selection, balance, fast turn around and extensive interviewing. In one, two or three days the event is over and there are no repeats, so you have to work fast and know what you are doing! The procedures Pat has developed in this work provide a good starting point for any photographic evaluation.

Finally, on a practical note, if you use photography as a research or evaluation method and technique lets you down, don't throw away photographs that you think are failures! One of the most interesting displays I have seen was at my daughter's primary school following a school trip. The teacher had assembled all the 'failed' photographs taken by the children — heads cut off, no-one in the

Rob Walker

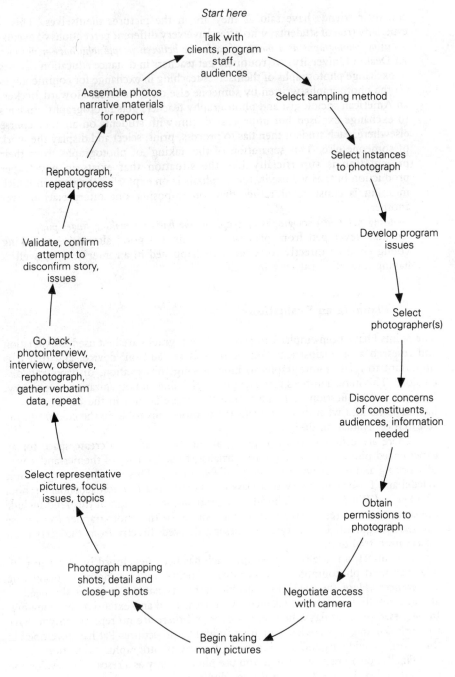

Start here

Talk with clients, program staff, audiences

Assemble photos narrative materials for report

Select sampling method

Rephotograph, repeat process

Select instances to photograph

Validate, confirm attempt to disconfirm story, issues

Develop program issues

Go back, photointerview, interview, observe, rephotograph, gather verbatim data, repeat

Select photographer(s)

Discover concerns of constituents, audiences, information needed

Select representative pictures, focus issues, topics

Obtain permissions to photograph

Photograph mapping shots, detail and close-up shots

Negotiate access with camera

Begin taking many pictures

Figure 5.1

(Source: Templin, 1979; see also Templin, 1982)

frame, the heron (Well, it was there when I took the picture!') . . . The children had used these for developing collages which mixed prints and drawing, so that the picture with no heads had the heads drawn in, the heron appeared walking out from behind the frame and the empty frame appeared in a picture frame on a living room wall.

An Example

All the ideas I have outlined concern ways of using photography within a research or evaluation study as a way of working rather than as a means of illustrating other data. My claim is that photography has the capacity to provide a distinctive qualitative 'voice'. Here is an example, these pictures are taken from a study of a secondary school by Jon Prosser. Jon used photographs as a means of developing an understanding of the culture of a school that had undergone amalgamation and reorganization. Approaching the problem visually rather than verbally gave him access to understandings of the school that are at a level of some subtlety and complexity. What is interesting in the present context is that Jon did the reverse of what is normally done in using photographs. He worked from the pictures to words, rather than using pictures to illustrate what had already been written.

'Parents' Evening: a formal occasion. Following the head's words of welcome, parents move quickly to the rows of chairs provided. I was always shocked by the intensity of interaction between parents and teachers. After introductions and hand shakes, it is a complicated routine of hand flapping, usually by teachers, and intense eye contact, reminiscent of the mating ritual of Great Crested Grebes. Both teacher and parent put on a 'performance'. It is an evening of ritual.

The title of this book presents an important challenge to qualitative research, for in some ways the terms 'research' and 'voice' seem at odds with each other. In the sense that research is systematic enquiry made public (Rudduck and Hopkins, 1985), researchers are under some obligation to establish conventions, principles and procedures that make what they do accessible, which in turn implies a degree of consensus and conformity, and even uniformity. On the other hand, the notion of 'voice', carries the contrary expectation of a personal view. When we read a

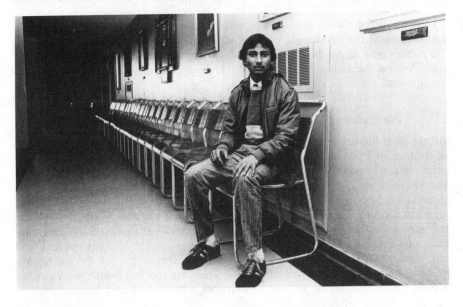

Mohammed's First Day. Mohammed had only just arrived in the school and was 'parked' in the main hall, among the cultural symbols of an old grammar school with a history going back to 1564. Mohammed could speak very little English and could not read. His native language was Bengali — he was from Bangladesh. I took the photograph because I felt unhappy for him. It wasn't the huge cultural difference between him and the school, but the realization that he was entering an institution — the row of chairs, the plastic floor tiles, the gloomy darkness in the distance — that's what bothered me. I followed him for nine months, taking shots of his 'integration'. Things worked out well for him.

case study by a particular author we come to it with certain expectations about the interests, preoccupations and style of the writer. If we were able to replicate case studies or ethnographies by sending multiple observers into a single site, we would expect marked differences in the results that derived from the author as much as from the site.

The assumption that the ethnographer is inscribed in the ethnography is not a new one. Anthropologists often quote a classic instance in cultural anthropology, where two researchers studied the same Mexican village (Redfield, 1930; Lewis, 1951). Time and other variables apart, the images and preoccupations that emerge from each study are very different. Where one author found harmony, the other found conflict. Oscar Lewis (1951) writes:

> The impression given by Redfield's study of Tepoztlan is that of a relatively homogeneous, isolated, smoothly functioning, and well integrated society made up of a contented and well-adjusted people. His picture[3] of the village has a Rousseauan quality which glosses lightly over evidence of violence, disruption, cruelty, disease, suffering and maladjustment. We are told little of poverty, economic problems or political schisms. Throughout his study we find an emphasis upon the cooperative and unifying factors in Tepoztecan society. Our findings, on the other hand, would emphasise the underlying individualism of Tepoztecan institutions and character,

the lack of cooperation, the tensions between villages within the municipio, the schisms within the village, and the pervading quality of fear, envy and distrust in inter-personal relations. (pp. 428–9)

Oscar Lewis explains part of the difference in view between himself and Redfield in terms of history and social change, part in terms of their focus on different questions and part on the different degree of intimacy they each had with the site, but some of the difference can be seen in terms of different voices. Redfield, Lewis (1951) points out, chose to ignore some things at the expense of others:

Redfield presented only the positive and formal aspects of inter-personal relations . . . he failed to deal with some of the negative and disruptive aspects of village life, such as the fairly high incidence of stealing, quarrels and physical violence. An examination of the local records revealed that in the year Redfield lived in the village there were 175 reported cases of crime and misdemeanors in the local court. Most of these cases were offences against persons and property. Since not all cases reach the local authorities, this number is indicative of considerable conflict. (*ibid*, p. 450)

Furthermore, it is not just selective reporting that leads to the formation or support of a viewpoint: it is built in to the language of description, notice the use of the word 'picture' in the initial quote above. Lewis observes:

Redfield described local politics as a game, but we found that politics was a very serious affair which frequently led to violence. The year Redfield was there, the political schisms culminated in open violence bordering on civil war, and it was this situation which finally resulted in Redfield's leaving the village . . . (*ibid*)

Generally, it is clear that selection at a number of levels, including identifying a site, locating reliable informants, finding social situations in which one can engage with ease, through to the language of reporting, are all factors in the construction of 'voice'. And, despite its apparently mechanical nature, photography is free of none of these. As well as having a grammar of its own, photography has a specialist set of sources of judgment including framing, cropping and the elusive concept of the 'proper moment'. As Susan Sontag (1979) put it:

The photographer was thought (in the early days of photography) to be an acute but non-interfering observer — a scribe, not a poet. But as people quickly discovered that nobody takes the same picture of the same thing, the supposition that cameras furnish an impersonal, objective image yielded to the fact that photographs are evidence not only of what's there but of what an individual sees, not just a record but an evaluation of the world. (p. 88)

Once we start to look on photographs as having a 'voice' (or more accurately a 'view' or a 'vision'), then it becomes possible to ask questions about the relation of the photographer to both the object and the subject of the picture. Such questions quickly lead to questions that are familiar to social scientists, questions about objectivity and subjectivity, representativeness, reliability, validity and generalizability. These questions are often described as though they were simply technical problems, capable of reasonable resolution, but in practice they often appear as moral dilemmas, concerned with selection, framing, judgment, risk and making one interpretation rather than another.

Real Schools

As researchers, we have a tendency to assume that questions about the reliability or validity of voices are essentially technical, not moral, questions. We too easily forget the achievements of ethnomethodology, and its demonstration that they are issues for us all, and not so much technical as close to defining our sense of identity (classically in Garfinkel, 1967). Photographs, exemplify the ethnomethodological processes of 'remedying' and 'filling-in', for they exist on the boundary between what is familiar and what is unknown. When we look at a photograph the picture acts as a window to a dictionary of meanings, a picture of a school or a classroom causes us to search a range of memories in order to locate this specific instance which is essentially unknown to us. We are aware, in looking at a photograph at possibilities that lie just beyond our horizon of recognition and familiarity.

Susan Sontag has pointed out that the taking of a photograph is not simply the mechanical process it sometimes seems but is capable of generating surprises. Likewise, photographs are not just about the things that they portray but also about the ways in which we make sense of them. Looking at pictures of schools and classrooms challenges the assumptions we make about what a 'real' school or classroom looks like.

The notion of 'real school' as a significant concept in educational debate has recently been described in a novel and interesting way by Mary Haywood Metz (1990). In a study of the ways in which eight schools were responding to attempts to introduce change through policymaking, Metz points out that educational reformers 'assume a common script'. They write about schools as though they were single and singular institutions, and indeed, in her research, it appeared true that schools were very similar in many ways; in the work of teachers, in the use of textbooks in instruction, in the ways in which they organised time and space. But equally, there were many respects in which the schools were idiosyncratic, especially as a result of their need to adapt to local circumstances.

Metz found this puzzling, for while her overwhelming impression from the fieldwork data was of the differences between schools this seemed unrecognized by many of those trying to bring about change:

> . . . this variation riveted our attention as we moved from school to school
> . . . (but) . . . we puzzled over the discrepency between our diverse experiences and the reformer's assumption that schools are standard . . . (p. 76)

Metz came to explain the discrepency between aspiration and achievement in the schools in terms of the notion of 'real school'. 'We felt we were watching a play. The title was *Real School'* (*ibid*, p. 83) The common script, she argued, held together a symbolic system and a crucial set of values, even in the face of real variations in provision, experience and achievement. The notion of 'real school' allowed teachers and others to live with a singular image of schooling in the face of local adaptation within a system that is ideologically unified (the US, unlike Australia and Britain, generally has public faith in public education). Whenever she pointed up ways in which particular schools did not appear to be meeting general standards, people would say things like, 'You have to be realistic'.

Looking at photographs creates a similar sense of contradiction between image and appearance. A tension is created between the image and the picture, between what we expect to observe and what we see. 'Real school', in Metz' research is not just an artifact of qualitative methods but provides the images that make it possible to maintain a rhetoric or an institutional facade of equity in the face of significant evidence to the contrary. Images, we need to remember, are not just adjuncts to print, but carry heavy cultural traffic on their own account.

Notes

1 This paper derives from a research project 'Schooling the Future', funded by the Australian Research Council. The research team includes Richard Bates, Chris Bigum, Lindsay Fitzclarence and Bill Green. It is an extended version of a paper commissioned by the Arts Council (UK).
2 Perceptive readers will also note parallels with the notions of 'emic' and 'etic' description as formalized in anthropology by Kenneth Pike. For an accessible account of Pike's terms, see Harris (1964) pp. 133–50.
3 Note the visual allusion!

References

BARTHES, R. (1982) *Camera Lucida: Reflections on Photography*, London, Cape.
BERGER, J. (1978) 'Ways of remembering', *Camerawork*, **10**, London, Half Moon Gallery.
BERGER, J. (1980) *About Looking*, London, Writers and Readers.
BERGER, J. and MOHR, J. (1982) *Another Way of Telling*, London, Writers and Readers.
CHARLESWORTH, M. *et al.* (1989), *Life Among the Scientists: An Autobiographical Study of an Australian Scientific Community*, Melbourne, Oxford University Press.
COLLIER, J. (1967) *Visual Anthropology: Photography as a Research Method*, New York, Holt, Rinehart & Winston.
GARFINKEL, H. (1967) *Studies in Ethnomethodology*, Englewood Cliffs, NJ, Prentice Hall.
GOULD, S.J. (1990) *Wonderful Life: The Burgess Shale and the Nature of History*, London, Hutchinson Radius.
HARRIS, M. (1964) *The Nature of Cultural Things*, New York, Random House.
ISHERWOOD, C. (1945) *Goodbye to Berlin*, Harmondsworth, Penguin.
LEWIS, O. (1951) *Life in a Mexican Village: Tepoztlan Restudied*, Urbana, University of Illinios Press.
MACDONALD, B. (1974) 'Evaluation and the control of education' in MACDONALD, B. and WALKER, R., (Eds) *Information, Evaluation, Research and the Problem of Control*, Norwich, University of East Anglia.
METZ, M.H. (1990) 'Real school: A universal drama amid disparate experience' in MITCHELL, D.E. and GOERTZ, M. (Eds) *Educational Politics for the New Century*, Lewes, Falmer Press.

PROSSER, J. (1989) *Classroom Processes*, Multimedia Course Materials, Geelong, Deakin University Press, **ECT** 401.

PROSSER, J. (1991) *The Nature of School: An Ethnographic Study*, School of Education, University of York.

REDFIELD, R. (1930) *Tepoztlan — A Mexican Village*, Chicago, IL, University of Chicago Press.

RUDDUCK, J. and HOPKINS, D. (Eds) (1985) *Research as a Basis for Teaching: Readings from the Work of Lawrence Stenhouse*, London, Heinemann.

SONTAG, S. (nd) *On Photography: A Film*. BBC TV, London.

SONTAG, S. (1979) *On Photography*, Harmondsworth, Penguin.

STASZ, C. (1979) 'The early history of visual sociology' in WAGNER, J. (Ed.) *Images of Information: Still Photography in the Social Sciences*, Beverley Hills, CA, Sage Focus Edition.

TEMPLIN, P. (1979) *Photography as an Evaluation Technique*, Monograph no. 32, Research on Evaluation Program, Portland, OR, North West Regional Educational Laboratory.

TEMPLIN, P. (1982) 'Still photography in evaluation' in SMITH, N.L. (Ed.) *Communication Strategies in Evaluation*, Beverley Hills, CA, Sage.

WALKER, R. (1985) *Doing Research: A Handlook for Teachers*, London, Methuen.

WALKER, R. and ADELMAN, C. (1975) *A Guide to Classroom Observation*, (photographs by Janine Wiedel), London, Methuen.

WALKER, R., INGVARSON, L. and BORTHWICK, A. (1981) *History Teaching at Karingal School: A Photographic Case Study*, Geelong, Deakin University Press.

WALKER, R. and WIEDEL, J. (1985) 'Using photographs in a discipline of words' in BURGESS, R. (Ed.). *Field Methods in the Study of Education*, Lewes, Falmer Press, pp. 191–216.

WITKIN, R. (1976) *The Intelligence of Feeling*, London, Heinemann.

Chapter 6

Why I Like to Look: On the Use of Videotape as an Instrument in Educational Research

Hugh Mehan

When I started conducting research on schools in 1969, the US was in the middle of the Civil Rights movement, protesting the war in Vietnam and still reeling from the assassination of JFK. The civil rights movement had shifted from marches in the deep South to the streets in the North. The legal agenda moved forward under the crafty leadership of Kennedy's successor, Lyndon Baines Johnson. The Great Society, with its 'war on poverty'[1] produced significant social legislation extending civil rights into new domains.

Some of these programs addressed the poor school performance of America's poor students. The most notable of these was the Head Start Program. Adopting a sports metaphor, Head Start accepted uncritically America's belief in life as a race, a competition, in which people get ahead by hard work and individual effort. What made Head Start unique was its acknowledgment that white middle and upper income kids had an advantage in the race for success. In order to level the playing field for poor and minority groups, the government provided considerable amounts of federal money to school districts. Programs all over the US sprang up to compensate for the presumed deficiencies in the family and cultural arrangements of poor and minority students.

Right in the middle of this considerable governmental intervention launched in the name of equality of opportunity came an unprecedented article by Arthur Jensen. The *Harvard Educational Review* devoted an entire issue to Jensen's analysis of differences between black and white school performance (Jensen, 1969). The lead sentence of the article said 'compensatory education has been tried, and it has failed'. Jensen went on to argue that attempts to close the gap between black and white school achievement were doomed to failure because blacks had a genetic deficiency in intelligence. This article sent shock waves through academic and political circles. Blacks and liberals were incensed by the racism underlying Jensen's argument. Government officials were angered because the interventionist assumptions of the Great Society were undermined by Jensen's biological determinism.

The liberal agenda to close social divisions by governmental intervention, especially in schooling, received another blow about this time. James Coleman reported the results of a massive government sponsored project examining the influence that the quality of schooling had on students' school achievement. Instead of reporting the expected finding that schools with better trained and better paid teachers, well stocked science labs and elaborate facilities were better than schools with poorly trained and underpaid teachers and poor facilities, Coleman shocked liberal educators with his conclusion that 'schools don't make a difference, family backgrounds do' (Coleman *et al.*, 1966). Coleman, like Jensen, cut to the heart of America's optimistic achievement ideology. They questioned whether a person can work hard to get ahead, whether the environment can be modified to overcome limitations imposed by quirks at birth, such as gender, race, family socioeconomic position and ethnicity.

In addition to a common ideological orientation, these studies had methodological elements in common. Both were large-scale surveys. Jensen relied on the results of massive IQ testing; Coleman used the results of a national survey of high school students.

I entered this scene with a number of convictions. One was a disquiet about the methodological approach beneath work like Jensen's and Coleman's. Like many others who would later occupy the interpretive space in educational research, I felt that large scale surveys and experiments masked important theoretical and policy issues, were ill-equipped to uncover the root causes of inequality and did not enable us to hear the voices of the disenfranchised. I thought that it was necessary to look much more closely at social life and listen to the voices of the dispossessed to understand the complex processes composing inequality. A second was policy oriented. Despite Coleman's and Jensen's attack, I still believed schools could make a difference in the lives of the children who attended them. A third was theoretical. As a result of studying with Cicourel (1964, 1968 and 1973) and reading Garfinkel (1967) and Schutz (1962), I was convinced that notions like 'intelligence', 'school success' and 'school failure' were social or cultural, not natural or given. That is, cognitive skills don't reside in the head of people, including children in schools, they reside in social situations which are composed of people and often technology such as the IQ test. Talent (or the lack of it) is not given in the nature of things, it is the product of social arrangements, which often have an institutional framework and a long cultural history (Mehan and Wood, 1975).

The Construction of Students' Intelligence in Social Interaction

These ideas converged in my first study (Mehan, 1973 and 1974), in which I compared kids in lessons, tests, and at home. Like Labov (1972) and Philips (1972), I reported a finding which later became a staple observation in the 'situated cognition' literature (LCHC, 1983; Lave, 1988; Rogoff and Wertsch, 1984): kids' performance varied as a function of the type of situation they were in. Students who had difficulty with linguistic constructions (for example, the locative) on standardized tests had little difficulty when these same prepositions were contextualized as part of classroom lessons or instructions.

I uncovered this variation through a close analysis of discourse in testing, home and lesson activities, facilitated by videotapes of tests and lessons at school and play at home. Like the other investigators on this project (Cicourel *et al.*, 1974), I taped events, transcribed and analyzed the interaction. When I looked at the tapes and listened to the children over and over again, I began to see the way in which behavior which we attribute to children as their private possession emerged from the interaction between the tester or teacher and the student.

Let me illustrate what I mean from examples of testing interaction. The protocol for intelligence tests directs testers to ask questions in a mechanical, routinized way. They are to ask a question, pause, let students respond, record the answers and go on to the next question. This protocol, and the theory of intelligence that underlies it, assumes that talent is inside the student and the test 'taps' or extracts that talent. The way in which the results of testing are presented, i.e., in the form of test scores which presumably represent that individual effort, reinforces that theory. When we examine tester-student discourse, however, we get a different, a much more social view of talent.

Testers and students collaborated in the production of test results. This collaboration was visible in each and every tester-student exchange. It was particularly visible when testers inquired about students' answers rather than going on to the next question. A question on the Wechsler Intelligence Scale for Children (WISC) in use at the time of my study was: 'What is the thing to do if you lose a ball that belonged to one of your friends?' After the tester asked this question, the following exchange took place:

Student: 'Might get another one for her?'
Tester: 'Yeah. Is there anything else you might do?'

That is, instead of asking the next question, the tester questioned the student's answer. The tester's intervention led the student to modify his answer:

Student: 'Tell her the truth.'

I saw this pattern over and over again in tests I videotaped and analyzed (Mehan, 1973 and 1978). Importantly, this kind of interaction influenced students' test results. Depending upon whether a tester recorded the first or subsequent answers after these interventions, a student's test score could vary by as much as 25 per cent (Mehan, 1978).

The collaborative construction of test answers was also visible when students started to answer before a tester completely answered a question. A question on the Basic Concept Inventory, used in the school at the time of my study, is supposed to be read by the tester this way:

Tester: There is a ball in one of these boxes (touches a box on a page with a picture of two boxes on it). Which box is the ball in. Tell me what you know, don't guess.

The child is supposed to indicate the box which the tester had not touched because she can infer its presence from the information given. In one particularly poignant exchange, 'Jenny' started answering the question before the tester completed her question. The exchange went like this:

Tester: Jenny, there is a ball in one of these boxes (touches page)
Jenny: (touched one of the boxes)
Tester: Which box is the ball in?

> *Jenny:* (touched the box again)
> *Tester:* Tell me what you know. Don't guess.
> *Jenny:* (shook her head 'no.')

At this point, Jenny has responded to the tester's question three times; twice before the question was completed. The child's multiple responses pose an interpretive problem for the tester: Which of these three *responses* is the child's *answer*? The answer to that question is not inherent in Jenny's behavior; the tester must interpret the child's behavior, choosing one of three responses. In this case, the tester chose the third response (the child's head nod) because (as she told me in an interview after the test) this was the only response which occurred after the question had been read completely. That interpretation meant the child got this question wrong.

The very next question on the test asks the exact same question, but presents the child with a page with three not two boxes on it. Now the child is to answer 'I don't know' because there is no empirical evidence upon which to locate the ball. The exchange between the tester and Jenny went like this:

> *Tester:* There is a ball in one of these boxes (touches a box on a page with a picture of two boxes on it). Which box is the ball in. Tell me what you know, don't guess.
> *Jenny:* I'm not guessing
> *Tester:* Good girl. There's no way of knowing is there?
> *Jenny:* Uh uh (shaking her head 'no').

The tester interpreted Jenny's statement ('I'm not guessing') to mean she chose not to touch the page, i.e., she knew the difference between knowing and guessing. The tester reifies this interpretation in the next exchange where Jenny's agreement with the tester's proposition was treated as confirmation. The tester scored Jenny as answering this question correctly.

A different interpretation of this sequence, one which enables us to hear Jenny's view of things, became available by watching the testing tape carefully. Just as the tester started to complement Jenny for 'not guessing', her right hand had started moving toward the page on the table. Jenny arrested this movement just as the tester said 'good girl', apparently realizing that any other action would be incorrect. This means that Jenny's correct answer on this question is jointly produced. Following out this logic, Jenny's incorrect answer on the previous question is the result of combined action between the tester and the student. The tester's statement 'don't guess', which from the point of view of testing protocol was to implore the child to act on empirical evidence, was interpreted by the child as a command 'don't touch the page anymore'.

In sum, listening closely to tester-student discourse, afforded by videotape of actual testing encounters, along with test scores, produces a different view of intelligence than an examination of test scores taken alone. Intelligence, that talent which we attribute to individuals, emerges from a social nexus, the interaction between testers, students and the piece of technology called the test. Tester-student exchanges constitute an answer; a summary of students' answers-to-questions constitutes their scores. Test scores, when presented as a numeral, are an individualized product which is divorced from the social means which produced them.

The Socialization of Students into Implicit Classroom Culture

A fortuitous circumstance led me to explore further the use of videotape as a tool to hear students' voice and to better ground my theoretical notions. Courtney B. Cazden, a noted authority on child language and education on the faculty of the Harvard Graduate School of Education, wanted to return to the classroom in order to reaquaint herself with the real world of elementary school teaching. After I made arrangements with the San Diego City Schools for a year of teaching responsibilities, we planned a comprehensive examination of classroom discourse. Based on work that was unfolding simultaneously (McDermott, 1974; Erickson and Schultz, 1977), I had some speculations about what counted as success in elementary school classrooms. McDermott, Erickson and Schultz were displaying in elegant presentations delicately choreographed teacher-student and counselor-student routines. They were locating the structures of interactional synchrony in head nods and elbow bends.

Suppose students' success in classrooms had this social foundation? That is, in addition to learning to read, write, compute, master natural science and social science 'facts,' etc., students have to learn that there are interactionally appropriate ways in which to cast their academic knowledge, that certain ways of talking and acting are appropriate on some occasions and not others. Could we see and hear students learning the classroom culture as a school year progressed? Would students who a teacher considered 'successful' display a finer sense of interactional synchrony than students judged less successful?

In order to document the skills and abilities that students needed to display in order to be judged as competent students, we videotaped an hour of activities in Cazden's classroom at regular intervals throughout the school year. A close examination of these classroom lessons showed they had a recurrent structure: the teacher initiated a round of questioning; students replied to the teacher's initiation and then the teacher evaluated the students' replies:

	Initiation	*Reply*	*Evaluation*
8:5	T: . . . where were you born Prenda?	P: San Diego.	T: You were born in San Diego, alright.
8:6	T: Um, can you come up and find San Diego on the map?	P: (goes to board and points).	T: Right there, ok.

Although this segment is brief, it contains the main ingredients of classroom lessons (Mehan, 1979). First is their sequential structure. While everyday conversations seem to be organized in two part sequences (Sacks *et al.*, 1974), classroom lessons are organized into three-part sequences; a teacher's initiation act induces a student's reply, which in turn invokes a teacher's evaluation. This three-part structure seems to be the function of the kinds of questions teachers ask. Teachers' questions often test students' knowledge rather than seek new information. These 'known information questions' are responsible for the presence of the evaluation act in the third slot in the syntax of classroom lessons. Also note that the initiation act not only specifies an action to be taken (answering the question), it also identifies the person who is to take the action. That is, the normative order of the classroom includes a set of procedures for allocating turns and gaining access to the floor. Some of these (like the example above) select an individual to speak. Others (for example, 'raise your hand if you know the answer') enable students to select themselves as next speaker; still others (for example, 'what's the answer to this one?') facilitate a group response. Thus, while access to the floor is governed by rules, the rules proscribe different behavior. There are occasions when students can reply directly and others when they must first receive permission to reply. This means that students have to determine when the rules apply, a difficult task because the rules are seldom stated directly. Because the rules governing turn taking are tacit, students must infer the appropriate way to engage in classroom interaction from the ongoing flow of discourse.

Distinguishing the special features of classroom lessons is an important part of the socialization of students into the culture of the classroom. Students need to learn that teachers will ask them questions even when they know the answers. They need to learn that teachers control the floor, which means that students cannot offer their opinions or volunteer their ideas whenever they want. Furthermore, teachers not only parcel out the floor; they take it back after a student replies.

Gumperz (1982), Philips (1982), Erickson and Mohatt (1982) and Heath (1982) suggest that the discourse features of the language spoken in the home of low income and linguistic minority youth does not match the discourse features of the language used in the classroom. And this mismatch is responsible for their poor academic performance. Our description of the unique features of classroom lessons contributed to this line of thinking by calling attention to the special challenge students face when they enter the school and confront the implicit rules of classroom discourse.

The 'cultural discontinuity' account challenges the determinism in class based theories (for example, Coleman, Bowles and Gintis, Jencks) and Jensen's hereditary deprivation account of differential school performance by shifting the focus of attention away from the characteristics of students, their families, their cultures. Researchers who have documented the subtle features of classroom discourse, tester-student interaction and home-school language say that the source of school difficulties is not to be found between the ears of low income children or under the skin of black and Latino children. It is to be found in the relationship between the social organization of the family and the social organization of the school.

The Construction of Educationally Handicapped Students

A number of researchers were studying the social organization of classroom discourse, teaching/learning and drawing the implications for the education of students from underrepresented groups during the 1970s, including Michael Cole, Roger Shuy and Peg Griffin, Cazden and Erickson. These 'schleppers' (so named because we hauled video equipment from place to place) met as frequently as possible to 'watch tape', in which we presented findings, demonstrated techniques of analysis, drew implications. An underlying goal of these meetings was to see whether it was possible to generalize beyond the individual cases we had studied.

Despite these efforts to generalize, the entire enterprise was subjected to criticism. Interpretive studies were dismissed by Karabel and Halsey (1977) for focussing too much on 'micro' processes, thereby ignoring 'larger' social forces (for example, the constraints imposed by capitalism, social class, bureaucracy). Ogbu (1981) took Erickson and others to task for not explaining the success of ethnic groups which shared similar circumstances with blacks, Latinos and native Americans. More recently, interpretive studies have been criticized for a consensual world view, one which overlooks the exercise of power and the presence of conflict (Foley, 1990).

It was with these criticisms in mind that I designed a study to describe the process by which students' identities in school were constituted. I firmly believed that the process of examining events closely would reveal social structure in the making. As my friend and colleague Ray McDermott was fond of saying, 'if you grasp enough of the social interaction, then you have the social structure'. I also believed that discourse analytic techniques, though tedious, could be applied beyond the boundaries of a single event. It was not necessary to abandon close analysis of social interaction in order to grasp social structure; it was only necessary to extend the analysis, to link events together. Therefore, in order to show the power of constitutive or constructivist theory, I decided to follow students through some of the crucial events in their school lives. The result was a study which focussed on a school district not a classroom, situated the school district in relationship to its community, state and federal laws and utilized data from many sources including students' records, interviews, observations, videotape.

To carry this off, I capitalized on a recurrent feature of school life: the referral of students from classrooms for special help. After a summertime of consultations with teachers, principals, and (most importantly for the practicalities of the research) school secretaries, I arranged to be called if a teacher referred a student for special help, I would be notified. Then either me or one of my graduate student assistants observed in the classroom and videotaped key events. We analyzed the lesson structure, looking for the form/content distinctions that guided our previous work. We also interviewed teachers about the 'referral student' in relation to other students. If students were referred for educational testing (and if we were able to secure parental and tester permission), we videotaped testing encounters, looking especially to see whether testers' contributions to test scores were distributed differentially across ethnic groups. Finally, we observed (and as often as possible videotaped) the committee meeting in which a decision was made to place students in 'special education' or the regular classroom.

This study, then, took the form of case studies, in which the construction of students' profiles across key events was documented (Mehan *et al.*, 1986). Let me illustrate what we did and what we found by summarizing one student's case.

The process by which a child became 'educationally handicapped' usually began in the classroom when a teacher referred a child by completing a referral form. Completing the form does not automatically make the child educationally handicapped; but unless that bureaucratic step is taken, the child can not be eligible to achieve that status. As we followed students' cases through the referral system, we found that fiscal, legal and practical circumstances influenced the construction of students' identities. For example, 'Ms. Payne' referred 'Shane' during the second week of September for his 'low academic performance' and his 'difficulty in applying himself to his daily class work.'[2] At its first meeting in October, the School Appraisal Team, a committee of educators at the 'Desert Vista School' charged with the responsibility of assessing referrals, instructed the school psychologist to test Shane. The recommended assessment did not take place, however, until December and January because the school psychologist had difficulty in obtaining permission to test from Shane's parents (who were separated at the time) and obtaining records from Shane's previous school district.

It was not until 2 February, four months after the referral was initiated, that the committee heard the testing report. The delay was exacerbated by the itinerant nature of the school psychologist's work assignment. Responsible for a number of schools in the district, she rotated testing. Because of her rotating schedule, the psychologist could not simply test the next day; she had to wait until she cycled through that school on her next round, a practical circumstance which led to the delays we see in Shane's case.

The psychologist reported that Shane had a verbal IQ of 115 and was reading at a fourth grade level. His arithmetic and spelling tested at 3.0 and 3.5 which put him 'below grade level'. His test age on the Bender-Gestalt was 7.0–7.5, while his actual age (at the time) was 9.0, which put him 'considerably below his age level'. Based on this assessment, the SAT recommended that Shane be considered by the 'Eligibility and Placement' (E&P) Committee for possible placement into a special program.[3]

Here we hear a general call for help become refined in official language. The teacher's vague observation, Shane 'has difficulty in applying himself to classwork' became a technical assessment expressed in numerical terms (IQ of 115, test age of 7.5). He is compared to a normative standard: he is 'behind grade level'. No longer is he a child 'who needs help'; now he is a candidate 'learning disabled child'.

When the E&P Committee met on February 16 to discuss Shane's case, the following dialog took place:

EDM #33
92 **Psychologist:** Does the uh, committee agree that the, uh learning disability placement is one that might benefit him?
93 **Principal:** I think we agree.
94 **Psychologist:** We're not considering then a special day class at all for him?
95 **Special Education Teacher** I wouldn't at this point//
96 **Many:**   =No.

The Committee decided to place Shane into an LD group, a pullout educational program in which students spend a part of the school day in the regular classroom and the other part of the day in a special program.

This dialog was typical of the fifty-five placement decisions which occurred during the year of our investigation. First of all, the placement decision was brief, occupying only a minute or two in a meeting which generally lasted an hour.

Second, although there was a range of some fifteen placement options available, the Committee rarely considered more than one of them. Fiscal, legal and practical circumstances united to constrain these placement decisions. PL 94–142, 'the Education for all Handicapped Students' act, specified that 12 per cent of the school age children would be eligible for special education but provided funds for only that percentage of children. This federally mandated guideline limited placement options at the school district level. In order to get the business of education (as they saw it) done, the school psychologist took into account the number of students in various educational programs when recommending place-ment decisions. In this particular case, the range of options was limited to two closely related programs. The others had been eliminated by administrative fiat (because they were too costly) or because they were 'full' (no more state or federal funds would come to the district if Shane were placed into those programs). These constraints can be heard in the exchange between the principal and the school psychologist in the dialog above.

Third, there is a prevailing way of representing children in these meetings and the other occasions which led to the construction of an educationally handicapped student. The prevailing mode of discourse is dispositional; it places the problem inside the child. The dispositional mode of representation dominates two other languages spoken in the meeting. One is a sociological idiom, voiced by the teacher, the other is a historical idiom, spoken by the student's mother. The contrast can be heard in the interaction at the beginning of the meeting:

3 **Psychologist** Shane is ah nine years old, and he's in fourth grade. Uh, he, uh, was referred because of low academic performance and he has difficulty applying himself to his daily class work. Um, Shane attended the Montessori School in kindergarten and first grade, and then he entered Carlsberg-bad in, um, September of 1976 and, uh, entered our district in, uh, '78. He seems to have very good peer relationships but, uh, the teachers, uh, continually say that he has difficulty with handwriting. 'kay. He enjoys music and sports. I gave him a complete battery and, um, I found that, uh, he had a verbal I.Q. of 115, per-formance of 111, and a full scale of 115, so he's a bright child. Uh, he had very high scores in, uh, information which is his long-term memory. Ah, vocabulary, was, ah, also, ah, considerably over average, good detail awareness and his, um, picture arrangement scores, he had a seventeen which is very high//

At the end of this presentation, the psychologist asked the student's teacher to provide information:

8 **Classroom Teacher** Um. Probably basically the fine motor types of things are difficult for him. He's got a very creative mi:ind and expresses himself well ( ) orally and verbally and he's pretty alert to what's going on. (2) Maybe a little bit [too] much, watching EVERYthing that's (hh) going (hh) on, and finds it hard to stick to one task. And [mostly] I've been noticing that it's just his writing and things that he has a, a block with. And he can rea:ad and comprehend some things when I talk to him, [but] doing independent type work is hard for him.

9 **Principal** mhmmm, putting it down on paper . . .

10 **Classroom Teacher** Yeah::, and sticking to a task//

11 **Principal**   =mmhmmm//

12 **Classroom Teacher**
   =and getting it done, without being distracted by
   (hehhehheh)

13 **Special Education Teacher** How does he relate with what the other kids do?

14 **Classroom Teacher** Uh, very well. He's got a lot of frie:ends, and, uh, especially, even out on the playground he's, um (3), wants to get in on the games, get on things and is well accepted. So:o, I don't see too many problems there.

The classroom teacher started to present some of the conditions under which Shane has trouble (8), was interrupted by the principal (9), then the special education teacher took the floor (13). From that point on, the special education teacher asked the classroom teacher a series of questions about Shane's peer relations, reading level, and performance in spelling and math. Next, the questioning shifted to the mother, who was asked about her son's fine motor control at home:

46 **Special Education Teacher**   How do you find him at [home] in terms of using his fingers and fine motor kinds of things? Does he do//

47 **Mother**   =He will, as a small child, he didn't at all. He was never interested in it, he wasn't interested in sitting in my lap and having a book read to him, any things like that//

48 **Special Education Teacher**: =mhmmm//

49 **Mother**   =which I think is part of it you know. His, his older brother was just the opposite, and learned to write real early. [Now] Shane, at night, lots of times he comes home and he'll write or draw. He's really doing a lot//

50 **Special Education Teacher**   ( )

51 **Mother**   =he sits down and is writing love notes to his girl friend (hehheh). He went in our bedroom last night and turned on the TV and got out some colored pencils and started writing. So he, really likes to, and of course he brings it all into us to see//

52 **Special Education Teacher**   =mhmmm//

53 **Mother**   =and comment on, so I think, you know, he's not [NEGAtive] about//

54 **Special Education Teacher**   =no//

55 **Mother**   =that any more//

56 **Special Education Teacher**   =uh huh

57 **Mother** He was before, but I think his attitude's changed a lot.

The psychologist characterized Shane as having trouble: 'he has difficulty applying himself to his daily work', 'he has some fears and anxieties'. The verbs 'have' and 'is' attribute the 'difficulties' to Shane; they are beneath his skin, between his ears. The psychological language included absolute and categorical statements about the student's abilities. The result was a 'context free' view of the child, one who had a general disability which cuts across situations.

The classroom teacher saw the student's problem varying from one classroom situation to another: 'If he studies his spelling and concentrates on it he can do pretty well.' His performance varies according to the kinds of materials and tasks: 'It's hard for him to copy down [math] problems . . . if he's given a sheet where he can fill in answers and work them out he does much better.' The result was a 'context bound' view of the child, one who had specific problems which appeared in certain academic situations, but who operated more than adequately in other situations. The mother's language contrasts with the psychologist's even more sharply, for she spoke about improvements and changes for the better. This provided an alternative explanation about the source of Shane's problem. The locus of difficulty was not within him ('it's not physical', 'it's not functional'); it was in his past experiences and prior situations. The mother's language added a historical dimension, for she spoke about changes and improvements through time. This provided an explanation of Shane's difficulties which contrasted with the school psychologist's. The locus of difficulty was not within him ('its not physical', 'its not functional'). It was his past experiences and prior circumstances that led to his difficulties.

The recommendations voiced in a psychological idiom were accepted by the Committee without challenge or question, while the recommendation voiced in a sociological and historical idiom were routinely interrupted with requests for clarification and further information. That is, representations of the child expressed in dispositional terms prevailed over representations expressed in contextual or historical terms. The psychological language was bolstered by a technical vocabulary. While the classroom teacher reported information she had gained from first hand observation over a school year, she did not provide specific data. So, too, the mother reported on first hand information, obtained over the student's lifetime, but it too was formulated in general terms. The technical, quasi-experimental mode of representing Shane helped defeat the competing modes of representing him and contributed to the construction of his identity as a 'learning disabled child'.

This study was responsive to criticisms of interpretations of interpretive studies in education because it showed how power and authority are worked out and voiced in the discourse of the school. Students' institutional identities were shown to be constructed in the interactive dynamics between social forces which operated outside the school and local practices within the school. State and federal law directed public schools to place students in certain educational programs, but provided only limited funds for this additional requirement. This arrangement placed school officials in an administrative bind, which they resolved by adapting federal policies to meet local contingencies.

Conclusion

So, these are the reasons why, like Chance in Peter Sellers' great movie, *Being There*, I like to listen and watch. When we listen to and look at social life closely, which is what a videotape or film record enables us to do, we see and hear a different version of social life than is otherwise possible. We are able to examine more critically the factors which have played a dominant role in explanations of school performance. 'Social class', 'heredity', 'ethnicity', and other important concepts which have been said to determine school success do not operate as simply and as directly as we are lead to believe by much of prevailing social theory.

By listening to the language of groups of educators as they engage in the work of teaching, testing and sorting students, I have tried to demonstrate the situated relevance of social structures in the practical work activities performed by people in social interaction. Educators carry out the routine work of conducting lessons, assigning students to ability groups or special programs, administering tests and attending meetings. The notion of *work* stresses the constructive aspect of institutional practice. Educators' work is repetitive and routine. Its mundane character should not overshadow the drama of its importance, however, because steps on students' career ladders are assembled from such practice. The enactment of routine bureaucratic practices structure students' educational careers by opening or closing their access to particular educational opportunities.

Notes

1 The war metaphor in domestic politics is still with us. Today we have a 'war on drugs.' Both are equally ineffective. Washington politicians have apparently not learned that waging a war on a social problem is not the way to solve it.
2 *Source*: Referral form in Student's school record.
3 *Source*: School Psychologist's Assessment Summary. This report was also read to the E&P Committee on 16 February, (see below for my discussion of this report in the context of the E&P meeting).

References

CAZDEN, C.B. (1988) *Classroom Discourse*, New York, Heineman.

CICOUREL, A.V. (1964) *Method and Measurement in Sociology*. New York, The Free Press.

CICOUREL, A.V. (1968) *The Social Organization of Juvenile Justice*, New York, Wiley-Interscience.

CICOUREL, A.V. (1973) *Cognitive Sociology*, New York and London, MacMillan.

CICOUREL, A.V. *et al.* (Eds) (1974) *Language Use and School Performance*, New York, Academic Press.

COLEMAN, J.S. *et al.* (1966) *Equality of Educational Opportunity*, Washington DC, US Government Printing Office.

ERICKSON, F. and MOHATT, G. (1982) 'The cultural organization of participant structures in two classrooms of Indian students' in SPINDLER, G. (Ed.) *Doing the Ethnography of Schooling*, New York, Holt Rinehart & Winston, pp. 132–75.

ERICKSON, F. and SCHULTZ, J. (1977), 'When is a context?', *IHCD Newsletter*, 1, 2, pp. 5–10.

ERICKSON, F. and SCHULTZ, J. (1982) *The Counselor as Gatekeeper*, New York, Academic Press.

FOLEY, D. (1990) *Learning Capitalist Culture: Deep in the Heart of Texas*, Philadelphia, PA, University of Pennsylvania Press.

GARFINKEL, H. (1967) *Studies in Ethnomethodology*, Englewood Cliffs, NJ, Prentice Hall.

GUMPERZ, J.J. (1982) *Strategies of Discourse*, Cambridge, Cambridge University Press.

HEATH, S.B. (1983) *Ways With Words*, Cambridge, Cambridge University Press.

JENSEN, A.R. (1969) 'How much can we boost IQ and scholastic achievement?', *Harvard Educational Review*, 39, 1, pp. 1–123.

KARABEL, J. and HALSEY A.H. (1977) *Power and Ideology in Education*, Oxford, Oxford University Press.

LABOV, W. (1972) *Sociolinguistic Patterns*, Philadelphia, PA, University of Pennsylvania Press.

LAVE, J. (1988) *Cognition in Practice*, New York, Cambridge University Press.

LCHC (1983) 'Culture and cognitive development' in MUSSEN P. (Ed.) *Handbook of Child Psychology*, New York, John Wiley and Sons, pp. 295–356.

MCDERMOTT, R.P. (1974) 'Kids make sense', unpublished PhD dissertation, Stanford, Stanford University.

MEHAN, H. (1973) 'Assessing children's language using abilities' in ARMER, J.M. and GRIMSHAW A.D. (Eds). *Methodological Issues in Comparative Sociological Research*, New York, John Wiley and Sons, pp. 309–43.

MEHAN, H. (1974) 'Accomplishing classroom lessons' in CICOUREL, A.V. *et al.* (Eds) (1974) *Language Use and School Performance*, New York, Academic Press, pp. 76–142.

MEHAN, H. (1978) 'Structuring school structure', *Harvard Educational Review*, **48**, 1 pp. 32–64.

MEHAN, H. (1979) *Learning Lessons: Social Organization in the Classroom*, Cambridge, MA, Harvard University Press.

MEHAN, H., HERTWECK, A. and MEIHLS, J.L. (1986) *Handicapping the Handicapped: Decision Making in Students' Careers*, Stanford, CA, Stanford University Press.

MEHAN, H. and WOOD, H. (1975) *The Reality of Ethnomethodology*. New York, Wiley-Interscience.

OGBU, J.U. (1981) 'School ethnography: A multilevel approach,' *Anthropology and Education Quarterly*, **12**, 1, pp. 3–29.

PHILIPS, S.U. (1972) 'Participant structures and communicative competence' in CAZDEN. C.B., JOHN, V.P. and HYMES, D. (Eds) *Functions of Language in the Classroom*, New York, Columbia Teachers College Press, pp. 370–94.

PHILIPS, S.U. (1982) *Invisible Culture*, New York, Longman.

ROGOFF, B. and WERTSCH, J.V. (1984) *Children's Learning in the Zone of Proximal Development*, San Francisco, CA, Jossey Bass.

SACKS, H., SCHEGLOFF, E.A., and JEFFERSON, G. (1974) 'A simplest systematics for the organization of turn-taking in conversation', *Language*, **50**, pp. 696–735.

SCHUTZ, A. (1962) *Collected Papers I: The Problem of Social Theory*, The Hague, Martinis Nijhoff.

Chapter 7

Crosscultural, Comparative, Reflective Interviewing in Schoenhausen and Roseville

George and Louise Spindler

Voices

'Voices', for us, means the voices of our 'native' informants in the Schoenhausen and Roseville elementary schools, the sites of our comparative research. The voices include those of the administrator, the children, and, most importantly in this exercise, the voices of two teachers teaching in comparable schools, one in Germany, the other in the United States. The voices in our study are elicited by using evocative stimuli in the form of films taken by us in the Schoenhausen and Roseville schools. We have arranged for textual space so that informants have their own voices, and made the dialogue between ethnographer and informants explicit, as appropriate to a study in modernist format. Our analysis is directed at culturally phrased assumptions apparent in the voiced discourse of the informants. The voices of the ethnographers, ourselves, are heard in the quest for assumptions in the discourse phrased by the natives, but our voices are muted, since we try to elicit the discourse in such a manner that it is self/other reflective. Our method is therefore called the 'Crosscultural, Comparative, Reflective Interview'.

The Research Sites

Schoenhausen is a village of about 2000 in a semi-rural but urbanizing area in *Land* Baden Württemberg, southern Germany. Schoenhausen was known, and still is to some extent, as an ausgesprochener Weinort (emphatically a wine-making place). The native-born are swaebisch and protestant. Most of the 'newcomers' originally migrated from the former east zone, Sudetenland, or other areas from which Germans were expelled or from which they fled after World War II. They are somewhat more urbanized as a rule, and more often than not Catholic (Spindler, 1974). The Grundschule (elementary school) is charged with the responsibility for educating all of the children and preparing them for a changing Germany and world. Its 127 children are distributed in four grades staffed by six teachers and a Rektor (Principal), and various other special services personnel. The Schoenhausen Grundschule has enjoyed a good relationship with the community and with the parents whose children attend it. Partly, at least, this relationship is due to the benign influence of the Rektor (Principal) who has been in that position since the beginning of our study in 1968.

The Roseville elementary school, located in central Wisconsin, includes kindergarten through eighth grade and is somewhat larger than the Schoenhausen school, but is comparable in every other respect. The school district is rural but has many commuters that work in nearby towns, some of them as much as forty or fifty miles distant. The majority of children attending the school come from small dairy farms. This school also enjoys good relationships with its community and with the parents who eagerly attend school functions whenever possible. The Principal is himself a farmer as well as an educator and is well-liked. The predominant ethnicity of the Roseville School District is German (Spindler, 1987a, 1987b and 1990).

Purpose

Our purpose in this chapter is to demonstrate one particular kind of research technique and the text that it produces — the crosscultural, comparative, reflective interview (CCCRI). The technique has been discussed only briefly in our own publications and demonstrated somewhat more extensively in a study in which a Japanese and an American pre-school furnished the cultural 'brackets' in the form of films (or video) from each location, for interviews with teachers (Fujita and Sano, 1988). Our research in Schoenhausen began in 1968, and continued in 1977, 1981 and 1985. In each of the field visits we had specific research objectives that are discussed in 'Schoenhausen Revisited and the Discovery of Culture' (Spindler, 1987a). Our overall objective was to explore the role of the school in culture change in comparable areas in Germany and the United States.

As with all instruments or special techniques used in our research, the CCCRI developed out of field experience *in situ*. It was fully applied for the first time in 1985 though we had used films as evocative stimuli (Collier and Collier, 1986) in interviews before that, though not in an explicitly comparative and reflective framework.

The interviews conducted with teachers, children and administrators were directed at cultural differences and similarities, both between Schoenhausen and Roseville and among the named 'audiences'. The diagram below expresses the overall relationship in both sites.

The diagram shows us that all three kinds of natives in the Schoenhausen and Roseville elementary schools shared some perceptions and assumptions and diverged in others. The divergence appears to represent positional differences. Both the 'shared' and 'divergent' sectors may be considered cultural phenomena. The anthropologist is not a native, but participates in the situation, perceives, and assumes. His and her (G. and L. Spindler) perceptions and assumptions are no less influenced by position as well as by shared experience and participation in the dialogue of the two research sites.

The CCCRI are designed to stimulate dialogue about pivotal concerns on the part of natives in comparable cultural systems. Some form of audiovisual material (in this instance films of classrooms) representing two cultures (conceivably more) is used to 'bracket' the interview. That is, the interview is conducted as an inquiry

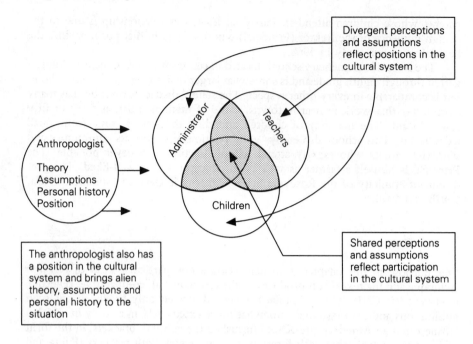

Divergent perceptions
and assumptions
reflect positions in the
cultural system

Anthropologist

Theory
Assumptions
Personal history
Position

Administrator

Teachers

Children

The anthropologist also has
a position in the cultural
system and brings alien
theory, assumptions and
personal history to the
situation

Shared perceptions
and assumptions
reflect participation
in the cultural system

Figure 7.1: The cross-cultural, comparative reflective interview (CCCRI)

into the perceptions, by the native, of his/her own situation and that of the 'other',
and the assumptions revealed in reflections about those perceptions. We regard
both the perceptions and assumptions as cultural phenomena.

We believe that a 'complete' ethnography should include explicit recognition
of this complex dialogue in both its shared and divergent aspects.

The Crosscultural Comparative, Reflective Interview (CCCRI)

The basic procedure for the CCCRI is simple — we filmed in Schoenhausen and
we filmed in Roseville and we showed the teachers, the children, and the administrators in both sites the films from both places.[1] We conducted interviews
about what they saw in their own classrooms and in those of the 'other' and how
they interpreted what they saw. These interviews are of a different quality than
anything that we had collected previously. They are *reflective* in depth and with a
subtlety that had heretofore been lacking, and they are cultural translations by
natives. The observed differences in the action in the two settings, Schoenhausen
and Roseville, caused teachers and children to reflect back on their own behavior
at the same time that they were pronouncing perceptions of the behavior of the
other. In a sense they were experiencing what we have experienced as ethnographers. After working in the Schoenhausen school in 1968, 1977 and 1981 our
visits to the Roseville school, beginning in 1983, caused us to reexamine what we
were observing in Schoenhausen. This reorientation was fully implemented in our
1985 visit. We had come to accept the Schoenhausen school and community as

'normal', as familiar, and it had become increasingly difficult to 'see' what it was we were observing. The Roseville experience sharpened our perceptions and caused us to think about them in a different way. In order to observe anything, anywhere, it seems necessary to make it a little 'strange' (Spindler, 1988).[2]

The rest of this chapter will be devoted to an examination of some texts produced by the crosscultural, comparative, reflective interviews. Though we have extensive interview material from all of the teachers, the administrator, and from the children in both school settings, we will present only two interviews from teachers, one in Schoenhausen and the other in Roseville, provide some excerpts from the perceptions of the children when they saw the films of their counterparts and provide a brief excerpt from a longer monologue by a high official in the school district of which Schoenhausen is a part, when he saw the Roseville films. The reactions of the children follow, excerpted from group interviews conducted in the Schoenhausen and Roseville schools. The children will be followed by the administrator, and finally the two teachers, Mrs. Schiller (Roseville) and Frau Wanzer (Schoenhausen).[3]

Diverse Reflections

Children's Reactions to Films

Schoenhausen

We showed the films of Roseville classrooms to the first and second grades combined and the third and fourth grades combined, in separate screenings, in the Schoenhausen Grundschule. These are the same films that the teachers and administrators viewed. The Schoenhausen first and second graders seem barely able to control their enthusiasm at the prospect of spending an hour looking at films from America. The teachers keep saying 'still!' and 'ssshhh!' and 'wiederstill!'. The noise level is very high and one has the impression of tremendous vitality. The teacher and then George Spindler describe the kinds of films they are going to see and what we would like them to do. The first film shown is of a first and second grade class in Roseville on the history of exploration in the United States. Some of the children are seated at a table in the front of the room with the teacher discussing the exploration of the Mississippi River Valley while other children are seated at their desks or moving quietly about the classroom as they pursue individual tasks. After the film is shown the Schoenhausen children bounce up and down on their seats, snap their fingers, and shout for attention. 'What did you notice?' says the teacher. The children respond, 'Some of them could work at a table with a teacher and others could sit alone'. 'They could work with another person if they wanted to.' 'They could go to the closet and get things to use if they wanted to and there were some of them listening to tape recorders.' The teacher admonished them, 'I can't hear unless you're a little more quiet!' — but the noise level continues at what to us seems a very high level. The second film, is shown, also of a first and second grade classroom in Roseville. The children are shown working on preparations for Thanksgiving so they are moving about the classroom a great deal but in the subdued way in which children move in Roseville classrooms. The Schoenhausen children are beside themselves! 'Waaagh!' 'Wooooo!' 'Huhuhuuuuuu!' They are shouting, jumping up and down, and snapping their fingers. The teacher again attempts to still them, but with only moderate success. 'Some of them are black-haired!' 'The children are not fighting with each other!' 'There's nobody tripping anybody else when they move around!' 'There's 'keine Streiten' (no fighting).' 'The teacher stays up front with the group.' 'She doesn't even look at the others!' 'Doch, doch!' 'The seats are all rooted to the floor!' 'They could run around anytime they wanted to!' 'They were at various places.' 'They were rühig (quiet) even though they run from place to place (verscheidene Zonen).' 'What were they doing with the paper?' 'What's in those bags?' (We explained that the film had been taken on 'popcorn day' when children could buy popcorn for ten cents a bag if they wanted to and that the colored paper being cut up was in order to make tails for Thanksgiving turkeys that would be put up on the bulletin board). 'They picked up all the paper that they dropped on the floor!' 'They were quiet in the classroom all the time.' 'They talked only in English.' 'They didn't fight at all.' 'They weren't loud.'

Films of comparable classrooms in Roseville were shown to the Schoenhausen third and fourth grade classes. We went through the same procedure of explanation and then showed the first film. The reactions to the films were very similar to those furnished by the first and second grade children though the older children were somewhat more reflective. They felt that the Roseville system would not work for them because there would be 'too much fighting' in the Schoenhausen school. They would not learn as much without a teacher present to help them 'at all times'. 'Learning with a teacher is much simpler than having to learn by yourself.' 'You couldn't have somebody walking around the classroom anytime they felt like it because somebody would be sure to trip them.'

Roseville

We followed the same procedure in the Roseville school, showing the children films of their grade counterparts in Schoenhausen. We had already showed them films of their own classrooms. The children filed into the gymnasium where the film showing was to take place and where bleachers had been set up for grades 3 through 6. They took their places quietly and talked to each other in whispers. The teachers did not have to call upon them to be quiet or to focus their attention on the films. We showed three films in sequence and we present here only a few of their comments. 'I'd rather live away from school. I like riding on the bus!' 'We have more recesses and they are a lot of fun and we have a gym — did they have a gym?' 'I like having desks like ours where there is a special place to keep one's own things. I wouldn't like to get a table with other kids.' 'I like being in school a long time each day.' (We had explained that the German school day was much shorter than theirs). 'We like staying in school for lunch, it's fun.' 'It's too noisy in those (Schoenhausen) classrooms. How could you learn anything if it was so noisy?' 'I couldn't work by myself if there was so much noise all the time.' (A few said that they would like to be able to talk out loud and run around the room sometimes and make more noise in general but the consensus was that the Schoenhausen classrooms were too noisy). 'I like being able to choose things that I want to do.' 'The teacher isn't always telling us what we have to do.' 'None of them wore hats!' 'Two of them looked like Bernie and Travis (children in Roseville).' 'The top of their desk was messy, there were markers lying all over.' 'The moving chalkboard is really neat.' 'I wouldn't want to live so close to the school. I like to ride on the bus.' 'It would be nice to have sinks in the classroom like that.' (The Schoenhausen classrooms all have sinks towards the front). 'Our school is more modern and has a nice gym.' 'The town is very old.' (We had showed one film of the Schoenhausen environment). 'I like modern buildings.' 'I'd like to be able to make all the noise I want!' (chorus) 'No way!' 'My ears would go woof woof!' 'There is just too much noise.'

Interpretation

Children notice the same features that adults notice, but from a different perspective, quite naturally, since they are children, but they are natives of the same system that the teachers are. The Roseville children perceive the noise level and activity of the Schoenhausen children as greater than in their own classroom and most place a negative value on it. They appreciate the long school day, the lunch period, and living out in the country not 'packed in' with other families in houses. They also recognize the facilities such as the gymnasium and the modern school building as being positive attributes. They are, surprisingly, not particularly attracted by the route of apparent freedom to talk out loud or to engage in vigorous physical activity at times and felt that this could actually be injurious to learning. They do not reflect in the same way that the teachers do on the significance of these differences but merely accept them as given. They are much more attentive to details of the environment and details of behavior. Schoenhausen children attend to the popcorn day, the black hair, the desks, picking up paper, and not fighting when they move around. They perceive the quiet order of the Roseville classrooms and feel that it would not work that way in their own school.

These are the real conditions of the childrens' lives in the school. These conditions are perceived through cultural screens provided by life in Roseville and life in Schoenhausen. How far this goes into what we could think of as 'American' culture or 'German' culture is beyond the scope of our intent at the present. What is most important for our purposes is that there is, as will be seen, considerable similarity in teacher perceptions, administrative perceptions, and those of children of the same situations, but there are important differences that reflect the positions of the teachers, administrator, and the children respectively.

The reflections of the Schulamtdirektor (Superintendent of Schools) follow.

The Schulamtdirektor Speaks

We showed the films we have described to the Schulamtdirektor, his staff and the Schoenhausen teachers the third evening that we were in Germany in 1985. The Schulamtdirektor had expressed his strong interest in seeing the films when we explained our mission on the first day of our presence in Germany. We excerpt, following, a few translated statements from his much longer reaction.

It is difficult for me to see whether these films (of either Roseville or Schoenhausen) are typical of either the school or of other schools in a broader area. If they are typical we come to a situation. I must say that there is between the school in Roseville and that in Schoenhausen a clear difference. A decisive difference. Our teachers, our understanding about school, are situated in a specific system. This system is influenced directly from above, from the school system viewpoint. One always understands that there is a curriculum plan prepared beforehand from above that is binding. And it gives a clear statement of what instruction means. A very clear statement. Instruction is, as we understand it, as a rule joined with a certain theme. Instruction is joined with a certain class. Instruction is linked to a certain preparation, a certain goal and a certain realization of these goals. Indeed there are always variations but these variations are always within the framework of these intentions. It binds the teachers and the school children in their relationship. The teacher is always at the front. The children sit before him. That can vary of course but as a rule that's the way it goes. The teacher instructs everyone at the same time. There are certain themes that can be followed in groups but these are brought together in a successive sequence. One hears what has been done and what will be done. It is the art of the teacher to bring together these results in order to bring all of the children along, insofar as possible, in the same way. The teacher brings everything together under the same label, tries to reach the same goal, so that in every hour a little piece of the mosaic (of learning) is laid down. And so goes the work in a given hour and in the next hour, week for week until finally the teacher with the children reaches a specific goal. This is characteristic for German instruction and for our understanding of instruction. If I am to take these pictures of (Roseville) that we have seen as typical, and you say that they are, then it is very difficult for me to understand how instruction and progress can move together. There are many questions, many. For example, are the children able to reach, to proceed in similar steps towards learning goals? We have certain disciplines, as in Deutsch, in Mathematik, in Sachuntterickt. Is there something like that comparable here? How does the teacher handle the problem of having one group further along and the other hanging along behind? I am not one to think that there is only one way to get to Rome. But without doubt for us a goal (Ziel) is a goal and without doubt a goal is to be attained. The overall goal is to maintain regular progress in the class. When a child, for example cannot reach the goal then there is a possibility to repeat or to go to a special school. Naturally one will in instruction always seek to stimulate and follow children's personal motivation, but Leistungsfähigkeit (productive efficiency) for the group is the purpose — not the self-purpose of the individual. Everything goes back again into the group. This is certainly the art of the teacher.

The Schulamtdirektor goes on at length about the relationship of goals for the school, for instruction, for each hour of instruction. He points out that there have been changes in this curriculum plan through the years in Germany but that there always is a plan and it is given to the teachers. He feels, paradoxically, that he had greater freedom as a younger teacher than teachers have today. He is particularly impressed with the apparent freedom of the teachers in the Roseville school to teach at their own pace and manner and that the curriculum plan is generated by the teachers themselves.

It is clear that the Schulamtdirektor perceives the Roseville classrooms in ways parallel to the way the Schoenhausen children do and in the same general frame of reference as Frau Wanzer does in the following interview (and Frau Wanzer represents quite well the other teachers in the Schoenhausen school). This convergence of perceptions from children, teachers and the higher administration impresses us. If we think of culture as a screen through which one perceives 'reality' then a part of this screen is shared by these participants in the Schoenhausen and Roseville process. At the same time, however, it is important to recognize that the teachers, children, and the administrator are each speaking from their particular positions. Their perceptions converge, but they are not identical. The positions, and the perceptions flowing from them, are also culture. Diversity and commonality are both subsumed by cultural structure and process.

Our next step is to present the text from interviews of two teachers, one from Roseville, the other from Schoenhausen.

Two Teachers

MRS. SCHILLER, Roseville Elementary School

The interview begins with a summary, by us (GLS) of what we had seen and filmed in Mrs. Schiller's classroom yesterday (and later showed in Germany). As usual, there were a group of children (twelve) at the big table at the front of the room, in this instance, learning how to tell time. Mrs. Schiller seemed completely absorbed in this activity and didn't even glance at the children in the back of the room working at their desks or moving quietly about the room to get materials or books from the big closet or shelves lining the walls. Four children, in two pairs, were using flash cards for drill in arithmetic, two others had headsets on and were listening to tapes. Some were pasting paper 'feathers' on the tails of paper turkeys (it is close to Thanksgiving). Yet others appear to be working on workbook lessons.

Mrs. Schiller has seen some of the same films of Schoenhausen and Roseville as the children, other teachers, and the Schulamtdirektor had.

GLS: It's remarkable that the children work on their own as they do. How do you prepare them to do this?

MRS. SCHILLER: I'm not sure I do prepare them. They have to trust me. We try to develop a relationship, that has to happen first. Then I try to figure out which kids won't get along — there are some I would never put next to each other. I separate those — but basically we have really good kids.

GLS: How do they know what to do?

MRS SCHILLER: Well, you're probably thinking of the silent reading period that is never silent at this grade level. They want to share. They can move around, use the flashcards, whatever. I'm just glad they want to come to school and share in the activities like that.

GLS: They seem so, so independent. They are teaching each other! How do they know how to do that?

MRS. SCHILLER: I suppose some need help and others know when they need it so they just do it.

GLS: It's not something you establish?

MRS. SCHILLER: No, I don't. It begins as soon as they grow up a little (in first grade). This one needs math, this one reading. You know, we're pretty high in math here, but low on reading pretty much in the whole area. Jack (the Principal) has ten of his students (from the seventh and eighth grades) come in and each one takes one of my children and reads a story to them, and the little ones read back, too. It is a great help. I can tell when we discuss the readings later. They are well informed. (Mrs. Schiller spoke at length about one problem child and his mother who won't come to school to consult with her.)

GLS: Now, with respect to your underlying objectives as a teacher, that is Linda Schiller as a teacher, not necessarily what you get in the education courses, what would you say your basic purpose is?

MRS. SCHILLER: To teach them to be an individual, to be all they can, to the limits of their abilities and if I can get them to be a happy person, as well as get them to do their best, then I think I have done my job. (Mrs. Schiller talks more about the problem child and his mother. The mother was going to sue because Mrs. Schiller had him repeat the first grade. What she tried to do was to help the child to learn all he could in order to overcome his reading difficulty.)

GLS: Now let's go back a little to this management process. It strikes me (GS) as rather incredible that you have some kind of understanding that they are supposed to go about their activities on their own — individually — and pick up on the things they do without wasting a great deal of time or being disruptive in the class. It seems to me that there's something pretty deep going on here. It doesn't work that way in Schoenhausen.

MRS. SCHILLER: You don't feel that if I went to Germany I could operate a classroom the way I do now here? If I got them at the same age level?

GLS: It would be remarkable experiment! The kids tend to act up when adults are not around. But here in Roseville wouldn't you be able to walk out of the classroom, go down to the office, leave your class for five minutes or more?

MRS. SCHILLER: Well, yes. I left the first graders alone up in front without any assignment just the other day and Jeremy grabbed the pointer and started 'A,B,C,D,' etc. and the whole class repeated, and then went on through the alphabet several times. And I said, 'That was so nice. You did not waste time!' And then I had to go to the art room and Christopher, my repeater, (a child who was 'held back' a year) called all the children in the first grade to the desk to get their math books out and be ready and he stood at the board to write names down if they were talking, so they were all ready, waiting for the class to get started. When they do things like that, I praise. We don't have any time to waste and so I was happy to have the first graders ready to go when the bell rang.

GLS: There were so many different things going on in the class we observed yesterday. It was fascinating to try and film them — this little group here, this one here, another some place else. I (GS) have a logistics question. How do the children know when and how to find what they need?

MRS. SCHILLER: Well, it would be great if we could do more of this kind of free choice, but a lot of it is more structured. The head office would like us to do more of the things the kids want to do themselves.

GLS: But how do they know, when they do, what they do?

MRS. SCHILLER: Well, it's just the choice. The flashcards, are there somewhere, the charts, the tape recorders, — you know they're, they're really all little teachers, it's just built in. They come up and ask, 'Can I do the flash cards? Can I use the charts? Can I use the tape recorder?' Especially if it's a first grader that needs help and then a second grader can teach them. They love to do that.

GLS: But you arrange the materials for their use somehow?

MRS. SCHILLER: Well, they ask if they can do it.

GLS: But you keep the materials in the classroom and they know where they are? Access to them is just them asking you?

MRS. SCHILLER: Yes, and it's their choice of friends that they want to work with or whoever they want to share with.

GLS: Where have you taught before? (Mrs. Schiller named several places — all larger and more urban than Roseville.) Do you think it was this way in those communities also?

MRS. SCHILLER: Yes, I really do. I have a lot of faith in kids. I think kids are neat! If you have high expectations, 98 per cent of the time they will fulfill your expectations.

GLS: What would you feel like if you went out in the hall or someone called you to the phone and you came back after five minutes and found things in considerable disorder?

MRS. SCHILLER: Well, I would tell them right out, 'I am *very* disappointed! I had this important phone call and you couldn't sit for five minutes while I answered it.' I would let them know it hurt me personally. It's a kind of personal thing. Oh, yes! You start building that up the first day of school. Then they feel 'we can't hurt our teacher'. Oh, yes, that happened today! I had to take a workbook to a parent who was taking her little girl to the dentist so she could work on it if she had to wait and the class had the same assignment. When I came back to my room they had all finished that page that was assigned and they went right on to the next one. I praised them again 'it was *really* nice that I could count on you, and I could come back to a nice quiet class'. And of course they all beamed. They just love praise!

GLS: Do you think you are different than other teachers here or elsewhere?

MRS. SCHILLER: Perhaps. I have so many sisters that are all teachers and my mom is a teacher. I have my own philosophy. I don't think children need to finish every page of the workbooks, etc.

It's so important for these children living in a rural area to socialize with each other so I try never to keep a child in during recess or after school to do make-up work on a workbook. They need socialization. And I will *not* be a grouch. I'm not really strict. Some people would probably say that I was lax.

GLS: Were you struck with any special feature when you looked at the German films?

MRS. SCHILLER: Well, one thing was the discipline. When they were running around the room and making a lot of noise it was going further than it would here. But I do feel like we can learn even though we're a little noisy.

GLS: You know, we found that each of the teachers in the Schoenhausen school had a regular sequence of operations that they planned out in every classroom and every hour. Would you say that there was a sequence here and in your classroom?

MRS. SCHILLER: Well, we have a curriculum, but we can handle it any way we want. I don't go through the same sequence every day. It would be too boring!

GLS: You mentioned a 'curriculum' — in Germany the teachers have a 'Lehrerplan', that defines subjects and sequences and amount of time that should be spent on certain themes. Is that what you mean by curriculum?

MRS. SCHILLER: There is a little book here on the shelf that happens to be for the third and fourth grade (she hands it to us).

GLS: Where does this come from?

MRS. SCHILLER: The teachers put it out.

GLS: You mean — the teachers here?

MRS. SCHILLER: The whole district of Arcadia (the larger area around Roseville) — teachers from Roseville had input.

GLS: Does it tell you how to teach?

MRS. SCHILLER: No, it doesn't tell you that. We are still queens in our own classrooms and there's plenty of freedom.

GLS: Now we have seen a number of reading books and some periodicals that are used in your classes. Where do these materials come from?

MRS. SCHILLER: One is the *Weekly Reader*, and there's *Sprint*, and we pick our own books — there's a Reading Committee, a Math Committee, and so forth, appointed from teachers. We look over the books that the various publishers furnish and pick out the ones we want. We pick, say, three books. They are sent out to schools and then the teachers all vote on them. The ones that get the most votes are the books that we use.

GLS: Well, thank you very much for your time and all the insight you've given us. It's been a real pleasure to talk with you and we'll be doing it again, we hope.

MRS. SCHILLER: It's been very enjoyable for me and I've learned a lot looking back on my own teaching practices and classroom management. Looking at the Germans, at the films from Germany, really stirred up my thinking.

FRAU WANZER Schoenhausen Grundschule

For the first few minutes we talked about what we wanted to do in her classroom, indicating that we would like to present a systematic view of her classroom on film, to the Roseville teachers, in our exchange activity. To help do this, we suggested that she spend some twenty minutes before the class that we were to film explaining her procedures and goals, and that we, in turn, would explain this to the Roseville teachers. She had seen the Roseville films at the same time as the Schulamtdirektor.

FRAU WANZER: Ja! It would perhaps have been good if for the films you showed us (of the Roseville classrooms) they had this introduction. Fyr Yurich in jedeur Fall (for me in any case), it was really difficult to see what was intended. Perhaps that was also the ground for the feeling that many of us had, 'Was lernen sie eigentlich?, (What are they learning really?)'

GLS: We explained that the films shown were typical for this class and that the 'friewillig' (free will) character of the classroom activity was indeed characteristic.

FRAU WANZER: I can scarcely understand how the teacher working at the table with some of the children would work on without looking to see what the other children were doing in the rest of the room. How do the children working alone know what they are supposed to do? But it had to function well — they were seemingly satisfied and they weren't causing any difficulties. Bei uns gibt es (with us there are) Schwierigkeiten (difficulties) und Streiten (strife or fighting). This was apparently not the case (in the Roseville school)! Probably they (the children) are accustomed to this.

GLS: 'Frau Schiller is very proud that her classroom is productive. The 'freiwillig' character also impressed us.' 'How do the children know exactly what there is for them to do?' we asked Frau Schiller. She answered 'I do nothing — the materials are there and the children seek them out for themselves, but they usually ask me if they can use them.' 'Naturally, the children have specific lessons, but when they are finished — they can do what they will.'

FRAU WANZER: Sie können tuen was sie wollen! (They can do what they want!)

GLS: They have various opportunities — such as tapes, computers, the library, flash cards, charts and posters, etc.

FRAU WANZER: Da ist natürlich ein grosser Unterschied (There is naturally a great difference) to our school. They (Roseville) have much more time to work, much more. With us one hour equals forty-five minutes and one must in this time reach a goal. In America they have so much time and so when they are finished with their lessons they can do what they want, but with us there is no time. The more gifted children finish, but many do not and then they must be helped to reach the goal for the lesson. (She talks about helping the slower children and how the more gifted children get less attention than they deserve. She also talks about the learning-disabled children — how some of them can reach only minimum goals defined in the curriculum plan [Lehrplan]).

GLS: To go back a little, so there is for every hour a specific goal you must reach?

FRAU WANZER: Ich habe in mein Lehrplan (I have in my curriculum plan) the goal that I must reach — the goals that I must reach. Every hour has a part goal. I must find out as the hour progresses if I'm going to have enough time to reach that goal. It depends on whether the hour goes well or badly — how much time I will spend. For example, there is the topic of 'Where do we get our water?' It's fascinating. In the Lehrplan there are ten hours given for this subject, but the children are so begeistert (enthusiastic), they want to know so much! It takes much more time than the ten hours foreseen in the Lehrplan. Then I must narrow down the amount of time spent on other subjects such as plants or animals, all within the Sachunterricht (home, community, civic affairs, etc.) curriculum.

GLS: You speak of a Lehrplan. Is that local or Baden Württemberg?

FRAU WANZER: Ja, the Baden Württemburg plan.

GLS: The Lehrplan appears to be very tight. If you had more time would you have freiwillig (free choice) periods?

FRAU WANZER: Ja, bestimmt (Yes, certainly).

GLS: How would you handle it?

FRAU WANZER: I would arrange materials beforehand that zu eine bestimmten Thema gehört (that belong to a specific theme). But in the framework of this theme, the children could do what they wanted. But I wouldn't just leave it up to them to choose from unorganized material. I would have the fear that they would choose things that were just play. And I have the impression that the children are so müde (tired), so lustlos (without drive) that they wouldn't do anything strenuous. They spend all afternoon and evening before the TV. This is very practical for the parents, but not good for the children. I am afraid that if I ask them to do whatever they wanted they would do gar nichts (nothing at all)! For instance, I told them 'Everyone bring a favorite book and we'll make a big library and we'll have a free reading period'. Well, two-thirds of them read with pleasure and one-third did nothing at all and disturbed the others.

GLS: So how would you proceed? Would you have them work in groups?

FRAU WANZER: Ja, for example, with respect to animals that we don't have in Germany, such as camels and lions, etc., I would have four tables arranged and I would furnish each of them with books and materials, such as pictures, before the children arrive. And then they could work on whatever they chose — a lion or a camel or whatever — of the four possibilities. And then ten minutes before the end of the period I would have them report, each group, to another group. This kind of procedure will work, but völlig frei (fully free)? Das macht nichts (that makes nothing — that's of no use)! We have a time problem and when I only have three hours per week for Sachunterricht, there is simply too little time for this kind of free-choice situation.

GLS: We would like to ask another kind of question. We have the impression that here in the Schoenhausen Grundschule, or for that matter in any of the schools in the nearby towns that we have visited, that when you leave the classroom, Sie erwarten dass die Kinder unruhig und eben chaotic werden (that you expect that the children will become restless and even chaotic).

FRAU WANZER: Erwartet (expect)! Ich hoffe sie bleiben ruhig! (I hope they remain quiet!). But there are always those two or three children that are poorly socialized and get everyone else stirred up. There is, for example, in my class, a child that has terrible personal problems. He strikes out and shouts at other children and they tell him he's crazy and, he's very sensitive. He comes from a family with no father — a damaged home environment — he is terribly sensitive and disruptive.

GLS: Would you expect the children to work on their lessons when you leave them?

FRAU WANZER: This is my goal!

GLS: How often is it reached?

FRAU WANZER: In the course of the school year — in the first grade — hardly. In the second year it goes somewhat better. By the fourth year they can work for longer periods. You have to handle this sort of thing in little doses.

GLS: What would you do if you heard a disturbance in the room when you returned?

FRAU WANZER: I would talk to the class. I would attempt to reach an understanding. Scolding does no good. Sometimes I have said that I am traurig (sad).

GLS: Would you say you were beleidigt (hurt)?

FRAU WANZER: No, never beleidigt, nur (only) traurig.

GLS: Do you make the children feel guilty (schuldig)?

FRAU WANZER: I feel that guilt is not understandable for children of this age. How can they understand who is guilty, the one who started the trouble or the one who responded to the trouble and carried it on further?

(We carried on discussions of this kind with Frau Wanzer several times and her interpretation of her own behavior in the classroom and that of the Roseville teachers that she had seen on film was consistent. She saw the Roseville classrooms, as did the other teachers, as tending towards being directionless and without specific goals and not organized for the attainment of whatever goals existed. She did find the quiet orderliness of the Roseville schools impressive and as exhibiting good 'teamwork'.)

Interpretation

Frau Wanzer and Mrs. Schiller are two experienced teachers of about the same age, teaching the same grades, about many of the same things, in quite similar schools in parallel communities in Germany and in the USA. And yet their handling of their classrooms and the assumptions that guide their behavior are significantly different at some critical points. And their perceptions of each other's classrooms reflect these differences. Mrs. Schiller's classroom is relaxed, quiet, low-keyed, and diverse. Children carry out various activities on their own, in addition to those carried out by the teacher and the small group she is leading through a specific learning task. There is little or no disruptive behavior. These qualities, confirmed in many sessions of observation by us, are apparent in the films we showed to all of the Schoenhausen teachers, the Principal, the Schulamtdirektor (Superintendent of Schools) and his assistants.

Frau Wanzer perceives Mrs. Schiller's classroom as undirected, as almost goal-less. At the same time, she acknowledges that there appears to be good 'teamwork', but that this method would be unlikely to work this well in Schoenhausen Grundschule.

These perceptions are apparent in the interview. Frau Wanzer's assumptions are apparent: that if children are undirected they, or at least a significant proportion of them, will do nothing at all, become disruptive, or will choose to play rather than work. She also reports that when children have clear directions on an interesting topic they can become very enthusiastic about learning and will work hard at it.

Frau Wanzer explains the differences observed in terms of time, which is short in Schoenhausen, and the fact that the curriculum plan there defines the goals to be reached quite precisely. She does not see these as *cultural* attributes, but as given, practical, preconditions to whatever she does, and the children do, in her classroom.

The differences run deep. Mrs. Schiller assumes that her goal is to help each individual develop to his or her fullest degree — to the limit of their individual capacities. Frau Wanzer assumes, as does the Schulamtdirektor, that her purpose is to help each child attain the standards set forth in the Lehrerplan — that some will meet them fully and others only minimally. Frau Wanzer takes for granted the existence of a Lehrerplan and that it is furnished to the school by the State school system, and that it will guide her management of her instruction directly. Mrs. Schiller takes for granted the fact that teachers from the school district develop their own curriculum and that it is only an approximate guide. Frau Wanzer assumes that the children eventually learn to continue working when she leaves the classroom, but that one can't expect too much of the younger first and second graders. Mrs. Schiller expects her first and second graders to be responsible for keeping a quiet, on-task classroom when she is gone for a few minutes. Frau Wanzer would 'talk' to her class if there were a disruption, but she would not act 'hurt', only 'sad', and she would not try to make her children feel 'guilty'. Mrs. Schiller would develop personal liking and trust with her children, would be 'hurt' if they misbehaved, and would leave them all feeling guilty if they did. And the two teachers have quite different conceptions of guilt. For Frau Wanzer guilt has to be established — there is a perpetrator, a reinforcer, and perhaps a victim. For Mrs. Schiller there is a feeling state — guilt is internalized. The children feel guilty about their irresponsible behavior and hurting their teacher.

These are the assumptions, as we see them, that lie behind both the behaviors of the two teachers in their classroom, and their perception of each other's behaviors *in situ*. These are cultural differences, we believe, that are expressed in, and derived from, the German and American historical experience respectively. The case for this extension would have to extend substantially beyond the scope of this chapter. We, therefore, confine ourselves to the observation that in Schoenhausen and Roseville respectively, these are assumptions that we regard as cultural, in the sense that they are pervasive within the dialogue of the school and school system and antecedent to the operations of the specific teachers and children we have observed.

Conclusion

The cross-cultural comparative reflective interview procedure furnishes clear evidence that the various audiences viewing the action all saw the same things in the films of classrooms. The children and teachers in Roseville saw the children in the Schoenhausen classrooms as noisy and enthusiastic. The children and teachers in Schoenhausen saw the Roseville classrooms as quiet and orderly. Each acknowledged that their own classrooms were more 'noisy' or more 'quiet', as well as seeing the other in those terms.

The crosscultural comparative reflective interviews also gave us clear evidence of the ways in which position affects perceptions. The Schulamtdirektor, the children, and the teachers 'saw' the same features of behavior in the 'others' setting, but emphasized these features differently, and the children actually 'saw' some things the adults did not. The Schulamtdirektor viewed the action from the top down, from the perspective of a system. The children interpreted the classroom action and setting from their perspective — desks, lunch, clothes, popcorn day, teacher's position in the classroom, blackboards, and so forth, but still 'saw' the quiet and order in the Roseville classroom and the noise level and boisterous activity in the Schoenhausen classrooms. The teachers, represented by Mrs. Schiller and Frau Wanzer, interpreted behavior in their own and the other's classroom with clearly different assumptions about what each expected of children and what their purposes as teachers were. These assumptions, we hold, are cultural.

All of the principals cited above are 'natives', and they tell their 'story' in their own way. The foreign observers, ourselves, the ethnographers, also 'saw' and 'interpreted'. We 'saw' the same features of classroom activity and our interpretations are not wildly different from those of the natives at any point, but they are influenced by our anthropological goals, our persistent search for 'culture', in its various expressions. The interested reader may find confirmation of the above in our publications (Spindler, 1987a and 1987b).

What we have presented in this chapter is, in contrast to a 'realistic' text, a modernist text. Modernist texts are designed to feature the eliciting discourse between ethnographer and subject or to involve the reader in the work of analysis. 'The experience represented in the ethnography must be that of the dialogue between ethnographer and informants, where textual space is arranged for informants to have their own voices (Marcus and Fischer, 1986, p. 67). We have featured both the eliciting discourse and involved the reader in the work of analysis.

Doing this (above) is regarded by Marcus (and others) as a 'radical shift' in perspective — as a 'derailment of the traditional object of ethnography'. Part of its challenge to traditional ethnographic realism is that it avoids the assumption of shared cultural coherence. The texts we have presented in this chapter both demostrate shared culture and culture differentiated by position. We believe that an adequate ethnography must represent both. We do not feel, however, that this 'derails' ethnography, but, rather, enhances it, by making ethnography a more accurate representation of social and psychocultural reality.

In all of our ethnographic work we have paid attention to differences in culture in relation to gender (Spindler, 1990), sociocultural adaptation (Spindler, 1978), social class and ethnicity and cosmopolitan/hinterland differences (Spindler, Trueba and Williams, 1990) and we have consistently tried to let the voices of informants, of the 'natives', be heard. What we have done differently in the research leading to this chapter is to place the dialogue between informant and ethnographer in the framework of an 'own' and 'other' reflection upon audiovisual representations of similar situations (classrooms) in our two field sites. The dialogue is thus culturally bracketed and the conversation becomes reflective, but the reflectivity is not focussed on the ethnographer, as it often is in the 'new' ethnography, but on the informant. The 'native' is doing his/her own cultural analysis by engaging in discourse about the self and other. Under ideal conditions the ethnographer is almost a bystander.

What is left unresolved for us is how the elicited dialogues represent 'German' culture and 'American' culture. We have recently represented the latter as a 'cultural dialogue' (Spindler *et al*, 1990) and we can understand certain of Mrs. Schiller's inter-pretations as expressions of (for instance) individualism, achievement and internalization of authority and guilt, that are a part of this dialogue. We can understand some of Frau Wanzer's discourse, and that of the Schulamtdirektor, as expressing certain aspects of a long-term German dialogue about authority, efficiency, collective effort and the attainment of standards. To claim that the little elementary schools in Roseville and Schoenhausen somehow express that the national *Zeitgeist* goes further than most of us want to go, and yet there are some tantalizing connections. The action in these classrooms and the interpretations by the 'native' seem to be the 'tip of the iceberg'. The part of the iceberg under the water is the enormous complexity of the national whole and its history. Just how to make the analytic connections remains unresolved. Neither our concepts, nor our vocabulary are sufficient. However, the value of methodology we have presented here does not rest on being able to solve this problem.

The results of our research also have some implications for the debate swirling in anthropological circles about objectivity, positivism, humanism, and the effect of the position of the ethnographer on observation and interpretation (O'Meara, 1989; Spaulding, 1988; Rosaldo, 1989; Marcus and Fischer, 1986; Clifford and Marcus, 1986). The agreement about what is observed ('seen') is greater than one would presume from the doubts cast on the possibility of objectivity in ethnography. Irrespective of position in the situation (for example, child, teacher, administrator, or anthropologist) we all 'saw' the same basic features of action and setting. At the same time it is important to acknowledge that position of the observer *vis a vis* the action, actors, and setting, as well as training and personal experience, do affect the interpretation (and cultural translation) represented in the writing of ethnography.

Acknowledgments

We wish to thank the faculty and staff of both Roseville and Schoenhausen Elementary Schools and the Schulamtdirektor and his staff, of the Schoenhausen area. They could not have been more gracious or more helpful. We also wish to thank Mimi Navarro and Diane Johnson for their indispensable help in the development of the article from a voice on tape to a finished product. We are grateful to Hector Mendez, University of California at Santa Barbara, for his expert use of the computer in producing figure 7.1. We appreciate the perceptive readings of the first drafts of this chapter by Christine Finnan, Ray McDermott, and Bernard Siegel, and the responses of the many who attended a conference on education in a multicultural world sponsored by the Division of Education at the University of California at Davis, organized by Marcelo Suarez-Orozco and Henry Trueba, where we first presented this paper on 12 October 1990. And we are beholden to the Spencer Foundation and the Center for Educational Research at the University of Wisconsin, Madison, for crucial funding.

Notes

1   We used super 8 mm sound and color film rather than video and though we have converted some of the films to video cassettes we still use film for most viewings in our own classroom, since resolution and screen size are so much better.

2   In some recent reading in education we found to our surprise that there is a well developed 'reflective teaching' orientation that has developed in educationist circles (Ross and Weade, 1989). As we briefly explored this literature we had the feeling that one way of enhancing the desired reflective process on the part of teachers would be to create cultural 'brackets' for the reflection in some manner similar to the procedure we carried out for Schoenhausen/Roseville. Even the relatively small differences in classroom management between Germany and the United States caused teachers to 'stand on their heads' to look again at their own practice. In both of our research sites it was rewarding to hear teachers say that they felt that they had gained insight into their own practice as a consequence of this crosscultural reflective activity. Though improvements in practice were not one of our explicit objectives, it is always good to feel that beyond merely not doing harm one may be doing some good with one's research activity. Another effort to help teachers to reflect on their own activity in the classroom is represented by 'cultural therapy', as conducted with individual teachers in conjunction with ethnographic studies of their classroom (Spindler, 1989).

3   Our first reflective interviews were conducted in Schoenhausen in 1985 and had been preceded by interviews in Roseville, before we had read Marcus, Clifford, or others engaged in 'post-modernist' criticism of traditional positivist realist ethnography. We have been influenced, however, by our recent reading of their critical writings in the interpretation of what we were doing.

References

CLIFFORD, J. and MARCUS, G. (Eds) (1986) *Writing Culture: The Poetics and Politics of Ethnography*, Berkeley, CA, University of California Press.

COLLIER, J., JR. and COLLIER, M. (1986) *Visual Anthropology*, Albuquerque, NM, University of New Mexico Press.

FUJITA, M. and SANO, T. (1988) 'Children in American and Japanese day-care centers: Ethnography and reflective cross-cultural interviewing' in TRUEBA, H. and DELGADO-GAITAN, C. (Eds) *School and Society: Learning Content Through Culture*, New York, Praeger, pp. 73–97.

MARCUS, G.E. and FISCHER, M. (Eds) (1986) *Anthropology as Cultural Critique: An Experimental Movement in the Human Sciences*, Chicago, IL, University of Chicago Press.

O'MEARA, T. (1989) 'Anthropology as empirical science', *American Anthropologist*, **91**, pp. 354–69.

ROSALDO, R. (1989) *Culture and Truth: The Remaking of Social Analysis*, Boston, MA, Beacon Press.

ROSS, D. and WEADE, G. (Eds) (1989) 'The context of reflection', *International Journal of Qualitative Studies in Education*, **2**, pp. 273–5 (special issue on reflective teaching).

SPAULDING, A.C. (1988) 'Distinguished lecture: Archaeology and anthropology', *American Anthropologist*, **90**, pp. 263–71.

SPINDLER, G. (1973) *Burgbach: Urbanization and Identity in a German Village*, New York, Holt, Rinehart & Winston.

SPINDLER, G. (1974) 'Schooling in Schoenhausen: A study of cultural transmission and instrumental adaptation in an urbanizing German village' in SPINDLER, G. (Ed.) *Education and Cultural Process: Toward an Anthropology of Education*, New York, Holt, Rinehart & Winston, pp. 230–73.

SPINDLER, L. (1978) 'Researching the psychology of culture change and modernization' in SPINDLER, G. (Ed.) *The Making of Psychological Anthropology*, Berkeley, CA, University of California Press, pp. 174–98.

SPINDLER, G. and L. (1987a) 'Schoenhausen revisited and the discovery of culture' in SPINDLER, G. and L. (Eds) *Interpretive Ethnography of Education at Home and Abroad*, Hillsdale, NJ, Lawrence Erlbaum Assoc., pp. 143–67.

SPINDLER, G. and L., (1987b) 'In prospect for a controlled cross-cultural comparison of schooling: Schoenhausen and Roseville' in SPINDLER, G. and L. (Eds) *Education and Cultural Process: Anthropological Approaches*, Prospect Heights, IL, Waveland Press, pp. 389–400.

SPINDLER, G. and L. (1989) 'Instrumental competence, self-efficacy, linguistic minorities, and cultural therapy', *Anthropology and Education Quarterly*, **20**, pp. 36–50.

SPINDLER, G. and L. (1990) 'Male and female in four changing cultures' in JORDAN, D. and SCHWARTZ, M. (Eds) *Personality and the Cultural Construction of Society*, Tuscaloosa, AL, University of Alabama Press, pp. 182–200.

SPINDLER, G. and SPINDLER, L. (1988) 'Roger Harker and Schoenhausen: From the familiar to the strange and back again' in SPINDLER, G. (Ed.) *Doing the Ethnography of Schooling: Educational Anthropology in Action*, Prospect Heights, IL, Waveland Press, pp. 20–46 (first published in 1982 by Holt, Rinehart & Winston.)

SPINDLER, G. and L. with TRUEBA, H. and WILLIAMS, M. (1990) *The American Cultural Dialogue and its Transmission*, London, Falmer Press.

STOCKING, G.W. (1983) *Observers Observed: Essays on Ethnographic Fieldwork*, Madison, WI, University of Wisconsin Press.

Part 3

Keeping Authentic Voices Alive and Well

Understanding the Incomprehensible: Redundancy Analysis as an Attempt to Decipher Biographic Interviews

Dietmar Larcher

The voice of redundancy does not speak at top volume. It makes itself heard only to those who have learnt to listen carefully to the subtle and often hidden messages in speech containing traces of social structure and social experience. Utterances and verbal interactions of people in everyday situations abound in such redundant, but hidden messages. Actually redundancy is a most prominent quality of communication. Whatever we say is conveyed in various channels and in different codes. Thus one message is not only transmitted once, but over and over again in the course of conversation. The problem is, however, that on the surface of speech we are often not aware of redundancy despite the fact that we all seem to have a well developed sub-conscious competence of noticing it in the utterances of our partners in conversation.

In order to perceive the voice of redundancy better than in everyday conversation, we need to have some systematic approach enabling us to increase our conscious perception. Redundancy analysis slows down the process of ordinary understanding and tries to transform the sub-conscious competence we all have into a conscious quality. It aims at making audible and even visible (in the case of a written text) what passes unnoticed by the conscious mind in everyday conversation. By systematically experimenting with the social context of an utterance, the social message incorporated in an utterance and in a person's text is explored. By systematically experimenting with variations of this utterance and of a person's text within a certain social context, the various shades of social meaning associated with one specific expression or utterance or text make themselves heard.

Listening systematically to the voice of redundancy means to test every single word in a variety of testing procedures. After a while redundancy makes itself perceptible and crops up over and over again. While any form of quantitative approach would try to test as many items of as many texts as possible in order to detect a common structure, redundancy analysis does its job the other way round: By testing very few items profoundly it tries to find as many variations as possible of speech and of social context in order to discover what is redundant in a person's speech. Usually it is not what he/she *intends* to verbalize.

Redundancy analysis is not a variety of psychoanalysis, but brings to the surface what might be called the individual's social unconscious. Education must be aware of this unconsciously transmitted/internalized social message since there is a lot of evidence that just because it is hidden to the conscious mind it plays an important part in any indivdual's identity formation.

Redundancy analysis has been developed in the course of a research project investigating the socialization patterns of bilinguals in order to provide an empirical base for theory formation in intercultural education. It owes its origin to the qualitative analysis of biographic interviews, but attempts have also been made to apply it to other fields of educational research.

Language as Social Institution

The approach of redundancy analysis is based on the general assumption that language — in the sense of 'parole', i.e., spoken language or language in use — is the best link between the objective and the subjective aspects of sociocultural life. In other words: each individual's personal use of language — in the sense of 'langue', i.e., language system — cannot help but mirror the sociocultural rules of his/her respective social system, however hard the speaker may try to express his/her very personal and unique point of view in a highly individualized language. The very nature of language (langue) is that of a collective symbolic construct which functions like a social institution and indeed it has often enough been called a social institution by linguists and sociologists alike (c.f., Berger and Luckmann, 1967). This means that language is responsible for a large-scale transaction of social rules and values between society and the individual. More precisely, language (langue) seen as a social institution is the most important device for experiencing, defining, and evaluating reality within the framework of a society's culture. It stores in its structure and lexicon all the collective experience of a social group.

The individual does not have to give up his/her individuality the very moment he/she makes use of this institution and begins to speak. Speaking (and also writing) is a social activity in which the speaker/writer seeks a compromise between the collective patterns of the institution called language and his/her prelinguistic intention (Searle calls the state of mind preceding any form of speech 'intentionality', c.f., Searle, 1983). By selecting from a variety of possible structures and/or symbols, by combining elements of speech in a new way, by adopting the symbolic medium to one's expressive needs, by trying to cope with a social situation and a partner, one handles language like an open institution. According to Goffman (1961), open institutions allow room for personal contributions from the individual to the structure and the functioning of the institution. Language virtually is such an open institution, combining collective rules and individual freedom. It depends on the speaker's skill whether or not he/she is able to make use of the openness that is inherent in language. His/her language use (parole) mirrors the extent to which he/she is a mere 'client' of the institution which allows him/her only to reproduce the symbolic representations of reality as shaped by model utterances (such as proverbs, common sayings, stereotypes, formulas, prejudice, etc.), or whether he/she takes an active part in symbolically organizing and structuring reality ('language making' instead of 'language taking', one is prompted to say in analogy to Turner's 'role making' versus 'role taking', c.f., Turner, 1962). However active he/she may be in this creative use of language, there is always — amalgamated with even the most subjective handling of language — an underlying current of objective meaning that is not intended by the speaker.

The research approach depicted here analyzes biographic interviews. It takes a close look at the individual's skill at handling the institution of language. This skill is not considered a natural gift, but a product of socialization. Socialization is thought of as a process of internalizing the sociocultural patterns of a society, or rather a segment of society, via the language of the respective society. The way in which this language is acquired, the degree to which spoken language shows deviance from typical patterns, the extent to which it allows individual experience to be expressed, the taboos it has, etc., make it possible for 'insiders' to estimate the degree of institutional freedom open to the speaker, i.e., his/her possibility of moving freely within the rule-governed system of language. 'Insider' is a common denominator for anyone who is a competent listener/speaker in the respective language. Being such an insider is an indispensable prerequisite for redundancy analysis. The insider's competence also includes everyday knowledge about which stratum of language is appropriate for which social situation and for which social role. Mere linguistic knowledge does not suffice to decide how language must be matched to a social situation and to a social role. At his very best, the insider shares the common sense knowledge of the 'man in the street' and is capable of actively taking part in everyday communication of the culture which he/she is exploring.

The researcher's aim is to find out as much as possible about the sociocultural patterns internalized by his/her interview partner. He/she has to reconstruct from this partner's use of language the sociocultural rules he/she has internalized. Through the analysis of 'parole' (= language in use), one reconstructs 'langue' (= the language system underlying actual speech). 'Langue', however, is limited here to the language system of a group (for example, a sub-culture), not to that of a whole nation (for example, English as opposed to Italian). The reconstruction of 'langue' reveals a lot about the sociocultural rules that govern a social group (c.f., Wittgenstein, 1971). Most of these rules embodied in the structure of speech are unconscious or, at least, the speaker is not aware of them and does not consciously refer to them while speaking. Their existence is independent of the speaker's will. He/she cannot avoid them and cannot get rid of them as long as he/she uses language. And what is more, these rules do not only crop up every now and then but are omnipresent. They are, in fact, redundant and are embodied in language in various different forms.

Redundancy analysis was developed out of an interest in laying bare the sociocultural rules of groups with dominating influence on individual socialization. By identifying these rules the hope is to identify also the objective aspects of subjective existence. The qualitative analysis of biographical interviews is supposed to bring out this objective quality in the subject.

This approach resembles in many ways Oevermann's 'Objektive Hermeneutik' (= objective hermeneutics, c.f., Oevermann *et al.*, 1979), which is also concerned with the sociocultural aspects of individual speech and also tries to make visible and audible the objective meaning underlying each individual speech act quite apart from any subjective intention to communicate a personal message in an individual language. Both redundancy analysis and 'Objektive Hermeneutik' try to reveal the sociocultural determination in any speech act (and any written text).

As far as this objective aspect is concerned they both differ from psychoanalytic interpretation methods, which are above all concerned with the reconstruction of an individual's unique life-history and try to find traces of old conflicts sedimented in language (c.f., Lorenzer, 1973). The only psychoanalytic approach which is related to 'Objektive Hermeneutik' and redundancy analysis is the one developed by Leithäuser and Volmerg (1979), which also focusses on the subject-object relations within the individual and also studies the social side of a person's psychology, based on the assumption that the psyche is also social and that language is the transmission belt between society and the individual. However, all psychoanalytic approaches, including Leithäuser/Volmerg, rely on transference and counter transference in order to understand a person's unconscious (be it individual or social).

The difference between redundancy analysis and Objektive Hermeneutik lies mainly within a different attitude towards the structure of interaction. This is considered to be essential in Objektive Hermeneutik, but it is ignored in redundancy analysis. This is due to the fact that an interview situation (which is the only method of data gathering in redundancy analysis) is more or less pre-structured by an interactive ritual; it is an unbalanced approach with more or less one person asking questions and the other answering so that the structure of interview interaction has little to reveal about an interviewee's reality. Objektive Hermeneutik, however, analyzes transcripts of interactions in 'natural' settings where the interactional structure is an expression of, and a cue to sociocultural rules. Another difference must be seen in the 'redundancy assumption'. While it is not of overall importance for Objektive Hermeneutik, the approach presented here assumes that the cues to sociocultural rules abound in any spoken (or written) text in various guises. Even if, at first glance, a person's language does not seem to be redundant, it always turns out to be as soon as one looks carefully enough for the sociocultural meaning of different features of the spoken (or written) text. Once the redundancies are identified, the unique and erratic elements of a text that do not yield to subsumption under the redundancy categories established before also become important because they too mark crucial points in a person's social identity.

As a matter of fact, the great model for this type of research is Peter Handke novel 'Wunschloses Unglück' where he analyzes his mother's suicide. He describes his narrative technique as follows: 'In the beginning I started out from the facts and tried to find words for them. Then I realized that by seeking words I was already departing from the facts. Then I started out from already existing formulas, from the social corpus of language instead of the facts. From my mother's life I sorted out all those events that had already been foreseen in these formulas . . . I compared the general stock of formulas for a woman's biography sentence for sentence with my mother's particular life; the actual writing activity stems from agreements and contradictions' (Handke, 1972, p. 42 f.).

Redundancy analysis tries to reformulate Handke's literary program in terms of social science. It is a qualitative approach to the study of man's social nature which compares the language (parole) of an interviewee with the language system (langue) of his/her sociocultural group in order to discover redundant patterns. These language patterns are considered symptomatic of sociocultural rules. Redundancy analysis is related to psychoanalytic approaches in so far as it studies the unconscious. It differs from any psychoanalytic approach because its main interest is in the social unconscious. It is more closely related to 'Objektive Hermeneutik' because of this interest in the objective aspects of subjective life. The greatest difference to Objektive Hermeneutik must be seen in this absolute confidence in language as the best guide to an individual that is not conceived as an entity confronting society but as an entity shaped by society to its innermost being.

Redundancy Analysis in Minority Research and Other Fields of Application

So far this approach has been applied successfully in the study of identity-formation in the bilingual region of Southern Carinthia where many people grow up with two languages and two cultures (German and Slovene), but learn sooner or later that one these cultures and one of these languages is not fit for public use. Almost everybody must, at crucial points in his/her career (for example, school enrolment, choice of friends, behaviour in public places, marriage, job) decide whether or not to be loyal to his/her bicultural and bilingual background. Hiding one's bicultural and bilingual identity or supressing it in favour of the majority language and culture is usually regarded as helpful to social climbing and professional advance. Regional history provides enough arguments as to why swapping identity is rewarded and why confessing to one's original identity makes another person suspicious. Human Rights and the Austrian constitution, on the other hand, provide the moral and political arguments for all those who insist on their bilingual and bicultural identity, even in public places, in spite of all the disadvantages connected with such confessions. These 'confessors' also quote history to prove how much they have been suffering from injustice for at least 150 years, during which time German nationalism has poisoned the social climate of the bilingual and bicultural country. Often enough families are divided over these identity problems. While one brother/sister confesses to having a minority identity, the other insists on belonging to the majority. Grandparents usually define themselves as minority members. Parents, however, say they are bicultural, while the young generation is again monocultural. But unlike their grandparents, their culture and language is that of the majority. A lot of people are caught in between the cultures and languages so that they have difficulties with a monocultural identity.

Redundancy analysis has been very helpful in defining different patterns of sub-cultures that have been internalized by people in this bicultural region. Thus it was possible, on a theoretical level, to differentiate between the rather vague identity-concepts obtained by research into minorities. But the results also allowed the development and implementation of educational programmes influencing the general local attitude towards bilingual and bicultural identity in favour of more acceptance of diversity and pluralism (c.f., Boeckmann *et al.*, 1987 and 1988).

At the present time there are three projects running, each of them employing the redundancy approach to explore sociocultural influence on individuals' biographies. The first analyzes interviews with three old partisans who had taken an active part in the resistance against Nazi-Germany and fought against German troops on Carinthian territory. By scrutinizing their language-use, redundancy analysis will test how much of their anti-fascist attitude has been able to survive in post-war Carinthia in spite of a sociocultural climate with latent sympathies for fascism. The second tries to reconstruct the ideology of the Youth Hostels Association in German-speaking countries via redundancy analysis of interviews with four leading personalities that shaped the organization in its decisive moments in Austria, Western Germany, the former German Democratic Republic and Switzerland. The project's goal is to find out to what extent authoritarian aspects can be identified in the culture of this important educational institution. The third project explores the identity-management of retired Carinthian teachers who were loyal servants of three different political systems, i.e., the authoritarian Austrian regime before 1938, the Nazi dictatorship between 1938 and 1945, and the democratic post-war Austrian Republic after 1945. In this project, redundancy analysis helps to investigate the sociocultural climate of Carinthian socieny, or rather a special segment of this society. It is not possible to reconstruct the real social life of bygone times with the help of this method, but using it enables the researcher to gain insight into those aspects of culture that have been internalized by individual teachers.

It must, however, be mentioned that all the projects described here do not use the redundancy approach exclusively. In fact, each of them has also included the collection of as much context information as possible, by whatever means, that could throw additional light on local history and local social structure. The construction of theory then has consisted of the formulation of basic sociocultural rules that according to the results of redundancy analysis must have been internalized by the members of a given society.

The educational interest in the social nature of the individual has traditionally been neglected in favour of the interest in the particularity of the individual. Redundancy analysis tries to make up for this one-sidedness of traditional educational research by focusing on the objective aspects of socialization. Thus it helps to realize the sociocultural dimensions of identity.

Any researcher who is interested in the reciprocal influence of subjective and objective factors is well advised to use some qualitative approach. It depends on the nature of his/her data and, of course, on his/her guiding questions whether he/she prefers 'Objektive Hermeneutik', some psycho-analytic approach or redundancy analysis. In case of redundancy analysis a lot of preparatory work such as an intensive study of the historical and socioeconomic context by means of traditional methods must also be carried out.

This approach should not be used in research that is only interested in the objective structures of the social system, such as the division of labour, unemployment rates, indicators of hierarchy in institutions, changes in family structures over the centuries, a comparative study of suicide rates in different regions, the number and percentage of working class children in grammar schools, etc. Whenever the individual in society rather than society in the individual is under scrutiny, redundancy analysis has little or no contribution to make.

Torn between Nazi Hero and KZ-Inmate — A Sample

As will be seen in the next section, data may be presented at different stages of processing. The 'raw material' — if any such raw material exists at all — is the tape-recorded version of the original interview. What comes next is the transcript.

Most transcripts, however, are longer than thirty type-written pages (the longest one consists of seventy-seven pages), so that there is not enough room for them to be presented here. A concise narrative summary of an interview (which has to be written by the interviewer) would, in fact, represent the surface content of the interview, but it would not allow the reader to gain any insight into the texture of the interviewee's language. The only possible solution to this problem of limited space is to present an abridged version of the narrative summary.

Narrative Summary of Tone's Biography

(In the original version, the story is five pages long; here it is not printed in full length; only some passages of great importance are picked out to illustrate what summary writing is about.)

Tone, 35, telephone operator in the largest Slovene (and bilingual) company of Carinthia:

In his early years, he says, his Slovene had even helped him. He had attended the Slovene grammar school in Celovec/Klagenfurt and afterwards had applied for a job at a Klagenfurt bank. They had taken him because of his bilingual competence. He did not work at the desk, but whenever a Yugoslavian customer came, he was asked for help. In the office he had never realized any bad feelings against Slovenes, since everybody had been very tolerant.

He interrupts the interview to answer the phone: 'Guten Tag! Dober dan! Buon giorno!'

Once, he says, he had even left earlier in order to take part in a demonstration for bilingual culture. He had, of course, not told anybody in the bank where exactly he was going, but he was sure that everybody knew. When the demonstration then passed by the bank, his colleagues came out and watched the procession.

He was certain they must have seen him. The next day, however, nobody mentioned this event except for one who said to him: 'Yesterday you had quite a demonstration, right?' But that was all.

Interviewer's comment:

I am somewhat surprised: There is a conscious, 'confessing' Slovene sitting right in front of me — one who is engaged in the struggle for the survival of his ethnic group —, but he seems to remember no real trouble, only positive experiences with the majority.

Since I keep insisting on the question of what happens when some family members begin to deny their identity he tells me that, in fact, some Slovenes see a conflict in that; but they should not, he thinks.

He tells me that such splits within families go back to the times of the Nazi regime, when quite a number of Slovenes changed their ethnic identity while others did not, even when they lived in the same family. Professing one's Slovene identity was dangerous, though.

Tone continues:

He says that in his own family there was this split of German and Slovene identity although both parents were of Slovene origin. His mother, for example, was in a concentration camp while his father was fighting with the German army somewhere in the North . . . (translated from Gombos, Narrative Summary 'Tone')

Toil and Trouble — The Heavy Labour of Redundancy Analysis

Redundancy analysis is a group method that requires a lot of time and energy as well as creativity as far as application of language skill is concerned. It cannot be applied by one researcher only, because each step of interpretation needs communicative evaluation, i.e. collective and communicative agreement on what is correct common sense social knowledge and what is everyday language in the interviewee's social group. Even one small utterance of only a few words keeps a group of interpreters busy for hours. One line of transcribed text thus produces twenty pages of interpretative text which have to be condensed into a short interpretation containing the chief ideas of the long version. Of course, such enormous quantities of interpretation cannot be printed here. Therefore I have chosen a short-cut: I will describe the individual steps of the approach, but will illustrate only the most decisive ones with exemplary passages of the group discussion.

Step 1: Collecting data. This is done by the researcher with the help of biographical interviews. Each of these interviews takes about two hours and consists of some very open stimuli for conversation. These interviews are taped. The tapes are then transcribed. The transcription becomes the starting point for any further activity.

Step 2: The interviewer has to prepare his/her interview — usually about thirty or forty type-written pages — for further treatment by the research-team. This preparation consists of the following:

— Description of the interview situation (Who speaks to whom? Where? When? Under which conditions? In which social context? In which atmosphere?)
— Interviewer's emotional reactions to interview situation. (Which impression did interviewee make on him/her? How did the interview develop?)
— Narrative summary of interview, not longer than three or four type-written pages.
— Macro-Analysis: Cursory reading for first impressions, second reading for text structure, especially for redundant, contradictory or unfinished passages, third reading for language use, especially for idiosyncratic use of words, metaphors and grammar, syntactical breakdowns, abrupt changes of structures, etc.

Example taken from 'Interview with Tone':
This language is characterized by a tendency to double, treble, even to quadruple dominating grammatical, syntactical and narrative patterns:
'look, look . . .; because he, because he . . .; and and; in order to improve that, in order to improve that; there, certainly, there
we shall have to struggle for some more years, have to stuggle . . .'
He takes four runs to get out an 'if-then construction'. As the interview goes on, all these symptoms crop up over and over again. The content of his speech is that of a dramatic conflict that seems to be so overwhelming that language no longer serves its purposes. In fact, Tone's speech loses its balance as he tries to talk about his mother being imprisoned in a Nazi concentration camp while his father is fighting for the glory of the same German Nazi regime. His repetitions sound like

stammering. The closer he comes to the central conflict the more he stammers until there is a complete grammatical and syntactical breakdown.

Step 3: Crucial Passage: The interviewer selects from his/her interview text a crucial passage, i.e., one paragraph of the interview text in which macro-analysis has identified an extraordinary number of symptoms.

Example taken from 'Interview with Tone':

> 'Depending on what sort of person one is confronted with, well, I think, we must not so much, so much get down to this problem, because in the war . . . I don't know, well, for example my mother was in the concentration camp, in Ravensburg, while my father was, was, eh, in, in, well, in the German war, you see . . ., he was up there in Norway or in Lapland. And I think that should, that should right now not be such a problem or such an issue for the bilinguals, should not be, I want to say, for bilingualism in our country. Well, I think this . . ., when two people live together here, or two people together, I want to say . . . that . . . nothing else but tolerance and on the other hand we have to respect. (excerpt taken from Gombos, Interview with Tone, transcript)

Steps 4 to 14 require the presence of the complete research team even for those steps carried out individually. They are done 'here and now' in a continuous sequence; sometimes group interaction is more important than individual achievement, sometimes it is the other way round. For each step I have marked which of the two, group or individual, is of greater importance for the respective activity.

Step 4, group: The interviewer confronts the group with the first utterance of the crucial passage, usually by writing it on a blackboard or on a flip chart. No mention is made as to the interviewee's identity, the social context, the text that precedes and that follows the passage chosen.

In the project mentioned above, fifty-two interviews were made, transcribed, and analyzed in the way described here. For the 'interview with Tone' the project group was confronted with the following utterance (without any knowledge as to who was talking, what had been said before and would be said after this utterance) that kept the group busy for about three hours. Of course, there is not enough room here for a full length coverage of the analysis of this one utterance.

Example take from 'Interview with Tone':

> . . . because in the war . . . I don't know, well, for example my mother was in the concentration camp, in Ravensburg, while my father was, was, eh, in, in, well, in the German war, you see . . .

Step 5, individual: Each member of the group tries to imagine as many social situations as possible in which this utterance would make sense with exactly the same words.

Example taken from 'Interview with Tone', passage quoted above:

— sensitivity training, third day
— psychoanalytic therapy, 145th session
— drinking company in a Slovene pub at Eisenkappel/Železna Kapla, three hours past midnight

— confession to a very close Slovene friend after emptying a bottle of wine together
— confession of a Carinthian Slovene to his German-speaking girlfriend after he has proposed to her
— Carinthian Slovene being interviewed by Catholic priest for an article in the Sunday paper

Step 6, group: All the situations found by the group are entered on a long list. The most improbable ones are sorted out by group consensus.

Step 7, individual: The biographic experience expressed in Tone's original utterance is now verbalized in as many different ways as possible. Each of them must refer to this experience and must be acceptable to at least one local reference group.

Example taken from 'Interview with Tone' (The question was: In which different versions might one hear this sentence in bilingual Carinthia?)

— It was my mother who was faithful to her Slovene identity and even went to the concentration camp for it while my father rather became German to fight in this terrible war.
— My mother and my father had different impressions of the Second World War.
— Well, yes, my mother was in custody at that time, you know, but my father did his duty for Germany. He even was in Norway.
— Don't let us talk about the past. It was a hard time for mother and father, for each one in his way.
— Let sleeping dogs lie. But I can tell you that it was not easy for either of them.

Step 8, group: The variations of the original utterance are entered on one long list. The most improbable ones are eliminated by group consensus.

Step 9, group: Matching of situations (step 5) and utterances (step 7). It is expected that by now a variety of sociocultural rules as to what to say when and to whom have been associated with the original utterance. Picking out only one as the correct solution is not allowed. The point is to bring to the surface a whole variety of usually unconscious or semiconscious sociocultural rules that are built into any utterance of everyday speech.

Example taken from 'Interview with Tone':

The way in which T. speaks illustrates that he is breaking taboos that are not usually talked about in everyday conversation in this region. There are neither communicative nor linguistic rules nor models for explanation in public speech about the fact that National Socialism corrupted family solidarity and group loyalty. It is just not good manners to talk about this in public except when you have a good excuse, say for example you are drunk in the company of Slovene friends (but rarely in the company of German speaking friends). If you do it all the same without being drunk you must do it in a black-and-white technique with 'good mother, bad father' — stereotypes for a Slovene audience, with 'bad mother and good father' — stereotypes for a German speaking audience ('German' here refers to those German-speaking former Slovenes who have purposely forgotten their ethic origin and over-identify with German nationalism although they have little

German background). However, even in the black-and-white technique such topics are rarely discussed. Only artificial situations similar to Catholic confessions may succeed in getting people to talk about such taboos. The sociocultural rules, however, seem to make it necessary for 'confessors' to minimize even the most dramatic conflicts and to moralize about rather than to analyze them. Conflicts are not good. Whoever has a conflict, is not a good member of the group. Forgetful harmony is better than a critical evaluation of history that might lead to conflicting views.

Usually the interpretation of only one utterance takes three or four hours. The transcriptions in most of the cases consist of more than thirty type-written pages.

Step 10, the interviewer in front of the group: The next utterance is written on a flip chart or on the black-board. Go on as above, steps 1 to 5.

Step 11, individual: The different steps are combined and translated into an interpretative text taking into consideration sociocultural meaning and expressing analytic insights into the social nature of the person who is the author of the utterance being analyzed. As a result of step 11, there will be five to seven different interpretations depending on the number of team members.

Step 12, group: Each interpretation is discussed. The group decides by way of critical discourse which elements of interpretation are acceptable and which are not.

Step 13, group: The group works on a collective interpretation that includes all the accepted elements of step 12.

Step 14, group: This interpretation is compared with all the context information available and, if necessary, modified.

Step 15: Interviewer only: The interviewer is left alone to write a concise interpretation of his/her interview.

Step 16: All interpretations of all interviews are studied for parallel and contrasting elements. Generalizations are made. A theory on aspects of bilingual socialisation and identity formation is conceived.

Example taken from project 'Bilinguism and Identity' (Boeckmann *et al.*, 1988)

One of the central insights of our research is that all identity-types that we have discovered have images of the others as enemies.

Being different is threatening for any group. The fact that others are different makes them a threat. One looks for unequivocal clearness by trying to create such unequivocal clearness in speech. Whoever fails to be clear-cut remains a dangerous outsider and must be labelled as such. Those who form their identity mainly by eliminating and casting out anything and anybody that is different, tend to feel permanently threatened. It seems that they build their identity on this threat. Therefore the concept of the enemy has an important function in identity management. No doubt this may be temporarily helpful for the individual. For a peaceful development of the regional society, however, it is disastrous. (p. 228)

Outlook

It is hard to say if redundancy analysis has, or ever will have, a chance of becoming a major approach in educational research. First of all, it is an inconvenient method. It is time consuming: for the first utterance of ten or twenty words it takes a group of five to seven researchers about three or four hours to come up with an interpretation; for the first paragraph (or passage, or scene — a unit of speech which is defined by consensus of the group; usually it consists of all the moves to cover a topic) it takes at least another three to four hours; for one complete interview, three or four days of continuous work are the absolute minimum. It cannot be done by one or two persons only. In order to achieve high quality (in the sense of validity and reliability), a group of competent researchers (each of them competent in the methodology of interpretative social research and in the rules of regional culture and vernacular) must cooperate. This requires extensive preparation, coordination, and training in discourse-techniques.

Second, redundancy analysis cannot be done by everybody who does social research. Members of research teams must have a triple qualification (see above!) to the extent that they must be able to naively participate in everyday symbolic interaction (of the local region and/or culture that is being explored), and they must be able to lay bare hidden meaning and sociocultural messages of texts/utterances that, according to the intention of the respective authors/speakers, are nothing but personal communication without any social implication. To combine both qualities, that of the participant observer and that of the analytic researcher, takes a lot of preparatory work. So does the competence of group interpretation, which is not only a research technique but also a group-dynamic experience. The project mentioned above had a period of about two years to qualify in all three aspects.

Redundancy research cannot be recommended to students in their first years for it requires close acquaintance with a number of methods. Even researchers who are not used to working in teams or who work under the permanent threat of 'publish or perish' should rather be discouraged from using this approach. There is little chance for a quantitative dissemination of this qualitative method.

However, for the study of subject-object dialectics redundancy analysis is an excellent approach. Professional research teams doing project work on any topic where the individual is the starting point for the exploration of the internalized social world within the individual (for example, oral history, evaluation of educational innovations, etc.) are encouraged to consider this method provided they can establish the research-culture necessary for its application.

References

BERGER, P.L. and LUCKMANN, T. (1967) *The Social Construction of Reality. A Treatise on the Sociology of Knowledge*, Harmondsworth, Penguin.

BOECKMANN, B., BRUNNER, K.-M., EGGER, M., GOMBOS, G., JURIĆ, M. and LARCHER, D. (1987) *Zweisprachigkeit und Identität*, Klagenfurts, Projektbericht.

BOECKMANN, B., BRUNNER, K.-M., EGGER, M., GOMBOS, G., JURIĆ, M. and LARCHER, D. (1988) *Zweisprachigkeit und Identität*, Klagenfurt, Drava.

GOFFMAN, E. (1961) *Asylums. Essays on the Social Situation of Mental Patients and other Inmates*, New York, Doubleday.

HANDKE, P. (1972) *Wunschloses Unglück. Erzählung*, Salzburg, Residenz.

LEITHÄUSER, T., VOLMERG, B. (1979) *Anleitung zur empirischen Hermeneutik. Psychoanalytische Textinterpretation als sozialwissenschaftliches Verfahren*, Frankfurt/M, Suhrkamp.

Dietmar Larcher

LORENZER, A. (1973) *Sprachzerstörung und Rekonstruktion*, Frankfurt/M, Suhrkamp.

OEVERMANN, U., ALLERT, T., KONAU, E., KRAMBECK, J. (1979) 'Die Methodologie einer "objektiven Hermeneutik" und ihre allgemeine forschungslogische Bedeutung in den Sozialwissenschaften' in SOEFFNER, H.-G. (Ed.) *Interpretative Verfahren in den Sozial- und Textwissenschaften*, Stuttgart, Metzler, pp. 353–434.

SEARLE, J. (1983) *Intentionality. An Essay in the Philosophy of Mind*, Cambridge, Cambridge University Press.

TURNER, R. (1962) 'Role-taking: Process versus conformity' in ROSE, A.M. (Ed.) *Human Behavior and Social Process. An Interactionist Approach*, London, Routledge & Kegan Paul.

WITTGENSTEIN, L. (1971) *Philosophische Untersuchungen*, Frankfurt/M, Suhrkamp.

Chapter 9

Voices of Beginning Teachers: Computer-assisted Listening to Their Common Experiences

Günter L. Huber and Carlos Marcelo García

The Voice Behind the Talk

One hundred and five beginning teachers talked about their experiences when they entered the classroom after their pre-service training. They described their observations, their preoccupations, their feelings, their activities in their subjective languages. Some spoke very clear and directly, some talked about their experiences in ambiguous everyday language, some used rather idiosyncratic formulations, others frequently expressed themselves by means of metaphor, however, there seemed to be several common tones. The problem was to tune to this voice behind the talk. Using traditional methods of qualitative analysis the task of listening hard to the common message in individual formulations is really a tedious and time-consuming work. By describing the practical application of a software package for the analysis of qualitative data, we want to outline basic features of computer assistance to qualitative research, and to demonstrate the contribution of computers to hear the voice behind the noise of a multitude of utterances.

General Orientation

A recent examination of research in teacher education (Tisher and Wideen, 1990) showed, among other deficiencies, a series of discrepancies between theory and practice. Above all, pre-service training courses are not always well related to the demands of classroom teaching, and the socializing effects of schools often contradict even well-choosen contents of pre-service training courses. From a methodological perspective, Tisher and Wideen (*ibid*, p. 256) summarize a similarly disconcerting state of research in teacher education, characterized among other flaws by poor anchoring to the practical, day-to-day problems in teacher education and by 'unwarranted statistical overkill with sophisticated statistical analyses'. They discern a general dissatisfaction among the contributors to their book about the state of conceptual frameworks of research in teacher education. Considering additionally the demand to foster 'teacher ownership' (*ibid*, p. 266) of training activities, we feel strongly reinforced in our general orientation to study teacher education and teacher socialization from the teachers' subjective points of view, following the paradigm of 'teacher thinking' (Clark and Yinger, 1979) or 'subjective theories' (Groeben et al., 1988).

Guided by this orientation we hope to circumvent one of the pitfalls of research in teacher education, which is to concentrate on isolated aspects of the overall highly complex process of teachers' professional development (c.f., Klinzing, 1990). Trying to get access to teachers' subjective conceptions of their own education and its significance for day-to-day teaching, however, does not guarantee *per se* to overcome the limitations of traditional research approaches. A collection of idiosyncratic experiencies may be impressive and colourful, but perhaps still nothing more than an aggregation of necessarily narrow and limited points of view. As the fundamental principle of 'Gestalt' states, the whole is more than an addition of its parts. What we therefore need is a comprehensive orientation in the field of scientific theories which should help us in comparing the single cases and in reconstructing a holistic understanding — as regards our approach — of beginning teachers' problems in the classroom.

This 'paradigmatic' orientation implies at the same time that we broaden the scope of research methods. If we want to integrate more components than a limited number of variables from instruments of doubtful ecological validity, at least from the teachers' viewpoint, we must not confine our study to standardized quantitative procedures. We need qualitative approaches, too, and reliable methods for the analysis of their produce. When using qualitative data, we have to handle texts from interviews, diaries, protocols of 'thinking aloud', field notes of participant observers and so on, in which individual perspectives are expressed in often colourful formulations. Unfortunately, they are often rather ambiguous, even within one and the same text. Qualitative orientation thus is faced with the fundamental problem of reducing a huge number of statements in hundreds of pages of transcriptions to units of meaning which are both well defined and comparable. This task takes a lot of time, great portions of which have to be spent on mechanical work, and it is rather susceptible to errors. A successful one-trial reduction is impossible, several repetitions of the whole process for control, correction and modification of interpretations are the rule. Qualitative methods therefore badly need support by tools that help to reduce the burden of work as well as to systematize the procedures.

Theoretical Orientation

The first months in a classroom are a most important experience for teachers. During this time a long and unpredictable process starts which transforms some beginners in the teaching profession into expert teachers. For some authors on this topic, the first year in school does not only represent an opportunity of learning to teach; it may at the same time set personal transformations going (Tisher, 1984). Insecurity and a lack of self-confidence are among the characteristics of teachers during this period. Johnston and Ryan (1983) state:

> First-year teachers are aliens in a strange world; a world that is both
> known and unknown to them. Though they have spent thousands of
> hours in schools watching teachers and involved in the schooling process,

first-year teachers are not familiar with the specific school setting in which they begin to teach. (p. 137)

Veenman (1984) made the concept of 'reality shock' popular, by which he describes the state from which many teachers suffer during their first year in the classroom. Following this Dutch author, this first year is characterized generally by three attributes: intensive learning (in most cases by trial-and-error), striving for survival, and acting according to the ethics of practicability.

According to Feiman and Floden (1981) and Feiman-Nemser and Floden (1986), there are three main theoretical approaches to explain the process by which teachers acquire teaching competencies. The first approach concentrates on teachers' concerns or preoccupations as indicators of different stages in their professional development. Another approach looks at teachers from a fundamentally cognitivistic point of view and explains learning to teach as a process of intellectual maturation. A third approach to analyze the process of introduction to the profession is focused on social and cultural aspects of being a teacher, and on their assumption by beginning teachers.

Developmental stages of concerns

Fuller and Brown (1975) identified three stages of teacher development, differentiated by teachers' main preoccupations. During the first stage, concerns about *personal survival* are predominant. It is a phase in which the teacher is above all trying to maintain the role of a teacher, to stay in control of the classroom, and to please the students. The second stage is characterized by preoccupations about the *teaching situation* itself, that is about materials and methods, and about didactical approaches. Finally, in the third stage the concerns are focussed on the *students*, on their learning, on their social and emotional needs (Veenman, 1984). In other words, this approach states that teachers, who are mostly concerned about themselves in the classroom, are on a low level of 'teaching maturity'. Learning to teach therefore consists in proceeding from stage to stage until the major concerns are directed towards the students.

Cognitive developmental framework

Feiman and Floden (1981) and Feiman-Nemser and Floden (1986) based their theory of teachers' cognitive development on the work of Sprinthall and Thies-Sprinthall (1983), who assume that human development is a consequence of changes in cognitive organization, changes which represent new ways of perceiving the world. Under this perspective, the teacher is conceived as an adult learner, and teacher training as the process by means of which teachers are assisted in gaining higher and more complex conceptual levels. The most important assumption is that people on higher levels of cognitive development function in a more complex way, own a broader repertory of didactical skills, have a more profound perception of problems, and are able to respond more precisely and emphatically to other persons' needs (Veenman, 1984).

Consequently, beginning teachers should differ from each other in their capacities of information processing, and this should at least partially determine their success or failure during the period of introduction to classroom practice. Therefore introductory programs should lay stress upon fostering the intellectual capabilities of beginning teachers.

Teacher socialization framework

Within the theoretical framework of teacher socialization the period of introduction is studied as a process by which new teachers learn and internalize the norms, values, customs, etc. which characterize the social culture of the school into which they are going to become integrated (Zeichner and Gore, 1990).

Methodological Orientation

In our investigation we had intended to describe beginning teachers' perceptions during their first year of teaching. We were interested in the elements that play a role in beginning teachers' socialization (see Lacey, 1977). We also wanted to learn about their problems (didactical, organizational, etc.) during the first year. Finally we wanted to find out how these teachers learn and by means of which cognitive mechanisms. These goals imply that we did not rely entirely on pre-structured quantitative instruments, but tried to get access to what is going through beginning teachers' minds. Therefore we had to find a way to cope with the problems of qualitative research.

As outlined above, these problems are manifold. Miles (1983) therefore characterized qualitative data as an 'attractive nuisance', and his description still seems to be true. Researchers using quantitative methods can rely for the majority of their studies on standardized instruments of measurement and then choose from a well assorted stock of analytical procedures. Qualitative researchers on the other hand can refer to a broad repertory of methods for collecting data, which help to disclose the uniqueness of specific social sites or the subjectivity of personal world views. The problem for qualitative researchers, however, is to cope with an already physically overwhelming amount of rich and colourful verbal data. Although this aspect may appear to be quite superficial, a closer look to the time management in qualitative projects reveals that at least one-third of the available time is necessary for marking, clipping, glueing, sorting printed paper — not too exciting mechanical work. Then there is the real problem waiting: How to make sense of all these data? 'Making sense' of qualitative data first of all requires reducing texts to meaningful, comparable units. Reduction, not just 'duplication' of phenomena is the fundamental task of every scientific endeavour. Second, the reduced items have to be structured and displayed. Third, we want to draw and confirm comprehensive conclusions with the aim of theory building. Miles and Huberman (1984) outline what they consider to be qualitative analysis by these three forms of activity, emphasizing that these activities together with data collection form an interactive, cyclical process. Finally, a fourth step is often necessary: we have to compare the results of a number of analyses of single cases; i.e., we have to complement 'within-text' analysis by comparative 'between-text' analysis.

Of course, there are many occasions for intuition to enter this process. This subjective component is necessary if we try to listen to other people's voices. On the other hand, we do not undertake such endeavours in order to satisfy some personal curiosity, but to communicate the results, and in our case also hoping to find ways how to optimize teacher training. Our interpretations therefore have to be carefully scrutinized for objectivity, reliability, and validity or corresponding criteria more adequate for qualitative research (c.f., Lincoln and Guba, 1985). As regards objectivity of qualitative methods, we totally agree with Tuckman (1990) who wrote in a different context: 'I am not suggesting that everyone study every-thing the same way, only that they go about it in a systematic and controlled way . . .' (p. 24) But how could we enhance system and control in qualitative research? Lisch and Kriz (1978) demanded that researchers themselves should be aware of their decisions when reconstructing social reality, and they should inform their scientific community about these decisions. This means above all that a publication should not only inform about problem, methods, and results, but be as complete as possible about all relevant decisions which led the researcher from his/her question to these results.

Our conclusion was that adequate software could contribute to solve the more superficial problems of 'data-overload' in qualitative research as well as to change the way in which qualitative research is mostly realized. In other words, a software tool is needed for computer-assisted analysis of qualitative data that supports researchers in maintaining an overview about their decisions, in modifying them easily, and in sharing their decision-making with their scientific community.

Areas of Software Application to Qualitative Research

Not only qualitative data but even more the methods to collect and to analyze qualitative data represent a multiplicity of perspectives, adapted to the varied ideas and intentions of researchers dealing with unique sites and subjects. Although the fascinating kaleidoscope of analytical approaches defies generalization, this checkered picture is not ruled by mere chance but responds to structural constraints. In the following, we will outline possible contributions of software to assist qualitative researchers in mastering central tasks of data analysis, and we will describe the main features of the software-package AQUAD 3.0, which we developed as a tool for the Analysis of QUAlitative Data (Huber, 1990).

In an overview upon types of qualitative analysis and software tools, Tesch (1990) distinguishes four categories of functions that are necessary for the quali-tative researcher: *preparatory functions* (for example, importing text from word processors, numbering lines, printing files) are used to make texts ready for subsequent elaborations; *basic functions* (connecting units of meaning in the text with codes; searching and assembling coded text segments) have to be available for structuring and interpreting the texts, later for retrieving the results of this work; *enhancement functions* (for detecting sequences of codes, hierarchical struc-tures, multiple coding, particular logical relations between several units of meaning) are extremely important for testing hypothesis — and if we want to take seriously the demands for control and communication of processes in qualitative research; *housekeeping functions* (for example, saving, deleting, renaming files; switching between directories) have to be available in software tools of all kinds. Since software for qualitative analysis always has to provide preparatory, basic, and housekeeping functions, we will concentrate here on the description of enhance-ment functions. It is in this domain that programs for qualitative analysis differ widely, and AQUAD 3.0 was developed especially with the goal in mind to assist those tasks beyond retrieving text and counting frequencies, which we like to address as 'higher order' analyses.

AQUAD 3.0 was originally developed for biographical interviews, but it can handle any type of qualitative data. Since its main accent is on enhancement functions, especially those for generating and testing hypotheses or even theory-building (c.f., Tesch, 1990), many of its functions are not necessary for studies focussed on structural features of texts, for example, the frequency of particular codes or words. Although this kind of analysis is supported by AQUAD 3.0, its speciality are the following four groups of enhancement functions:

(i) *Enhancement of systematic interpretation*

During the process of coding we have to answer a series of questions regularly: Did we use the interpretation rules consistently? Did we stay within the limits of our codes or did we produce overlaps of meanings during interpretation? Can the meanings represented by particular codes really be found in the corresponding text passages? Thus we question reliability and (content) validity of our interpretation. Without software support the answers are difficult enough to find if we apply a pre-constructed system of categories, but the problems are increased markedly if we used only a preliminary framework of interpretative concepts which has to be differentiated inductively. Even more complicated is the task if we reduce the data inductively and try to get hold of the participants' thoughts by means of categories which are developed during the coding process. Especially in this case we cannot expect consistent and valid coding after the first pass, rather we have to establish these criteria during a second, third or more passes with modified coding rules. The main questions here are: Do the same/different codes signify the same/different units of meaning? Did we apply several different codes to the same thoughts or did we on the contrary attach the same label to differing units of meaning? By the software we get support in elaborating a synopsis of critical passages from the complete text material in order to answer these questions.

(ii) *Enhancement of hypothesis construction*

As a heuristic of hypothesis construction we often would like to know whether a particular category of meaning is/is not related to a particular other category. Are these considerations valid in the light of our text interpretation? We are still unable to formulate a specific hypothesis, but some search strategies implemented in AQUAD 3.0 are suited to answer questions like this, at least by informing us about general tendencies. We could enter one particular code, then the program will look for sub-codes (i.e., codes embedded within the text segment that is 'interpreted' by the critical code), overlapping codes (i.e., units of meaning that overlap the text segment associated with the critical code), multiple coding (i.e., whether the same text segment was interpreted additionally with other codes), or look for all codes which appear in the text within a particular distance (expressed in terms of line numbers) before and after the critical code. Another support for hypothesis construction in AQUAD 3.0 is the matrix display of coded text segments (c.f., Miles and Huberman, 1984). If we want to get a well-structured overview about units of meaning, which fulfil the demands of two criteria (codes) simultaneously, we can define a two dimensional network for displaying the relevant text passages. Thus we could answer, for instance, questions like: Is there a difference/correspondence between female and male teachers as regards particular experiences during their first year in the classroom? We have to define column headers (codes for gender) and row headers (codes for critical experiences) for a retrieval matrix. Besides contributing to prove the validity of interpretations, the resulting matrix display offers at the same time a simple and efficient possibility for enhancing the construction of hypotheses in qualitative research.

(iii) *Enhancement of hypothesis testing*
The common task in testing qualitative hypotheses is to retrieve all locations in a text, where two or more units of meaning appear in a defined relationship. AQUAD 3.0 comes with twelve hypotheses structures into which the user enters codes and distances defining the hypothetical relation. In order to test, for instance, the hypothesis about beginning teachers' main concerns about evaluation (see below), we would choose the first option from a menu of hypothesis structures, enter the codes for concern, for evaluation, and the distance within which we expect to find remarks about evaluation after the interviewee mentioned something about his/her concerns. The program will then search in all our code files for this particular relation and print all the locations in the text, where this relation is true. We can use pre-constructed hypothesis structures of formulate our own hypotheses. Most frequently the following relations are of interest: Sequences of meaning units (for example, do beginning teachers describe their students' family background after reporting achievement or behavior problems?), clusters of meaning units, hierarchical structures (for example, are there reflections about their own experiences as students embedded in text segments dealing with the educational system?), dimensional structures (i.e., structures of meaning gained by combining correlated codes to quasi-factorial structures), and causal relations.

(iv) *Enhancement of comparisons*
After within-text analyses we know about specific patterns of meanings; now we may be interested, whether these patterns are similar for all participants in our study, or which of these patterns seem to be related essentially with a particular phenomenon, for example, 'reality shock' of beginning teachers. Ragin (1987) has suggested to use the procedures of Boolean algebra for this kind of qualitative comparisons. For this purpose, AQUAD 3.0 transforms interpretations into 'truth values'; i.e., it reduces them to binary statements 'condition true' (given) or 'condition false' (not given). In this way, we first represent the single cases as configurations of characteristics or conditions and then compare the patterns of configurations. This comparison is based on the Boolean concept of minimization. Minimization corresponds to the variable-oriented experimental design on the level of a comparison of single cases: If we find the effect Y in two cases, but in one case the condition X is given among other conditions, whereas X is absent in the second case, then this condition X can be eliminated as irrelevant from the

further analysis. The result is a simplified, that is, minimized configuration of conditions for Y.

Example of Data from the Study on Beginning Teachers

In the following we present a part of one of the interviews with beginning teachers. The lines are numbered in order to facilitate the identification of units of meaning.

```
 1  INI. 090
 2  What did you suppose regarding your first months
 3  of teaching?
 4  What did you suppose regarding yourself?
 5  //R.: The truth is that this was a totally new
 6  experience, that they phone you, that they send
 7  you a telegram, you become immediately member of
 8  a staff, you had no time to think, you have
 9  to become incorporated immediately, you come running.
10  They put you in a classroom with forty people.
11  Noise. (Calling at the door).
12  You don't know neither the subjects you'll have
13  to teach nor do they give you a timetable.
14  The first day, the second, the third, the first week,
15  if you stay for a week at this school, you need them for
16  orientation, some adaptation to the children, because
17  it is you who adapts to them, not they to you. They
18  do not consider you as their teacher, even if you want
19  them to, they really consider you as a substitute, not
20  as somebody to become teacher. Even if you are for a
21  long time at a school, as I am for instance now, they
22  do not consider you a teacher. Therefore there is an
23  obstacle you have to cope with, because the children
24  know that you are a substitute, and they treat you
25  like one; and with you they behave differently than
26  with the other teachers, whom they had already for
27  years. Well, that's the first thing, and the second
28  is that you come and you do not know the staff of
29  teachers. Often they do not assign you to your special
30  subjects, and therefore you have to improvise. (Noise.)
31  Above all, you have to improvise during the first days.
32  They don't give you timetables, nobody tells you
33  where to take things and where not to take them.
34  Your own students will show it to you.
35  The teachers only rarely offer to
```

This is the beginning of interview no. 90, taken from a series of interviews with 107 teachers in the South of Spain. They were chosen at random from a list of beginning teachers in this school district. About one-third of them teach on each level of the Spanish school system; forty-seven of them are men, sixty are women. Two interviews had to be omitted from further analysis.

The design of this study is of the type 'multi-site'. Firestone and Herrior (1984) identify as a particular advantage of multi-site qualitative studies that one can address the same problem in several places or settings and use always the same procedures for data collection and analysis.

The interviews were structured following the three theoretical orientations outlined above, i.e., we intended to get information about the teachers' concerns, level of cognitive functioning, and socialization (in terms of norms, values, etc.). For this purpose, we formulated 'descriptive questions', as recommended by Spradley (1979). For this type of questioning it is not necessary to know details from the interviewee's situation; one has to be familiar just with some of the essential aspects. In our investigation these were the school level and the general situation of beginning teachers. We used the method of structured interviews, because our goal was to obtain more specific information from these teachers (c.f., Bogdan and Biklen, 1982). The content of our questions corresponds with Spradley's (1979) categories.

With *experience questions* we asked the teachers to describe events, concerns, opinions:

    (i)   Could you describe shortly what these first months as a teacher meant for you? Please, comment upon your impressions, experiences, and changes during this period.

    (ii)   Could you tell me which were the most important of your concerns during this time?

    (iii)   What impressions do you have of the school where you are teaching? What about the facilities, what about collaboration with parents?

    (iv)   Are you satisfied with your relations to your colleagues at your school, especially with colleagues teaching the same subjects?

    (v)   Could you describe any aspect of your relation to the students that you think is interesting? How do you perceive them?

    (vi)   Concluding from your experience, which aspects of your teaching do you consider to be most problematic?

    (vii)   How do you evaluate your own educational and didactical training? In what respect was it useful for you?

With a '*Mini-Tour*' question we wanted to motivate the teachers to give us a narrative description of any everyday event:

    (viii)   Could you describe a normal lesson on a regular day?
           Native-language questions tried to instigate the teachers to respond in their own words, using a language that should give more direct access to their way of thinking:

    (ix)   Could you define yourself as teacher?

    (x)   Assuming there were counseling programs for beginning teachers, which aspects do you consider most important?

Of course, the order of questioning did not always correspond to this presentation. The interviewers were advised to modify the initial order of questions if necessary, depending on the development of the interview. The interviews were tape-recorded. All recordings were transcribed using a word processor (WordPerfect). The original files in WordPerfect format were transformed into ASCII (American

Standard Code for Information Interchange) format, thus making them accessible for further processing with AQUAD 3.0.

Procedures of Analysis

Before we can start the analysis, we have to get ready to use the text files within the environment of AQUAD 3.0 The program needs a list of all interviews. Using the text processing functions within AQUAD 3.0, we create an inventory containing the names of our text files, i.e., from 'ini.001' through 'ini.107'.

Reducing Data

The *first step* in interpretative qualitative analysis is the codification of texts. When coding, we attach abbreviations symbolizing our interpretation of particular text segments to the text. As another prerequisite for this work, we have to number the lines of the interview transcriptions (separately for each transcription) in order to get marks for beginnings and endings of significant text segments. The line numbering is done with one of the preparatory functions of AQUAD 3.0 (see above). Coding can be accomplished in either of two modes with our software: (i) we can print the line numbered interviews, mark units of meaning in the traditional way with a pencil and colours on the printout, and later enter the text boundaries (number of first line and last line) and the code for this segment into the computer; or (ii) we interpret the transcripts directly on the screen by adding a code together with the number of the last line of its corresponding text segment to the end of the first line of this segment. In both cases AQUAD 3.0 produces code-files which contain for every unit of meaning the number of the interview, segment boundaries, and the code attached to it. We can use several codes in the same line, and we are not forced to care about overlapping, nesting etc. of units of meaning.

Miles and Huberman (1984) distinguish three types of codes which are related to the researchers' intentions. There are *descriptive codes* which do not transport any interpretation by the coder (for example, codes representing sociographic data, gender, school level, etc.); *interpretative codes* require that the researcher uses some sort of inference; and *explicative codes* finally need high degrees of inference. In our study we use almost exclusively interpretative codes, corresponding to the type of information we have asked for in the interviews.

As a theoretical guideline for elaborating a system of codes we choose the model of Jordell (1987), because in this approach three major influences on the socialization of beginning teachers are considered at the same time. These influences are mapped on the dimensions of person, classroom, and institution. The *personal dimension* comprehends to the beginning teachers' former experiences as students (biographical data) as well as during teacher education, their actual experiences as a teacher, and references to personal beliefs. The *classroom dimension* includes statements referring to situations before, during, and after teaching. The students, classroom and teaching activities, planning and evaluation are aspects of interest on this dimension. Finally, on the *institutional dimension* we map those comments which refer primarily to the school, the educational system, and its ecological context.

When the research team started the process of codification, it combined a

Table 9.1: Primary code inventory

1 Personal Dimension ECA experiences as student (in school) EFP experiences in teacher education EDP previous teaching experience SIM self PRE concern APR learning CRE beliefs NEF needs of training CDO teaching load	**2.4 Subject Matter** CON **2.5 Interactive Teaching** MET methods ACT activities DIS discipline MOT motivation GES classroom management **2.6 Evaluation** EVA
2 Teaching Dimension **2.1 Classroom** RPA ratio teacher/students EFC size (of the classroom) EQU equipment AMB classroom atmosphere **2.2 Students** CON behavior REN achievement COM comprehension CNP previous knowledge REL teacher-student relations PAR participation EXP expectations PRO familiy background **2.3 Planning** PLA	**3 Institutional Dimension** **3.1 School** COL colleagues MAT materials and media AMC school atmosphere CUR curriculum IDE rules ORG organisation/administration **3.2 Context** PAD parents ENT relations to context **3.3 Educational System** ADM administration LIM limitations/rules

Note: The original codes are in Spanish, so the abbreviations are meaningful in this language; for instance, the first code 'ECA' stands for 'experiencias como alumno'

deductive and an inductive approach. We took Jordell's dimensions into account, and gradually developed a preliminary set of codes. According to a growing insight into the teachers' view of their world we elaborated on the initial coding system, incorporating new codes and deleting some others. As a result the team established a system of specific codes for each dimension, shown in table 9.1.

The research team then tried to come to terms with the definitions of these thirty-nine categories. In order to enhance the consistency of coding, every coder received an explanation for each of the categories, together with an example taken from the original interviews.

Equipped with this categorial system we continued by selecting ten interviews for codification by all of the research team's eight members. With the results of this step, we intended to control for reliability of coding as an essential condition of credibility for the results of this study in general. In our case, we could not compute a coefficient of reliability; instead, we proceeded by discussing the codifications suggested by different members with the whole team. Since all team members had been occupied with the same sample of interviews, these group discussions evoked interesting disputes among the team and comments from different members referring to units of meaning which were interpreted by means of different codes. Our goal was, above all, to agree in interpreting the statements, not in determining their frequencies (c.f., Goetz and LeCompte, 1988).

At the end of this process we could indeed find a higher level of internal agreement among the coders.

As the next step in the phase of data reduction we applied the just established category system to the coding of all 105 interviews. For this purpose, we distributed the interviews at random among the members of this research team. After coding, the team evaluated again the adequacy of the category system. We noticed that it was necessary to introduce some new categories not considered in the primary system. At the same time we found codes that could be deleted or regrouped, thus matching the demands of this particular study. For instance, a category labelled as 'beliefs' (CRE) was modified to 'opinions' in order to make it more comprehensive. Two new categories were introduced: 'reality shock' in order to include specific statements of beginning teachers, and 'problems'.

Changes like these led to a modified coding system of thirty-three categories. The majority of them were already used in the first system. However, following the recommendations of several authors (Miles and Huberman, 1984; Huber and Marcelo, 1991), we started to code anew all 105 interviews with the aim of adapting all earlier codifications to the new system.

Displaying Data

Already during coding the team got several hunches about typical influences on beginning teachers. Displaying data, i.e., printing excerpts from the interviews (or code files) according to some criterion is a simple way to gain better access to systematic occurences in the transcriptions. At the same time, this is a preliminary stage of hypothesis construction. Thus, displaying data demonstrates clearly the circular connections between different stages of qualitative analysis (c.f., Miles and Huberman, 1984; Shelly, 1986).

A simple, but efficient way of getting a structured overview is to use the function in AQUAD 3.0 for '*retrieving coded text*', i.e., all text segments which have been defined by a particular code. We will see all sentences which the teachers formulated referring to a particular dimension of meaning. In our case, we were interested especially in the teachers' descriptions of their colleagues. These descriptions contained comments on their relations, interactions in and out of school, compatibilities, interests, tensions, and friendships. Of course, a structured printout like this also allows us to check up on the content validity of coding. The display of isolated codings 'COL', i.e., without considering the context of these text segments, made a dependency prominent that existed between different school levels (elementary and secondary school) and relations between colleagues. Here is just one example of how beginning teachers in elementary schools talk about the other teachers:

> The relations? . . . quite well, from the first day on, because they knew
> I came just for two weeks, because they know about the situation of
> 'interim aids', the one more, the other less, isn't it? When they knew me
> better, well, they became more open . . . (INI.090, elementary school)

We found that beginning teachers at elementary schools highly accentuate relations of a personal type. These teachers usually stay only for a limited time as

Table 9.2: *Matrix of 'socialization determinants' by 'school level'*

primary level	secondary level
memory of own teachers	
0	9 'What I really do in the classroom is to follow what my teachers did with me, I treat my students the same way, maybe somewhat milder.'
well-known teachers	
1 '... because in my family everybody is teacher, this was something that I realized only slowly, now quite clearly ...'	0
students	
2 'The first day, the second, the third, the first week, if you stay for a week at this school, you need for orientation, some adaptation to the children, because it is you who adapts to them, not they to you.'	0
experience	
4 'I believe that a teacher develops, that for me in the school, if they give you some rules ... but nevertheless you develop by experience ... for example, I guess, I am much more patient than earlier, I believe, that I am always more patient, the more I understand them.'	8 'One learns something every day.' 'The only valid education is by experience.'
Other determinants	
0	5 'My pedagogical education was autodidactical ... I had to search on my own account ...' 'I joined some training courses in order to complete my education.'

'interim aids' at the school center, where they start to practice teaching. They are most preoccupied with making friends (in a professional sense), with 'behaving well', with being welcome, instead of asking for academic assistance or counsel. That is, beginning teachers at elementary schools perceive their colleagues at the school center mostly from a relational point of view, not as sources of experience that could facilitate their work.

Beginning teachers at secondary schools, on the contrary, looked at their colleagues as those people, whom they could ask for the orientation necessary for their work, as 'connoiseurs' of real life in school, and as those who would lend them a hand. Besides, these beginning teachers indicated affective ties, but they only rarely made them explicit. In their interviews we learn more about their academic than their personal life.

A most helpful tool for displaying data as well as for drawing not too complex conclusions is the *construction of matrices*. As Miles and Huberman (1984) state, this 'is a creative — yet systematic — task that furthers your understanding of the substance and meaning of your data base, even before you begin entering information' (p. 211). One of the aspects we were interested in, was to find out about the sources of socializing influences on beginning teachers. There seem to be six different agents of socialization mentioned in the interviews: (i) memory of ones own teachers during the years in school; (ii) well-known teachers (parents); (iii) students; (iv) experiences, (v) colleagues; and (vi) other influences (particular classrooms; in-service courses; autodidactic endeavours). In the following table we present a simplified matrix displaying determinants of socialization as mentioned by teachers from elementary and secondary classrooms. Table 9.2 does *not* show an original printout of AQUAD 3.0, but a summary containing only the frequencies of statements and one or two examples in each cell.

From the matrix in table 9.2 we could conclude that beginning teachers on the secondary level are very much influenced by their own former teachers. We can understand this if we take into account that teacher training for secondary schools in Spain does not take more than three months and is without any link to classroom practice. These teachers, therefore, have to remember their old teachers in order to find models to imitate. This does not happen to teachers in elementary school, who highly appreciate the weight of experience in learning to teach. These teachers, who have received a much longer pedagogical training (three years), attribute high importance to their training and to practical experiences. The latter is true for teachers in secondary schools, too.

Testing Hypotheses

Testing hypotheses (Shelly, 1985) or drawing conclusions (Miles and Huberman, 1984) is conceived of in qualitative analysis as stating systematic relations between particular units of meaning. As described above, our coding system includes three basic dimensions: personal, classroom, and institutional. Within the personal dimension there is a category 'problems' referring to difficulties, conflicts, obstacles, complications, which beginning teachers have faced during their first year of teaching. Our hypothesis was that there are beginning teachers who mention problems in their interview, and then, in close relation to this statement, talk about the school center, the parents of their students, or the educational system.

With AQUAD 3.0 we tested relations between text segments coded as describing 'problems' and text segments referring to the institutional dimension which could be detected within a maximal distance of five lines from 'problems'. On the basis of this analysis we present in table 9.3 the frequencies of associations between the code PRB (problems) and the different codes defining the institutional dimension. Our goal was to determine, which of these codes appeared in the interviews in the highest number of cases related to 'problems' expressed by the beginning teachers. Table 9.3 again is not the original printout, but a summary of

Table 9.3: Problems related to the institutional dimension

Institutional dimension:	COL	CDO	INF	AMC	CUR	ORG	PAD	ENT	LIM	Total
Problems:	9	1	10	3	33	1	8	0	9	44

the results from the analysis of all 105 interviews by means of the component for testing hypotheses in AQUAD 3.0. This component offers a choice between twelve pre-formulated hypotheses structures, into which we enter particular codes and distances while the program is running. (There is also a component to which the user may add her/his own hypotheses formulations.)

As tale 9.3 shows, there were forty-four problems mentioned in connection with the institutional dimension. In ten cases, in which the code INF (infra-structure) was detected in the transcriptions within a maximal distance of five lines from a text segment coded by PRB, the teachers addressed problems of equipment, facilities, and school materials at their schools. The second position in the rank order of problems related to the institution is occupied by LIM (limitations by the system), which the interviewees experienced regarding the teaching profession in general, substitutions, transfers, assignments to classrooms or subjects for which the particular teacher was not specialized, and these statements also included complaints and comments about the local, provincial or national administration.

When teachers mentioned — most frequently — infra-structural aspects of the institution in relation to problems, they complained about bad state, scarcity and total lack of materials and facilities. They also mentioned problems due to the poor state of old schools as well as due to the most recent opening of new schools, where materials were still lacking, or the installation of facilities like gyms or laboratories still had to be completed. Here is an example:

> Well, and then there was also another problem I was confronted with: the lack of material, the lack of adequate facilities. Lack of material in the sense that . . . well, in my school we had one overhead projector which was damaged. For three months I kept reporting this to the principal, but they still have not taken care of it. Of course, everything takes longer here, we know, this is not the problem of this school, but it is a problem of everybody. (INI.019, secondary school)

Outlook

We could only give some examples both of the results of this study on the socialization of beginning teachers and of the particular usefulness of software tools for qualitative research. Let us comment on the methodological approach first. The software tool proved to be very useful in our study. Because of its developmental history — it grew from the authors own needs for assistance in qualitative analysis and was adapted to particular demands of a number of other users — AQUAD 3.0 seems to be rather flexible for application to various approaches to qualitative research in the sense of text interpretaion as well as analysis of structural characteristics of texts (word frequencies, key-words-context, etc.;

c.f., Weber, 1990). It was, for instance, used for analyzing short answers to open ended quesitons, for assessing the level of cognitive complexity of subjects by means of a dictionary of particular suffixes (in German) as indicators of abstractness (defined by frequency of these suffixes), and to several studies using unrestricted text formats like interviews, diaries, or protocols of thinking aloud. The comparative component described above is still waiting for a serious test.

Because the software comes from computer-experienced researchers' own needs, it presumes some minimal acquaintance with computing for granted, for instance that the user is familiar with general terminology like files, directories, paths, file specifications and so on, and the corresponding operations on the DOS-level. Only thus could the manual be limited to about 150 pages. Familiarity with a word processor would be a good prerequisite for using AQUAD 3.0. At one point, however, the user should know something about fundamental principles of editing and compiling a program's source code, and he or she needs the Turbo Prolog (1.1 or 2.0) or PDC Prolog software in order to make the best of AQUAD's possibilities: by applying just five commands of Prolog, users can formulate their own hypotheses (beyond applying twelve built-in hypotheses structures) and integrate them into the program's source code. Eight to twenty hours of training were sufficient to prepare graduate students for this task.

On a more superficial level we should point to the limitation that AQUAD 3.0 offers only a minimum of error messages and warnings (because of memory limitations), and no online, context-sensitive help screens. To integrate these facilities appeared to the authors to be a time consuming luxury, but this is among the tasks listed for future revisions. On the other hand, AQUAD 3.0 behaves very user-friendly. The program is window-controlled, i.e., the user is not forced to memorize the large number of options it offers. We do not dare to say it is impossible, but at least we were not able to provoke a system crash with the latest version. In cases of missing files, erroneous path declarations etc., the program just returns to the main menu. Compared to the boring and time-consuming work which one has to invest in traditional text analysis, computer assistance proved to be a real progress, even considering the present limitations. Above all, we achieved systematization and controllability of our procedures.

As regards the content aspects of our research, we want to refer to Tisher and Wideen (1990) once more. Summarizing the articles on teacher education from all over the world in their book they conclude that this research

> . . . provides an impressive foundation on which to build. It tells us about successes and disappointments in teacher education programs, thereby providing information as to where consolidation, adaptation, reform or modification should occur . . . It . . . indicates areas where more understanding is required, and has the potential to inform practice and policy. (p. 257)

We think, too, that the beginning teachers in our study gave us valuable information about the impairing and facilitating influences on their professional socialization. We might not have noticed the most important details, had we not listened to them talking in their own language, or had we applied a methodological approach matching more the mainstream orientation of empirical research, instead of the complexity of life in classrooms. On the other hand, we have the same doubts that we read between the lines in Tisher and Wideen's text. Empirical results carry informative *potential* for change, changes *should* occur, but is there really the mass of research which 'now raises critical issues that policy-makers and course designers can no longer ignore' (*ibid*). By what means and for whom will these results become critical?

Since we rather want to look at our work from an optimistic point of view regarding its possible consequences, we suggest that a promising strategy will be to quit approaching educational issues on a most abstract level, reducing the vivid, colourful experiences of teachers, parents, students by the grey filter of pre-constructed quantitative scales. Those instruments are valuable complementary tools for answering particular questions. But if we want to further change of day-to-day conditions, we should start by staying as close to the phenomena as possible and assist people to speak in their own voice as well as assist those in charge for reforms to understand these voices clearly. If we manage to put this approach into action with methodological rigor as a prerequisite of credibility, the chance for change seems to be good.

References

BOGDAN, R. and BIKLEN, S. (1982) *Qualitative Research for Education: An Introduction to Theory and Methods*, Boston, MA, Allyn and Bacon.

CLARK, CH. M. and YINGER, R.J. (1979) 'Teachers' thinking' in PETERSON, P. and WALBERG, H.J. (Eds) *Research on Teaching. Concepts, Findings and Implications*, Berkeley, CA, McCutchan, pp. 231–63.

FEIMAN, S. and FLODEN, R. (1981) *A Consumer's Guide to Teacher Development*, East Lansing, MI, Institute for Research on Teaching, Research Series No. 94.

FEIMAN-NEMSER, S. and FLODEN, R. (1986) 'The cultures of teaching' in WITTROCK, M.C. (Ed.) *Handbook of Research on Teaching* (3rd edn) New York, Macmillan, pp. 505–26.

FIRESTONE, W.A. and HERRIOR, R. (1984) 'Multisite qualitative policy research: Some design and implementation issues' in FETTERMAN, D. (Ed.) *Ethnography in Educational Evaluation*, London, Sage pp. 63–88.

FULLER, F. and BROWN, D. (1975) 'Becoming a Teacher' in RYAN, K. (Ed.) *Teacher Education*, Chicago, IL, NSSE, pp. 25–52.

GOETZ, J. and LECOMPTE, M. (1988) *Etnografía y diseño cualitativo en investigación educativa*, Madrid, Morata.

GROEBEN, N., WAHL, D., SCHLEE, J. and SCHEELE, B. (1988) *Das Forschungsprogramm Subjektive Theorien. Eine Einführung in die Theorie des reflexiven Subjekts*, Tübingen, Francke.

HUBER, G.L. (1990) *Computer-assisted Analysis of Qualitative Data: Principles and Manual of the Software Package AQUAD 3.0*, Schwangau, Huber.

HUBER, G.L. and MARCELO, C. (1991) 'Computer assistance for testing hypotheses about qualitative data: The software-package AQUAD 3.0', *Qualitative Sociology*, 14, pp. 325–347.

JOHNSTON, J. and RYAN, K. (1983) 'Research on the beginning teacher: Implications for teacher education' in HOWEY, K. and GARDNER, W. (Eds) *The Education of Teachers*, New York, Longman.

JORDELL, K. (1987) 'Structural and personal influences in the socialization of beginning teachers', *Teaching and Teacher Education*, 3, pp. 165–77.

KLINZING, H.G. (1990) 'Research on teacher education in West Germany' in TISHER, R.P. and WIDEEN, M.F. (Eds) *Research in Teacher Education*, Lewes, Falmer Press, pp. 89–103.

LACEY, C. (1977) *The Socialization of Teachers*, London, Methuen.

LINCOLN, Y. and GUBA, E. (1985) *Naturalistic Inquiry*, London, Sage Publications.

LISCH, R. and KRIZ, J. (1978) *Grundlagen und Modelle der Inhaltsanalyse*, Reinbek bei Hamburg, Rowohlt.

MILES, M.B. (1983) 'Qualitative data as an attractive nuisance: The problem of analysis' in VAN MAANEN, J. (Ed.) *Qualitative Methodology*, Beverly Hills, CA, Sage, pp. 117–34.

MILES, M. and HUBERMAN, A. (1984) *Qualitative Data Analysis*, London, Sage.

RAGIN, C.C. (1987) *The Comparative Method. Moving Beyond Qualitative and Quantitative Strategies*, Berkeley, CA, University of California Press.

SHELLY, A. (1986) 'Life after coding — moving to higher levels of abstraction', paper presented at the annual meeting of the American Educational Research Association, San Francisco.

SPRADLEY, J. (1979) *The Ethnographic Interview*, New York, Holt.

SPRINTHALL, N. and THIES-SPRINTHALL, L. (1983) 'The teacher as an adult learner: A cognitive-developmental view' in GRIFFIN, G.A. (Ed.) *Staff Development* (82nd yearbook of the NSSE), Chicago, IL, University of Chicago Press.

TESCH, R. (1990) *Qualitative Research: Analysis Types and Software Tools*, Lewes, Falmer Press.

TISHER, R. (1984) 'Teacher induction: An international perspective on provisions and research' in KATZ, L and RATHS, J. (Eds) *Advances in Teacher Education*, 1, Norwood, Ablex, pp. 113–24.

TISHER, R.P. and WIDEEN, M.F. (1990) 'Review, reflections and reccomendations' in TISHER, R.P. and WIDEEN, M.F. (Eds) *Research in Teacher Education*, Lewes, Falmer Press, pp. 255–68.

TUCKMAN, B.W. (1990) 'A proposal for improving the quality of published educational research' *Educational Researcher*, **19**, 9, pp. 22–5.

VEENMAN, S. (1984) 'Perceived problems of beginning teachers' *Review of Educational Research*, **54**, pp. 143–78.

WEBER, R.P. (1990) *Basic Content Analysis*, Sage University Paper series on Quantitative Applications in the Social Sciences, series no. 07–049 (2nd edn), Beverly Hills, Sage.

ZEICHNER, K. and GORE, J. (1990) 'Teacher socialization' in HOUSTON, R. (Ed.) *Handbook of Research on Teacher Education*, New York, Macmillan, pp. 329–49.

Chapter 10

Empty Explanations for Empty Wombs: An Illustration of Secondary Analysis of Qualitative Data

Shulamit Reinharz

Adding a Second Researcher's Voice

Observation and interviews are the two major types of qualitative research methods, with many variations within each. The student learning to do qualitative research should expect to receive training in both types and in conducting literature reviews that synthesize and evaluate qualitative research. Whether doing interview, observation or literature reviews, the student will develop a researcher's voice that explains what was observed, what was said, or what the social science community believes. Unfortunately another, extremely useful type of qualitative research typically is not taught and may not even be recognized as an important method. The purposes of this chapter are to name that missing format, explain briefly why it is neglected, provide examples of those who have used it, and offer an original illustration.

The missing format is the analysis of qualitative data already collected by another researcher, a format I call 'secondary analysis of qualitative data'. Training people to analyze other people's qualitative data is essential if we are to correct the current imbalance that pays attention primarily to collecting, as contrasted with analyzing, qualitative data. By definition, in secondary analyses of qualitative data, researchers focus exclusively on data analysis, rather than on data collection. By naming and highlighting this type of study, I hope to make the secondary analysis of qualitative data a more standardized component of research methods training (see Colby, 1982). The researcher who collects primary data and then analyzes them may be said to add the researcher's voice to the voice of the people being studied. The researcher who subsequently does a secondary analysis of that data adds a second researcher's voice. This chapter explains the necessity of adding a second researcher's voice and illustrates how it might be done.

It is possible to mistake secondary analysis with meta-analysis. Meta-analysis refers to the integration of findings from various completed projects, whether conducted by a single researcher (c.f., for example, Powdermaker, 1966; Wax, 1971; Whyte, 1984) or by a variety of researchers (c.f., for example, Stein, 1960; Van Maanen, 1988). Meta-analyses are not the study of someone else's *data*; instead they are the reanalysis of a study's *conclusions*. Meta-analyses are done in order to increase the 'n' or number of cases, or to compare and contrast the conclusions of different studies (see Hossler, 1989; Miller, 1987). Meta-analyses basically are literature reviews of other people's findings. They are not based on a researcher's obtaining another person's data and trying to analyze them. My chapter illustrates this latter approach, i.e., the reanalysis of qualitative data.

I begin with a discussion of the way secondary analysis has become a dominant characteristic of survey research as contrasted with qualitative research. Next I present a few exceptions, i.e., instances of secondary analyses of qualitative data. I show that researchers who have conducted secondary analyses of qualitative data explain their use of someone else's data as an unsual, uncanny phenomenon. Finally, I provide an illustration from the field of miscarriage research in which I have been engaged for the last several years (Reinharz, 1987, 1988a, 1988b and in press). I display the data I obtained from other researchers (see table 10.1) and then undertake an interpretive analysis. My two-pronged conclusion to this chapter discusses my findings concerning explanations of miscarriages and then returns to the theme of secondary analyses of qualitative data.

Secondary Analysis in Survey Research

In survey research, in contrast with qualitative research, the analysis of data collected by others is popular, cost-effective and practical. According to methodologist Mark Abrahamson (1983):

> In sociology . . . approximately one-half of the journal articles published in the early 1980s utilized . . . already existing data. A similar and perhaps even higher percentage of graduate student dissertations and undergraduate projects also employ data collected previously and elsewhere. (p. 264)

The practicality of this approach arises from the fact that researchers and research organizations make quantitative data sets available for purchase to other researchers. Such data are available in an easily transferable form. Earl Babbie describes this process of data-transfer in his classic textbook, *The Practice of Social Research* (1983):

> With the development of computer-based analyses in social research, it has become easily possible for social researchers to share their data with one another . . . Once their own analyses were completed, the researchers made the data available to others for what is appropriately called secondary analysis . . . Beginning in the 1960s, the potential for secondary analysis was developed on an international scale. A consortium of research centers collaborated with one another to form a network of data archives, each of which would collect and administer data sets from various parts of the United States and the world. Decks of punch cards and magnetic tapes were shelved the way books are shelved in a conventional library, and the holdings were available for broad circulation and use. (p. 239)

Data typically subjected to secondary analysis include sample surveys, national tests, census reports and miscellaneous directory and personal documents

(Abrahamson, 1983, p. 265; Kasworm, 1990; Gleit and Graham, 1989; Soltis and Walberg, 1989; Auslander, 1988; Jones, 1988; Saris and Van Den Putte, 1988). All of these types of data can be used successfully for educational purposes. By advocating the secondary analysis of qualitative data, I am adding another tool to the educational researcher's repertoire.

Secondary research of quantitative data is not without its drawbacks, however. Commentators on the secondary analysis of survey research mention two inherent problems other than expense. First, the data are likely to have been gathered to focus on issues different from those of the current researcher; and second, the data may have been gathered originally for other than research purposes. In partial response to these concerns, some researchers believe secondary analysis of existing data should be combined with the collection of new data. The term devised for this format is semi-secondary analysis. Herbert Hyman (1972) wrote that secondary analysis refers to the analysis of previously collected data sets, whereas semi-secondary analysis combines this with newly obtained data. Whether combined or free-standing, the analysis of existing quantitative data sets is being described as a normative practice, at least in sociology.

Lack of Tradition of Secondary Analysis in Qualitative Research

By contrast with this normative practice in survey research, most books on qualitative methods do not mention the possibility of secondary analysis at all. Rather they start with the presumption that the student or researcher will collect new data. The researcher or student will do his/her own participant observation or interviewing and then analyze those data, rather than use pre-existing data gathered by someone else. For example, descriptions of fieldwork data typically state the following:

> Fieldwork usually means living with and living like those who are studied.
> In its broadest, most conventional sense, fieldwork demands the full-time
> involvement of a researcher over a lengthy period of time (typically un-
> specified) and consists mostly of ongoing interaction with the human
> targets of study on their home ground. (Van Maanen, 1988, p. 2)

This general rule of collecting one's own data can be seen in almost every case of fieldwork research. For example in a recent study of a town that was situated above a long-lasting underground fire, the researchers opened with the following statement: 'In planning a strategy to investigate the impact of the mine fire on the town's social fabric, we concluded that long-term, firsthand involvement with the problem was essential' (Kroll-Smith and Couch, 1990).

Instructions for doing qualitative research presume that researchers will collect the data they analyze. The following excerpt from a qualitative research methods text offers an encyclopedic array of data gathering techniques but excludes the analysis of previously collected data:

> The fundamental techniques relied on by qualitative researchers for
> gathering information are (i) observation and (ii) in-depth interviewing
> . . . Supplementing these are several specialized techniques (questionnaires,

film, street ethnography, psychological techniques, proxemics, kinesics, ethnographic interviewing, elite interviewing, historical analysis, life history, content analysis, and unobtrusive measures). (Marshall and Rossman, 1989, p. 79)

Locating and analyzing someone's else data is not part of this list. Secondary analysis thus challenges the unspoken rule that 'in qualitative methods, the researcher is necessarily involved in the lives of the subjects' (Bogdan and Taylor, 1975, p. 8).

Strangely, this unspoken rule actually is not completely adhered to. In particular, when more than one person is involved in a qualitative research project, team members actually may be analyzing other people's data rather than data they collected themselves. Furthermore, team research frequently involves supervisors or principal investigators who have to make sense of data collected by paid assistants. A classic example is W. Lloyd Warner *Yankee City Series* (1941–57), a project that involved eighteen fieldworkers. A contemporary example is Lenore J. Weitzman, *The Divorce Revolution* (1985), a project that employed a team of interviewers and an interview supervisor to conduct in-depth face-to-face interviews. Such research lies on the boundary between data collected and analyzed by oneself, and data collected and analyzed by others, since it represents qualitative data collected by others under one's own supervision for one's own purposes.

Despite these practices on the boundary, the unspoken presumption in qualitative research is that the researcher enters the field, develops rapport and relationships, records observations and then analyzes them. The assumption in interview studies is that the researcher interviews and then analyzes the transcripts; or that the researcher supervises the person doing the interviews; or supervises the supervisor. The assumption is that the data are newly gathered and under the researcher's control. It is my contention that these assumptions have had the effect of limiting the potential of the theory we can develop from qualitative data because our research is limited to the data we can collect or supervise.

Exceptions to the Rule of Collecting Your Own Data for Qualitative Analysis

By urging our students to engage in secondary analysis of qualitative data, we can underscore the significance of building theory rather than collecting data. Using other people's data, for example, sociologist Jack Katz developed a theory to explain why people commit crime. In the introduction to his book, *Seductions of Crime*, he thanked three classes of enthusiastic university students, two researchers (Franklin Zimring and James Zuehl), and the ethnographic research community all of whom provided him with data. The following is his account of the data he borrowed from the ethnographic research community.

The best data on robbery as a situational practice consist of narrative accounts of particular events by witnesses, victims, offenders, and co-offenders. Franklin Zimring and James Zuehl constructed such a data set from police records on several types of robberies that occurred in Chicago between September 1982 and October 1983. (Katz, 1988, p. 168)

Given that this was the best data set, Katz followed up on the opportunities to use it. In his words:

> When Zimring and Zuehl published a statistical write-up of their re-
> search, they added the provocative note to their qualitative characteriza-
> tion, 'recreational violence': 'If the term sounds frivolous or abstract the
> reader is invited into our files'. Indeed the category seemed so close to the
> patterns indicated by autobiographies I had been examining that I took
> up the invitation, which was graciously honored. (*ibid*, p. viii)

Finally, Katz made a general plea that material such as this be circulated among researchers. In his words:

> Although I use endnotes to acknowledge researchers by name, I would
> like to offer a generalized word of appreciation, and I hope a measure of
> encouragement, to those who do the groundwork for books like this.
> The fieldwork enterprise has become increasingly precarious in modern
> social science. Funding agencies, academic bureaucracies, and professional
> associations do not adequately recognize the enormous professional altru-
> ism of fieldworkers who take the pains to document poignant social
> action outside the auspices of formalized theoretical categories and con-
> ventionalized research methodology. But unless that work gets done,
> how can we expect new analyses to be broadly grounded in the lived
> experience of people in society, rather than in our personal experience,
> theoretical prejudices, or moral and political sentiments? A good part of
> the pleasure in working on this manuscript has come from a sense of
> recovering and reliving widely scattered, sometimes almost lost, mo-
> ments of fieldwork insight. (*ibid*, p. viii)

Katz seems to be suggesting a division of labor, with some ethnographers collecting data, and other, more theoretically inclined researchers analyzing them. True to his high regard for the sharing of qualitative data, he has made available to others the data collected by students in three offerings of his criminology class. These are filed as 'Autobiographical Accounts of Property Offenses by Youths, UCLA, 1983–1984, no. 8950, *Inter-university Consortium for Political Social Research*, Ann Arbor, Michigan'.

Another example is Elliot Mishler's research on doctor/patient relationships. In this case, too, the researcher did not collect the data, but analyzed, instead, data collected by another researcher. He wrote:

> I wish . . . to express my appreciation to John Stoeckle and Howard
> Waitzkin who offered me the sample of tape recorded medical interviews
> without which plans for this study could not have been realized. In giv-
> ing me free access to materials collected in their own investigations and
> through their encouragement of my work, even though our approaches
> differ, they demonstrated a spirit of true colleagueship . . . Waitzkin and
> Stoeckle's original corpus of nearly 500 interviews included a stratified
> random sample of physicians in private and clinic sessions in Boston and
> Oakland. For the present study, a small series of about twenty-five tapes
> was selected initially from the larger sample. Male and female patients

were equally represented in the series, and both single and multiple interviews of a patient with the same physician were included . . . (Mishler,
1984, pp. xi, 59)

Elliot Mishler then developed a theory of doctor-patient interaction based on
interviews done by the person who collected them for the third chapter of Howard
Waitzkin's *The Second Sickness: Contradictions of Capitalist Health Care* (1983).
Marianne (Tracy) Paget worked from this same set of recorded interviews and
produced her own publications (Paget, 1982, 1983, 1988 and 1990).

A third example of secondary analysis of qualitative data can be found in
Carol Warren's restudy in 1987 of interviews obtained thirty years earlier. She
writes:

The interviews on which the study is based — which are called, by those
who have worked with me, the 'Bay Area data' — were conducted between late 1957 and early 1961 by a team of researchers associated with
the University of California . . . The original study was designed to examine the impact of mental hospitalization on families over a thirty-
six-month period, beginning with the first week of admission and ending
as much as a year after discharge . . . Of these (seventeen) families all but
(five) were reinterviewed in 1972 . . . I came to the study by chance, as
a result of meeting one of the original researchers, Sheldon L. Messinger,
at a convention . . . I was interested in the mental health system; he asked
me if I would like to look at the interviews with these families. I was
indeed interested, and became increasingly so over the years. Following
a period of several months in which I commuted to Berkeley from Los
Angeles to examine the interviews, Shelly found the only way to get me
out of his office and shipped the transcripts to me in Los Angeles. Today
these approximately 15,000 pages of interviews live . . . in four filing-
cabinet drawers in my office . . . The original study focussed on the psy-
chodynamics of the mother-daughter-husband triad . . . as it served to
precipitate the crisis of hospitalization. By contrast, the focus of my study
is on gender, trouble and the husband-wife dyad . . . What I would argue
is that, from the perspective of the 1980s, the frameworks of gender
roles and trouble in the 1950s are particularly revealing . . . (Warren, 1987,
pp. ix–xi)

These highly successful exceptions to the generalized absence of secondary
analyses of qualitative data share the property of being based on interviews. Interviews may be more conducive to reanalysis than are fieldnotes. Fieldnotes pose
special problems not characteristic of interviews and interview transcripts. Many
ethnographers and fieldworkers think of their fieldnotes as personal materials
oriented primarily to jogging their memories, although some (for example, Simon
Ottenberg, Margaret Mead) arranged to have their fieldnotes deposited to make
them accessible to others (see Sanjek, 1990). Mark Fishman explains in *Manufacturing
the News* (1980), for example, that he had access to the fieldnotes of D.L. Wieder
taken roughly ten years earlier at a newspaper Fishman was studying. Careful
depositing such as this makes longitudinal and comparative study possible. Word-
processed fieldnotes can be reproduced easily in many different formats using
pseudonyms, thus making it possible to deposit notes without compromising the

anonymity and confidentiality of persons mentioned in the notes. In my next methodological study, I will examine the possibility of secondary analysis of observational data as recorded in fieldnotes in order to extend this discussion of the secondary analysis of qualitative data.

The Miscarriage Data

Although the study of miscarriage may not appear relevant to educational researchers, that is a mistaken view. The high prevalence rate of miscarriage (approximately 25 per cent of all women experience at least one miscarriage) and the high numbers of women among educational researchers suggest that miscarriage is likely to be part of the lives of the researchers themselves, the lives of female partners of male educational researchers, the lives of pre-menopausal adult females who are studied and the lives of parents of children who may be studied. Counsellors who work with sexually active adult women stand a strong chance of having to deal with this phenomenon. Advances in reproductive technology give many women and men the false impression that reproductive problems can be controlled. Yet many of these sophisticated techniques have a high failure rate. If people are going to use these techniques, they deserve to know the success rate and the likelihood that they will undergo a miscarriage. Unfortunately, this information is not readily provided.

Researchers in the field of the continuing education of women must be aware of women's psychological and biological health concerns. Miscarriage is one of these, particularly since middle-class women are delaying child-bearing, and the likelihood of miscarrying increases as one approaches and exceeds the age of 40. In addition, since miscarriage has received so little attention in the public and professional domains, and yet is so prevalent, many women (and men) have not had adequate opportunity to deal with their feelings about a past miscarriage. This incomplete state may affect their current circumstance. Recent advances in feminist scholarship remind us that many of women's experiences are poorly labelled, poorly understood, and receive insufficient attention. Educational researchers in a multitude of settings have an opportunity to improve our knowledge of women's lives and experiences. Practice innovations can be successful, however, only if they are based on the careful examination of people's lives. The miscarriage experience is only recently being explored, and one area that has received almost no attention is the relation between physicians' and miscarrying women's view of the phenomenon. This relation must be understood since the meaning of miscarriage is a socially constructed entity to which both the physician and the miscarrying woman (and others) contribute definitions.

The following is an analysis of previously collected qualitative interview data, meant to illustrate the case I have argued above. For this project, sixty-two women were interviewed who had had one or more miscarriages. All of the women were interviewed approximately two months following a miscarriage and were referred to the researchers by both private obstetricians/gynaecologists and hospital clinics. Thus the data reflect a very diverse group in terms of social class. The project was supervised by a sociologist and psychologist[1] and the interviews were carried out by several trained research assistants (see Lasker, Borg and Toedter, 1989; Toedter, Lasker and Alhadeff, 1988; Dunn, Goldbach, Lasker and Toedter, in press).

The interviews were semi-structured and averaged three-and-a-half hours in length, focussing on the circumstances surrounding the loss and the woman's response to it. When the woman was asked to describe her loss, her description was tape-recorded so that the interviewer could maintain eye contact and reduce distraction. The researchers' expectation that this would be an emotional part of the interview for most people was confirmed. The interviewers noted other information on sheets of paper, both paraphrasing and quoting the woman's words (the woman is referred to as R, or respondent; S or spouse is sometimes referred to). At the end of the interview guide, several topics were listed. If the interviewee had spontaneously brought up these topics, then the interviewer could simply check the question. If the interviewer had not brought up information pertinent to the question, the interviewer then asked the question specifically. After the interview the interviewer listened to the tape recording and wrote summaries of the woman's description of her loss.

I received photocopies of the interview guides on which the interviewer had written the women's responses and the summaries taken from the tape recordings. The names of the women were covered with white-out to protect their anonymity. I had not read any analyses of these data, nor did I know of the specific hypotheses or theories that underlay this project. I simply had qualitative data to analyze that I had not collected nor whose collection I had supervised.

My first step was to employ someone to make a word-processed file of each interview guide. My second step was to check these files against the originals to make sure there were neither errors nor omissions. A small amount of data 'clean up' was required before all the files were in order. I then read several of the interviews and realized that there was a great deal of interesting information on numerous themes. Finally, I decided to select two questions and try to interpret them. The two questions were how the doctor explained the miscarriage to the woman, and how the woman explains the miscarriage to herself. As mentioned above, these two points were not always asked specifically, because the women sometimes raised them spontaneously. For this reason, I cannot state the questions that elicited these answers. In the two columns I have listed a somewhat abbreviated version of what the women said about these two topics. It should be remembered that the material listed under the MD column is what the woman reports the MD as having said rather than quotations from interviews with the women's physicians.

The Secondary Analysis

Physicians' Explanations

Each of the sixty-two women interviewed for the study had been assisted by physicians in some phase of her miscarriage. All of the women remembered that their doctors had said something about the cause of the miscarriage. The women had either asked their physicians about the cause, or the physician had volunteered an explanation at the time of the miscarriage or shortly thereafter. 'Explanations' are thus an integral component of the miscarriage experience of these sixty-two women.

The explanations of the causes of these sixty-two miscarriages seem varied

Table 10.1: Sixty-two women's explanations of the causes of their miscarriages and their accounts of their physicians' explanations

MD	Patient
1 Egg genetically defective	1 Age, her husband exposed to arsenic, radiation and other chemicals at work
2 Just normal type miscarriage.	2 ABO problem was involved
3 No specific explanation, told her she didn't do anything wrong, it just happened	3 Honestly doesn't know, does feel guilty about her negative attitude and wondered if that had any influence on the outcome, but the doctor said, NO, it just happened
4 Blighted ovum	4 Accepts MD's non-explanation of blighted ovum
5 No data	5 No data
6 No definitive reasons other than high incidence.	6 While intellectually she knows that it was not caused by anthing specific, she feels pangs of doubt when she remembers she had been exercising prior to onset of spotting — most of the time she dismisses guilt feelings as unrealistic
7 No explanation	7 Feels she didn't get enough rest since she has three children and works from midnight to 7:30, four nights a week
8 No reason for loss, MD requested of P to test material and found chromosome deficiency; foam not a cause	8 Wondered if foam used as contraceptive could cause deformities; age; baby was cause. Not right, so her body got rid of it naturally
9 Things happen, usually something wrong to begin with, 20–30 per cent of pregnancies end in miscarriages	9 Felt she was on wrong side of odds, flu first week she was pregnant and still feels that contributed a certain amount. Doctor said NO, but in the back of her mind, feels that it may have contributed
10 R had an infection and this was blamed for the loss, mucus was infected. No idea how infection started	10 Wondered if having a mild cold during pregnancy caused the infection and blamed herself for missing her vitamin C one day, making herself susceptible to the cold, now isn't sure
11 Did not really have an explanation; something that happened; blood work showed nothing to indicate the cause of the loss	11 Probably something wrong with the baby, it was just meant to happen, not caused by anything she did or did not do
12 Fifteen per cent miscarry, something wrong with the egg	12 Intellectually knows that there was something genetically wrong
13 'Just something that happens' — he repeated statistics	13 Accepts doctor's explanation and seems comfortable with it; no further thoughts about it
14 Blighted ovum	14 Did think for a while that the bronchitis she had early on in the pregnancy may have caused it; then she felt guilty that her feelings may have caused it — worry over previous losses — now she is satisfied with doctor's explanation

Table 10.1 (Cont.)

MD	Patient
15 Doctor never did figure out the reason for the loss	15 R does have a theory; she says that she feels that it was just a very poor conception — not just a blighted ovum but also no sac being formed either
16 Chances are there was something genetically wrong with the foetus, but they don't really know for sure. Probably a defective foetus	16 She would like to have a more definite idea of the cause, but agrees with doctor at this point
17 Doctor told her he did not know why the miscarriage occurred	17 She 'has herself convinced' that it was not meant to be. She states that, at first, she felt some guilt. She wondered if she had done something wrong. Now she no longer feels guilt and says it was just one of those things
18 The doctor had no explanation	18 R can't imagine why it happened either; says when trying to get pregnant she stops smoking and drinking altogether, never does either to excess, and tries to live healthily, so she has nothing to blame. She had done the same thing with the first loss. 'I followed the rules by the book here and still had a miscarriage.' 'This is God's way to prevent having children who are deformed;' 'I'd rather have a miscarriage than bring a deformed child into the world, not that I wouldn't care for one if I did.'
19 There was no real reason for this having happened. It 'just happens sometimes'	19 R feels the loss might have occurred because of vaginal infections that she had had early in the pregnancy in July; she had a yeast infection, then a urinary tract infection, then a yeast infection again
20 The egg didn't develop the baby just stopped developing. Doctor mentioned odds — that many women have miscarriages — it's common.	20 No idea
21 He reassured her nothing she did caused the loss; sent remains of pregnancy to lab; felt loss was a freak of nature	21 No data
22 Blighted ovum	22 Agreed with doctor
23 He reassured R that these things happen and it was nothing R did. This happens when foetus is abnormal and the body gets rid of it	23 R feels the loss occurred because something was wrong with the foetus. However, R feels that with her next pregnancy, she is going to take better care of herself, such as not mowing lawn, taking time out to rest, eat better and not do a lot of strenuous exercise. R was questioning herself about whether it was something she had done

Table 10.1 (Cont.)

MD	Patient
24 Never gave R a definite cause for the loss. He just said the foetus died, and he was not sure what had caused this to happen	24 Even though they did not directly discuss it, she thinks he may have been wondering 'if they had removed the lesion, would the loss have been something that was going to happen?' R thinks of this often
25 It may have been septic miscarriage caused by the cervical lesion. Could have been infection	25 R tries not to think about the cause. She does often think perhaps if she had told them to remove the growth, things would have been different. But she does not want to dwell on this, and just tries to feel that it was something that was meant to happen and would have, no matter what had been done
26 Ninety-nine per cent of miscarriages are caused because of mismatch in chromosomes. He thinks that is probably what caused hers. Doctor told her if it would happen again, he would do a thorough test to find out why	26 R feels it happened because of her infertility problem. She is very afraid that her hormone levels are so 'messed up' that she may not be able to sustain a pregnancy
27 The doctor had no reason why it happened	27 R has no theories as to why it happened either
28 Everything appeared normal, and probably had something to do with the baby itself and that it was very common	28 R agrees, it was just nature's way of telling them the baby couldn't have made it through the pregnancy and birth. Something was probably wrong with the baby
29 It happens sometimes; in the first three months, sometimes things don't go properly	29 Agrees with doctor and also blames husband since all the arguments 'contributed to negative thoughts' about the baby, and greatly upset her
30 The doctors have no reason for the loss	30 R and S have no guess as to why it happened. In fact, R feels she did the utmost to ensure a healthy baby so she can't understand why it happened
31 The doctor said that a miscarriage is a quirk of nature. He reassured R and S that it was nothing they could have prevented	31 R says that she feels he knows more than he's telling because may be he's afraid she 'can't take it' if he tells her the real cause. R sometimes feels that she is to blame, because she had been working twelve-hour shifts the previous week. And she didn't eat properly and always forgot to take her vitamins
32 Doctor reassured R that she hadn't caused the loss in any way. If anything, he attributed the loss to chromosome abnormalities	32 R agrees with the doctor
33 The doctor never gave her any real explanation for her loss	33 Has no ideas

Table 10.1 (Cont.)

MD	Patient
34 Nature's way of getting rid of something that's not right	34 Really does not know
35 There was no baby — just a placenta that stopped growing	35 Agrees with the doctor
36 Blighted ovum	36 During process of D and C, R was trying to convince herself that it just wasn't meant to be; it was no one's fault
37 This is one of those things that just happens. Probably the foetus wouldn't have made it, or wouldn't have been healthy. There is no way of knowing just why it happened. Don't blame yourself	37 I don't know. I worried about having been to my high school reunion during the period before I knew I was pregnant, and really drinking heavily, and later I was coming down with a cold and I took cold medication. R says she would not have done these things if she had known she was pregnant. R wonders if these things were part of the problem. Feels guilty at times
38 She has a problem with the corpus luteum which is called a luteal phase defect. So the next time R became pregnant, he would prescribe something to help hold the pregnancy	38 R has a lot of faith in him and feels he is probably right
39 No explanation given, because nothing was conclusive. Wants R to have genetic testing	39 May be she had done something wrong to start the bleeding. May be overworking. Two jobs at the same time, not eating right. Now unsure. Looking forward to getting tests done in future to get some answers
40 He told her it was a very common occurrence for the baby to not start to develop; there was nothing wrong with her physically . . . the pathology report was 'ok' did not indicate there were any problems with her physically	40 Agrees with doctor's explanation of the loss
41 The baby never really developed. Tests didn't show anything but placenta. Doesn't know cause	41 R thinks perhaps it happened because she cut down on smoking but didn't quit. Although the doctor assured her this is not so, and she's trying to believe him. Also she wonders if the snow shoveling had anything to do with it, though the doctor says no. (R's spouse blamed the shoveling)
42 It was either an abnormal egg or an abnormal sperm. The pregnancy never progressed. No known reason	42 Her husband had been on acutane, for acne, when R got pregnant, and she at first was suspicious that this was involved, but the doctors assured her the acutane was not to blame. Now she says she accepts their word for this

Table 10.1 (Cont.)

MD	Patient
43 Reassured R nothing she did caused loss. Three options: low placenta; bacteria in placenta; no foetus in sac, the latter confirmed since tests done on what was left of placenta showed that there was no fetal tissue, but may be R lost tissue at home. Felt R had placenta but no foetus	43 R felt she had done something to cause miscarriage. May be lifting Angela caused it. R was wondering, 'Did I do too much?' 'Could I have done more?'
44 Doctor feels that there is a chromosome problem, although tests do not support that theory	44 R is totally confused and angry that by now she does not have an answer as to why it happened again. She has no theories either at this time
45 No explanation was given at the time. Doctor explained the next day that there could have been chromosomal abnormalities, that it was a blighted ovum and had never been developed	45 R has a lot of ideas about why it happened. (i) She follows the macrobiotic philosophy — yin/yang. She says she is too much yin — food wise — abused sugar when she was going to school. She says she ate a whole box of Godiva chocolates during the pregnancy on Valentine's day (she bought them), and she got a pounding headache. She says she never gets headaches; believes her body was rejecting the sugar because she was pregnant. Later she craved protein and she never eats meat, the yang foods. She believes the baby needed the protein but she didn't eat enough of it. (ii) Energy — she had a past abortion procedure which was a drawing out of the energy from her reproductive organ (went though she was not pregnant, she found out later). This left her organ weak. (iii) Emotional effects — she believes her being upset and unhappy affected her body chemistry — were detrimental to her health. She says now she was violently crying and upset at some point each day during the pregnancy, even though at times she was also happy — 'That can't be too good for you.' (iv) She wished at times she would have a miscarriage — even though she couldn't have the abortion, she wished the baby would die. She believes if you wish for something, it makes it more probably that it will happen. (v) She sort of believes what the spiritualist she went to see told her, that 'all souls pick a body . . . a soul picks a

Table 10.1 (Cont.)

MD	Patient
	mother to be born, It is around you and it goes into you around the third month. If the soul feels that something is not right or that it shouldn't be born, a miscarriage occurs.'R sort of believes that
46 Lab tests show no reason for foetal death	46 She had no idea why the loss occurred
47 It wasn't meant to be	47 Although the doctor couldn't really give a definite reason for the loss, R feels the untimely death of her father and the stress it caused her may have contributed to the loss
48 The miscarriage was just a case of no specific cause that was evident. They surmise that it was due to placental difficulties though, because R's uterus was the proper size for a foetus of twelve weeks	48 R and S agree
49 Dr gave no reason for the loss, only that it was common to miscarry with no apparent reason	49 R does feel somewhat uncomfortable with having been on the pill until three months previous to getting pregnant. She suspects it may have had something to do with the loss
50 Told R was not sure what caused the loss but it might be R has a curved uterus and doctor would like to do HSG on her to see if this was the reason	50 R unsure why loss occurred. Believes it might be her uterus, as doctor suggested
51 Miscarriage is a common thing — it just happens. He said there was some problem with the embryo — it was just not right genetically	51 Agrees with doctor's explanation
52 One out of every five lose their babies, she's a statistic	52 Feels there's something definitely wrong with her on the inside that's causing it; the pain she'd had all the time in between her pregnancies makes her feel there's got to be something wrong; she's going to another doctor now for tests and a second opinion
53 Offered them no real explanation for the loss	53 No answers; it just happened
54 Hydatiform mole	54 Fluke of nature
55 No real explanation given for the loss. The doctor just said that it was something that happens and that usually it's for the best because it's nature's way of telling you something's wrong	55 R feels it could have happened because she lifted her son who weighs forty-three pounds or because she and her boyfriend were going through a lot of arguing so that it could have been emotional stress
56 The conception tissues were starting to come out and the loss was inevitable. There was something wrong with the foetus itself, and it was incompatible with life	56 There was just something wrong, and the miscarriage was 'just meant to be'

Table 10.1 (Cont.)

MD	Patient
57 These things happen and no one knows why	57 No idea either
58 Doctor had no explanation for why the loss had occurred	58 R can't imagine why either
59 Doctor did not give R any specific reason for the loss	59 R feels strongly that this miscarriage was caused by the fall on the broken step on stairway to their apartment. R very angry about this
60 Neither doctor gave her any reason	60 Really doesn't know
61 None given	61 Doesn't know
62 No exact explanation of loss except may be baby wasn't right	62 May be it wasn't meant to be. R and S having marital troubles and financial troubles. May be God realized it was not a good time for a pregnancy. R feels God has a reason for the loss, even though R doesn't know what it is

when one first looks at the list of phrases. On closer examination, however, the 'explanations' offered by most of the physicians and many of the women turn out actually to be many different ways of saying one thing — 'I don't know'. These stand-in phrases are

> *straightforward declarations* such as
> 'no explanation' (numbers 7, 18, 33, 39, 53, 55, 58),
> 'no reason' (numbers 8, 27, 30, 42, 46, 49, 60), and
> no 'specific' or 'exact' 'cause, reason or explanation' (numbers 48, 59, 62) or

> *clichés* including
> 'it just happens' (numbers 3, 13, 19, 29, 51),
> 'these things happen' (numbers 9, 23, 37, 57), and
> 'something that happened' (number 11).

In the vast majority of cases the physician acknowledged not knowing the cause or stated that the cause was unknowable, using one of these phrases.

I refer to these phrases as 'empty explanations' — they have no content but are uttered as if they were explanations. The three types of 'empty explanations' these women remember hearing from their physicians are cliché-based, body-based and statistics-based. Some of the women accepted 'empty explanations' while others rejected them or simply let them exist alongside other explanations.

In about four of the sixty-two cases, physicians offered plausible medical reasons for the miscarriages — infection, corpus luteum problem, a curved uterus and a hydatiform mole. In all the other cases, the physicians used 'empty explanations' that sound like medical explanations of causes but actually are descriptions of outcomes or components of pregnancy. These pseudo-medical explanation of causes are 'body-based empty explanations'. The phrases include

'blighted ovum' (numbers 4, 14, 22, 36, 45),
'chromosome deficiency' (number 8),
'mismatch of chromosomes' (number 26),
'chromosomal abnormalities' (numbers 32, 45),
'chromosome problem' (number 44),
'defective or abnormal foetus' (numbers 16, 23, 56),
'the baby itself' (numbers 28, 62),
'problem with the embryo' (number 51),
'foetus died' (number 24),
'no baby or foetus' (number 43),
'abnormal egg or sperm' (number 42), and
'placental difficulties' (number 48)

Just as the cliché-based 'empty explanations' listed above, these body-based 'empty descriptions' do not explain the causes of miscarriage but function linguistically in the frameworks of a sentence and a conversation as if they do. The women remember these phrases as the way their physicians 'explained' their miscarriage.

The third category of 'empty explanations' is a set of phrases that deal with phenomena outside the woman's body. These include precise or vague statistical information (numbers 6, 9, 12, 13, 20, 28, 40, 49, 51, 52), 'freak of nature,' 'nature's way,' and 'wasn't meant to be'. None of these terms explains the cause of the miscarriage. Rather, they are linguistic devices that serve as surrogate explanations in place of 'I don't know'. Women remember their physicians using one, two or all three categories of 'empty explanations' for the event that in almost all cases they cannot explain.

Women's Explanations

The women's explanations of their miscarriages are similar and yet much more complex than those offered by their physicians. The ways in which their explanations are similar to their physicians' fall into three categories: (i) total agreement; (ii) ambivalence; (iii) eventual agreement. Only 20 per cent (or twelve out of sixty-two of the women agree with their physicians that there is no reason for the miscarriage or that the reason is unknown (numbers 4, 11, 13, 14, 20, 22, 27, 28, 29, 32, 35, 48). Some women reach this consensus with their physician only after initially accepting alternative ideas (numbers 16, 17). Other women employ the same linguistic strategies as do their physicians, using description to stand-in for causal explanation (numbers 15, 23, 56). Two of the physicians who offered physical explanations (numbers 38, 50) were believed, but in one instance the woman blamed herself for the physical problem (number 10) and in another the physical problem was itself attributed to a 'fluke of nature' (number 54).

Some women in this study harbor several contradictory explanations simultaneously. For example, one woman says

while intellectually she knows that it was not caused by anything specific, she feels pangs of doubt when she remembers she had been exercising prior to onset of spotting — most of the time she dismisses guilt feelings as unrealistic. (number 6)

In another case from a different study, a woman believes and does not believe the physical explanation her physician gave her for her six miscarriages that were followed by a normal birth and a current pregnancy:

Barbara Smith (pseudonym):   Interview by RG. 22 August 1989.

RG: You want to, um, talk a little about the previous pregnancies?

BS: Now that they're successfully solved, I'd be glad to talk about them. I had six miscarriages, all in the first trimester. And they really didn't have any idea, my immune deficiency, immune, auto-immune problems is what they finally came up with, but I had every test under the sun. And, um, so I had to take an awful lot of progesterone with F. (daughter), and that worked, and then that seemed to set the precedent. The next one has gone very smoothly . . .

RG: Did you ever get an explanation, about,

BS: The only thing that came up, the specialist came up with, by feeding my blood and my husband's blood to various rats, uh, and then breeding the rats, there was a higher incidence of miscarriage when my blood alone was mixed with someone else's blood than either of our bloods together or than his blood alone. The idea seems to be that I manufacture immuno-toxic factors myself . . . If I understand it in layman's terms, in pregnancy, the foetus is naturally a foreign body, and most people manufacture things which overcome the foreignness, they shut down the immune system . . . I didn't. So my body would recognize foreign tissue and say, oh, oh, let's do something about it.

RG: What was your response when you heard that this might be what was happening?

BS: Well there was, the only suggestion he had, and his method was to give progesterone in large doses early on. His sort of claim to fame was that it was earlier, and in larger doses. Now, we tried that three times, in increasing doses, and she arrived on the third one. However, on the last pregnancy, by the time I learned I was pregnant, I had done none of this and —

RG: You've carried —

BS: I've carried. So it's —

RG: There aren't explanations for everything, I guess.

BS: No, it could be that we've moved to the country. I mean, I'm perfectly, perfectly willing to accept that, that my lifestyle is less hectic here, that we got a dog and two pussycats, and may be it's up to them.

RG: Or her.

BS: Yeah, yeah. (p. 20)

In other words, some women who have miscarried work out an explanation and then rework it to fit new conditions and feelings. In some cases this 'mind-work' is very explicit (numbers 36, 41). This 'mind-work' may be a woman's attempt to relieve herself of guilt or accept some sort of explanation.

Several women also mention having believed in causes sequentially. They usually started with self-blame and ended with self-exoneration, e.g.

did think for a while that the bronchitis she had early on in the pregnancy may have caused it; then she felt guilty that her feelings may have caused it — worry over previous losses — now she is satisfied with Dr.'s explanation (number 14).

Aside from those women who agree with their physicians, there are many who harbor explanations that differ from those of their physicians. The contradictory explanations focus on behavior and emotions. The following are some of the behavioral and emotional causal explanations the women used:

negative attitudes (number 3),
stress (numbers 47, 55),
worry over previous losses (number 14),
worry over financial troubles (number 62),
inappropriate exercise (numbers 6, 23),
lack of rest (numbers 7, 23),
use of contraceptive foam (number 8),
drinking (numbers 18, 37),
snow shoveling (number 41),
smoking (numbers 18, 41),
taking cold medications, not taking vitamins, falling down a step, lifting a child, having a previous abortion, previously being on the pill, making poor medical choices, or simply 'doing something wrong' (number 39)

Although in no case did a physician suggest that the woman's behavior or emotions caused her miscarriage, many women believed that their behavior or emotions could have this result. The ideology that behavior or emotions can cause miscarriages persists despite physician's efforts to dispel it. In my view, the reason for the persistence of the belief in this form of causation is that many women consider the loss of life to be a momentous event that demands an explanation. For this reason, women develop their own behavioral and emotional explanations to fill the gaps left by the physicians' 'empty explanations'. Moreover, given that personal behavior is thought to have an impact on health in so many other arenas of life, it is difficult for the women to dismiss this belief even in the face of physician discrediting. The strength of this reasoning is evident in the ironic remarks of the women who avoided all of these 'dangerous' behaviors (numbers 18, 30) and yet miscarried nevertheless. Some women even stretched the domain of behavioral causes to include their husbands' behavior or use of medication (numbers 1, 29).

In other words, women were reaching for causes and needed more than 'empty explanations'. They adhered strongly to the widely accepted notion that stress is powerful in producing physical outcomes. In addition to this behavioral paradigm, they proposed physical explanations such as

age (numbers 1, 8),
blood type (number 2),
'messed up hormone levels' (number 26),

infections and illnesses (numbers 9, 10, 14, 19, 37),
'something wrong on the inside' (number 52)

that their physicians did not accept. They referred to a 'nature' that has processes to which they are subject (for example, a 'fluke of nature') and to spiritual beliefs that explain miscarriages in terms of outcomes — for example,

this is what God wanted (numbers 18, 62), or
this was 'nature's way of telling them' (number 28), or
this was just meant to be (numbers 11, 17, 18, 56, 62)

Thus, the occurrence of an unexplained miscarriage reinforced some women's belief in the logic of religion and nature. For other women, an unexplained miscarriage threatened their belief in sensible health precautions and in medical practice (numbers 31, 44).

The stories recorded on the interview sheets are tragic and emotional. They all begin with women telling that they had a little bit of 'spotting' early in their pregnancy (all were first-trimester spontaneous abortions), that they hoped would turn out to 'mean nothing'. In almost every case, the woman was shocked and dismayed when the miscarriage was confirmed. She was likely to cry intensely sometimes because of physical pain and almost always because of emotional pain. The experience of these women as they miscarried was the experience of shock — they could not believe what was happening to them. And yet the miscarriage continued inexorably to pursue its deadly course until the physician completed the procedure of scraping the uterus and the patient returned home — empty.

The story of these miscarriage experiences, however, did not end there. Instead the woman realized that her empty womb was matched by an empty explanation. For many of these women miscarriage is the first shock, the second shock is not having an explanation. A large number of these women simply could not bear the second shock — the empty explanation — and they filled it, instead, with something. Some filled it simply with the linguistic device their physician 'taught' them to use; others filled it with more substantive ideas relating to their behavior or beliefs. Given this conclusion it is not surprising to learn that in the last fifteen years there has been a proliferation of pregnancy loss support groups in which people 'search for and attribute meaning to the seemingly unexplainable event of miscarriage' (see Layne, 1990).

Concluding Statement on Secondary Analysis of Qualitative Data

The possibility of creating standardized computerized formats for qualitative data makes it more convenient than ever to analyze other people's data. The drawbacks in our not analyzing other people's data are manifold. We lose the potential of doing or having longitudinal studies (see, for example, Colby and Phelps, 1990); we lose the potential for diversity in types of population studied for a particular project; our research is seen as mysterious because our data are not produced to be shared; we do not do as many comparative analyses as we could; we do not replicate or build on each other's studies; we waste previously collected data that should be recycled; and we are unnecessarily obtrusive in settings where simply using someone else's data will do rather than collecting data all over again. By drawing on other people's qualitative data, we can utilize the demographic characteristics of researchers other than ourselves. Thus the secondary analysis of someone else's qualitative data makes it possible for an individual to study something to which they might otherwise not have had access.

This procedure would allow us to increase the 'n' and vary the 'n' of our studies. We would also benefit the original researcher by reevaluating the analysis which was previously reached, thus improving scientific procedures in general. I hope that this chapter encourages the publication of announcements by people who have collected qualitative data, stating that their data are available for additional analyses. I would also be pleased if qualitative data banks were created that could be used by novice and advanced researchers alike. Examples are Yale University's Human Relations Area Files and the resources of the Murray Center, Radcliffe College (see Herzog, Holden and Seltzer, 1989, appendix A.) Lykes (1983) is an example of an article that analyzes previously colleged oral history data. She writes:

> Transcripts used in this study were from a project entitled Coping and Adaptation in Older Black Women, co-sponsored by the Schlesinger Library and the Henry A. Murray Research Center of Radcliffe College and funded by the National Institute on Aging. The Black Women Oral History Project was sponsored by the Schlesinger Library. The data described in this paper are from the Coping and Adaptation Project; they are housed at the Murray Center and are available for additional analyses. (p. 79)

Resources such as these will make it possible for students to be trained in the analysis of qualitative data collected by others, thereby giving them an opportunity to focus on analysing rather than collecting data.

Educational researchers, counsellors and teachers who understand the cognitive, physiological and psychological confusion that accompanies many miscarriages will be better prepared to carry out their work. The tragic and emotional stories, to which I referred above, mean that women who have been given the chance to 'tell their stories' will likely provide information that is disturbing to hear. The guilt that some women experience may steer them in or away from the direction of working with children. The attitudes some will have to physicians are likely to be deeply affected as well. The widely experienced phenomenon of miscarriage, represents for some women the loss of trust in one's own body, or the loss of faith in a physician or the loss of security with one's partner, while for others it has little significance at all. Educational researchers must be attuned to the variations in people's attribution of meaning to their experiences. By learning how to do secondary analyses of qualitative data, one can explore these variations in meaning without being obstructed by the myriad of problems than can arise if one has to collect data from scratch.

Acknowledgments

I want to thank Egon Bittner, Peter Conrad, Lynn Davidman, Rosanna Hertz, David Jacobson, Elliot Mishler, Lisa Peattie, Stuart Pizer, Martin Rein, Helen

Reinherz and Robert Weiss for listening to my ideas and/or giving me helpful feedback on this chapter. I thank Judith Lasker for letting me use these data and giving me information about the data collection procedures of this project, and Robin Gregg for suppplying me with additional data from a different study. My thanks also to Danielle Greene and Barbara Winett for creating the computerized files. I would like to express my appreciation to Joanne Preston, Julie Shapiro and Laelia Gilborn for their thorough explanation of the purposes and procedures of the Henry A. Murray Research Center which is devoted to the secondary analysis of qualitative data concerning women's lives in the USA.

Note

1 The sociologist is Professor Judith Lasker, Lehigh University, and the psychologist is Lori J. Toedter of Moravian College and Research Scientist at Lehigh University. Three publications resulting from their study are Lasker, J., Borg, S. and Toedter, L. (1989); Toedter, L., Lasker, J. and Alhadeff, J. (1988) and Dunn, D., Goldbach, K., Lasker, J. and Toedter, L. (in press).

References

ABRAHAMSON, M. (1983) *Social Research Methods*, Englewood Cliffs, NJ, Prentice-Hall.

AUSLANDER, G. (1988) 'Social networks and the functional health status of the poor: A secondary analysis of data from the national survey of personal health practices and consequences', *Journal of Community Health*, **13**, 4, pp. 197–ff.

BABBIE, E. (1983) *The Practice of Social Research* (3rd edn), Belmont, CA, Wadsworth.

BOGDAN, R. and TAYLOR, S. (1975) *Introduction to Qualitative Research Methods*, New York, Wiley-Interscience.

COLBY, A. (1982) 'The use of secondary analysis in the study of women and social change', *Journal of Social Issues*, **38**, 1, pp. 119–23.

COLBY, A. and PHELPS, E. (1990) 'Archiving longitudinal data' in MAGNUSSON, D. and BERGMAN, L. (Eds) *Data Quality in Longitudinal Research*, New York, Cambridge University Press.

DUNN, D., GOLDBACH, K., LASKER, J. and TOEDTER, L. (in press) 'Explaining Pregnancy Loss: Parents' Attributions and the Search for Meaning', *Omega*.

FISHMAN, M. (1980) *Manufacturing the news*, Austin, TX, University of Texas Press.

GLEIT, C. and GRAHAM, B. (1989) 'Secondary data analysis: A valuable resource', *Nursing Research*, **38**, 6, pp. 380 ff.

HERZOG, A.R., HOLDEN, K. and SELTZER, M. (Eds) (1989) *Health and Economic Status of Older Women*, Amityville, NY, Baywood Publishing Company, Inc.

HOSSLER, D. (1989) 'Grounded meta-analysis: a guide for research syntheses', *The Review of Higher Education*, **13**, 1, pp. 1–ff.

HYMAN, H.H. (1972) *Secondary Analysis of Sample Surveys*, New York, John Wiley.

JONES, G. (1988) 'Integrating process and structure in the concept of youth: A case for secondary analysis', *The Sociological Review*, **36**, 4, pp. 706–ff.

KASWORM, C. (1990) 'Adult competence in everyday tasks: A cross-sectional secondary analysis', *Educational Gerontology*, **16**, 1, pp. 27–ff.

KATZ, J. (1988) *Seductions of Crime: Moral and Sensual Attractions in Doing Evil*, New York, Basic Books.

KROLL-SMITH, J.S. and COUCH, S.R. (1990) *The Real Disaster is Above Ground. A Mine Fire and Social Conflict*, Lexington, Kentucky, University of Kentucky Press.

LASKER, J., BORG, S. and TOEDTER, L. (1989) 'Report of new research on pregnancy loss' in BORG, S. and LASKER, J. (Eds) *When Pregnancy Fails: Families Coping with Miscarriage, Ectopic Pregnancy, Stillbirth and Infant Death* (rev. edn) New York, Bantam Books.

LAYNE, L. (1990) 'Motherhood lost: Cultural dimensions of miscarriage and stillbirth in America', *Women and Health*, **16**, 3/4, pp. 69–98.

LYKES, M.B. (1983) 'Discrimination and coping in the lives of black women: Analyses of oral history data', *Journal of Social Issues*, **39**, 3, pp. 79–100.

MARSHALL, C. and ROSSMAN, G. (1989) *Designing Qualitative Research*, Newbury Park, CA, Sage.

MILLER, S.I. (1987) 'Triangulation and meta-analysis: Narrowing the qualitative-quantitative gap', *Educational Foundations*, **3**, pp 80–ff.

MISHLER, E.G. (1984) *The Discourse of Medicine. Dialectics of Medical Interviews*, Norwood, NJ, Ablex Publishing Corporation.

PAGET, M. (1982) 'Your son is cured now: You may take him home', *Culture, Medicine and Psychiatry*, **6**, pp. 237–59.

PAGET, M. (1983) 'Experience and knowledge', *Human Studies*, **6**, pp. 67–90.

PAGET, M. (1988) *The Unity of Mistakes. A Phenomenological Interpretation of Mistakes in Medical Work*, Philadelphia, PA, Temple University Press.

PAGET, M. (1990) 'Performing the text', *Journal of Contemporary Ethnography*, **19**, 1, pp. 136–55.

POWDERMAKER, H. (1966) *Stranger and Friend*, New York, Norton.

REINHARZ, S. (1987) 'The social psychology of a miscarriage: An application of symbolic interactionist theory and method' in DEEGAN, M.J. and HILL, M. (Eds) *Women and Symbolic Interaction*, New York, Allen & Unwin.

REINHARZ, S. (1988a) 'What's missing in miscarriage?' *Journal of Community Psychology*, **16**, 1, pp. 84–103.

REINHARZ, S. (1988b) 'Controlling women's lives: A cross-cultural interpretation of miscarriage accounts' in WERTZ, D. (Ed.) *Research in the Sociology of Health Care*, Greenwich, CT, JAI Press, pp. 2–37.

REINHARZ, S. (in press) 'Miscarriage' in KATZ ROTHMAN, B. (Ed.) *Encyclopedia of Childbearing*, New York, Oryx Press.

SANJEK, R. (Ed.) (1990) *Fieldnotes. The Makings of Anthropology*, Ithaca and London, Cornell University Press.

SARIS, W. and VAN DEN PUTTE, B. (1988) 'True score or factor models: A secondary analysis of the ALLBUS-test-retest data', *Sociological Methods and Research*, **17**, 2, pp. 123–ff.

SOLTIS, J. and WALBERG, H. (1989) 'Thirteen-year-olds' writing achievements: A secondary analysis of the fourth national assessment of writing', *Journal of Educational Research*, **83**, 1, pp. 22–ff.

STEIN, M. (1960) *Eclipse of Community*, Princeton, NJ, Princeton University Press.

TOEDTER, L., LASKER, J. and ALHADEFF, J. (1988) 'The perinatal grief scale: Development and initial validation', *American Journal of Orthopsychiatry*, **58**, pp. 435–49.

VAN MAANEN, J. (1988) *Tales from the Field*, Chicago, IL, University of Chicago.

WAITZKIN, H. (1983) *The Second Sickness: Contradictions of Capitalist Health Care*, New York, Free Press.

WARNER, W.L. (1941–57) *Yankee City Series*, New Haven, CT, Yale University Press.

WARREN, C. (1987) *Madwives: Schizophrenic Women in the 1950s*, New Brunswick, NJ, Rutgers University Press.

WAX, R. (1971) *Doing Fieldwork*, Chicago, IL, University of Chicago.

WEITZMAN, L. (1985) *The Divorce Revolution*, New York, Free Press.

WHYTE, W.F. (1984) *Learning from the Field*, Newbury Park, CA, Sage.

ZIMRING, F.E. and ZUEHL, J. (1986) 'Victim injury and death in urban robbery: A Chicago study', *Journal of Legal Studies*, **15**, pp. 1–40.

An Epilogue: Putting Voices Together

Michael Schratz

A book on qualitative voices in educational research has to satisfy the different needs of a broad audience ranging from college student to university lecturers and researchers in education who are challenged by the new qualitative paradigm. Furthermore, it can also be a useful tool for the work of policy makers who are involved in evaluating educational processes, for teachers who attend in-service training classes to improve their analytical competence, for people who are involved in continuing education, as well as for educational professionals outside the immediate context of schooling (human psychologists, group leaders, facilitators, team leaders etc.). Therefore an epilogue is added in order to give the reader further guidance and assistance in getting the most out of this collection of articles. It offers questions and comments that may help to compare and contrast the individual contributions and brings together the different kinds of analytic procedures presented by the authors.

Comparing Qualitative Voices

Because of the complex nature of research work it was not an easy task for the authors to present their qualitative voices within the limited space of a chapter. Therefore when planning the chapters the authors were asked to draw their attention to the following questions that might also be a structuring device for the reader when comparing and contrasting the chapters.

(a) Frame of Reference

What is the philosophy of the respective author's research approach on a more general level? How does it differ from others? Is there a particular research tradition behind it?

(b) Areas of Application

What are the main areas of application of the research approach? Do certain areas provide better pre-conditions for specific methods than others? Are there any areas where your approach could not be applied at all? Does the political context matter in which the methodology is applied?

(c) Sample of Material

What sort of data do the authors use? Is it part from this material from their personal research work? How did the researcher collect that data? What methods did they use?

(d) Procedures in Data Analysis

What does the author do with the material represented in (c)? What are the individual steps or phases in the analytic processes of the data? Do they comply with the overall philosophy of the researcher's approach described in (a)? How is this philosophy reflected in concrete methodological steps?

(e) Outlook and Application

Does the chapter include an overall view on the application of the approach dealt with? Where else could this approach be used? What are its strengths and weaknesses? Are there any fallacies? How could this approach be improved? In the political context of education, how does it contribute to change?

Not all these questions can be answered by the information given in the chapters. By working out the similarities, differences and overlapping aspects on common grounds a better understanding of the voices expressed by the contributors can be achieved. One of the most important features in qualitative research methodology is the way how authentic voices gathered in field work are dealt with. As they contain the 'social breath' (Bakhtin) of the research subjects, they represent the most valuable asset in research. The different analytical procedures used are grouped together in two sections. In the first group the subjects' voices are given 'social breath' so they can be rendered more audible. In the other group the authors present ways in which they differently tuned the voices to make them better understood.

Rendering Voices Social Breath

The first group of approaches is characterized by very little interpretation given by the researcher in the analysis of data. The researcher's role is restricted to either stepping back and letting the subjects' voices speak for themselves or to give them a particular perspective for further interpretation. Their common background is a strong quest for democratizing the research process. It is no longer the researcher's voice that should be heard but that of the subjects under study.

In her presentation of school profile studies, Jean Rudduck shows how to leave room for pluralistic values by making the actors participants in the dialogic structure of the research process. When collecting data she tries to interfere as little as possible with the given situation. Driven by the quest for democratic evaluation and by giving the people the right to produce the data, gathered through observation, interviews and other methods of 'condensed field-work', the researcher becomes the active communicator in the feedback phase of the findings, the most sensitive part of the research process.

In a similar way, but with different methods, Rob Walker experiments with ways of communicating the voices of subjectivity. He uses photographs which not only captivate a particular moment within a longer research period but also offer the possibility to reflect on the process itself. The pictures build a relation between the photograph and the event and thus create a certain tension between the appearance of the outer world and the cognitive and emotive aspects of the inner world, between what is social and what is personal. This distinction between public and private uses of photographs gains considerable importance for evaluation and research. Since images are open to subjective interpretation, for the people involved deciphering their meaning becomes a cultural activity itself. Therefore for Walker it is not so much the use of pictures as records that matters but the way of engaging an audience in the process of evaluation.

George and Louise Spindlers' method of the cross cultural reflective interview, achieves the same effect to a different end. Various people involved within a school watch films from a culturally different perspective and thus engage in cross-cultural reflection. In this dialogue, again the research subjects are more involved than the researchers, whose voices become gradually muted. The subjects create 'modernist texts' which demonstrate shared culture, differentiated by the position of the actors involved. Thus a more accurate representation of social and psychocultural reality is rendered by such a research. The researchers come in during the last phase carefully unveiling societal aspects.

Self-reflection is also the topic in Michael Schratz's sociodynamic approach to the analysis of group processes. It is not an external evaluator who interferes with the interactions in the group but the collaborative effort of the group members to investigate into the psychosocial aspects of doing research. The data gathered from group interviews are primarily important for assessing the processes underlying the product orientation. On a secondary level, however, looking at the transcripts from collective phases of collective self-reflection opens up the inner world of collaborative work. Thus group processes can be better understood and evaluated. Moreover, paying closer attention to the interactive capacities of the people involved in research activities will enhance the organizational culture and stimulate institutional development.

Herbert Altrichter's chapter aims at bridging the levels of individual and institutional development. Setting up quality criteria in action research he wants to build on a concept of socially responsible professionalism and to develop a social field through action and reflection of the people concerned. Analyzing interview material on a secondary level, he discusses and exemplifies the value of these criteria and provides strategies through which the quality of practitioner research can be enhanced. He also proposes ways of implementing these findings in the research practice of action research programmes.

Tuning Voices for Understanding

Understanding schools as social institutions is the focus of Robert Burgess' chapter, which combines more traditional forms of fieldwork (observation and interview) with the use of 'event analysis'. He concentrates on critical phases in the professional world of a headteacher. By analyzing the interpersonal relations of the actors involved, he examines the psychosocial processes within the framework of a 'social drama'. Applying this data gained from interviews and observations of a teachers' dispute he identifies four phases of a social drama and examines one critical incident to exemplify how this method can assist in the understanding of headships. By pulling together the individual strings of the analysis he reaches a conclusion which shows both the formal relations among the conflict parties involved and the stresses, ambiguities and dilemmas of a headteacher during such a dispute.

In search of the significance of the social meaning in a person's discourse Dietmar Larcher uses the 'voice of redundancy' to listen to the subtle messages in speech containing traces of social structure and experience. By means of a laborious method of analysis, systematically experimenting with the social context of an utterance, he explores the social message incorporated in a person's conversation. Thus the researchers try to find as many variations of speech and social context as possible in order to discover the 'incomprehensible' in the redundant use of utterances. Since the application of this method is very demanding and time consuming, it can only be used in research teams. Satisfactory application requires an extensive preparation, coordination and training in the use of analytical discourse skills, as well as a suitable research culture.

Hugh Mehan's discourse analysis video taped in different educational settings points in another direction. By looking at various patterns of interactions on the micro level of educational practices he demonstrates the situated relevance of social structures in practical activities performed by people in institutional settings. Thus he uncovers how the social organization of educational settings can influence the school careers of certain individuals and underrepresented groups. Students' institutional identities are shown to be constructed in the interactive dynamics between social forces which operate outside the school and local practices within it. Comparing his data from different applications of discourse analysis he concludes that discourse analytic techniques can be applied beyond the boundaries of a single event illuminating the macro level of educational work.

Huber and García present a software tool for handling interview material in order to deal with the problems of 'data-overload' in qualitative research. Using data from biographical interviews with beginning teachers about their experience in the first teaching year they show how a computer program can help in making the analytical phase both easier to manipulate and wider in scope. The program can also be used for the enhanced constructing and listing of hypotheses by retrieving all locations in a text where two or more units of meaning appear in a defined relationship. Using extracts from their large study, they go through the procedures of the analysis showing how to reduce the data load, how to display them and how to draw conclusions from the coded parts of the interviews. As for the content part of their research they refer to the impairing and facilitating influences on the beginning teachers' professional socialization.

Another way of data handling is introduced in Shulamit Reinharz's chapter.

She does not deal with fieldwork at all but concentrates on the secondary analysis of qualitative data. Losing out on primary experience with the subjects might be regarded as a drawback of such an approach, but the author stresses its advantages in certain situations of qualitative research. Moreover, having other people doing the interviewing might increasingly become standard practice in field work as qualitative researchers spend less time collecting the data in their research programmes. It seems to be important though that the analysis is grounded in sufficient information about the circumstances of the field work. An interesting part of the presentation of the findings lies in the shift from the original quality of authentic speech (in the interviews) to a more quantitative listing of the occurrences of utterances related to the research questions.

Outlook

After more than two decades of experimenting with new approaches there have been several attempts to systematize qualitative methods in educational research. Such endeavours could only be unsystematic given the array of different cultural and educational environments where qualitative research methodology is applied. Summing up the different strands, however, is increasingly difficult as in the meantime there does exist a multitude of diverse voices in the field which are difficult to be kept apart from each other. It is in this context that this volume has tried to tune in to some of those qualitative voices in different educational settings in various parts of the world. Showing alternative ways of tackling research questions it represents an opportunity for exploring some current practices of qualitative work which link data analysis with a methodological framework. Thus this book tries to offer a systematic qualitative underpinning to educational research.

Such an endeavour would be sterile, however, if it did not relate to a connection to the everyday world of educational practice. Showing how the authors deal with authentic pieces of data is like inviting people to their research workshops and allowing them to look over their shoulders. This immediacy of presentation is a way of reflective exploration, appraisal and creation of theory in practice and thus a lively introduction into the particular author's tricks of the research trade. Nevertheless, not all the necessary steps in the long process of research work are always visible. This is not only due to the limited space available for each contributor but also shows that doing qualitative research is not a matter of simply stringently following a pre-set order of procedural steps but rather listening carefully to the diverse voices in the field and adopting one's research methodology accordingly.

Apart from the voices collected in this volume, there are many more available, which have not been included. For example, the one of an invited researcher who explained how his close observations gained from life among working class youth helped him gain insight into their daily life. This led him to propose major revisions in his theories explaining the reproduction of inequality in American society. After the deadline for the submission of the manuscripts he wrote: 'Now it appears impossible. The night before last, one of my students was raped by her stepfather. Both she and her mother (who is emotionally unstable at the best of times) have asked me for help. Emotionally, I am quite overwhelmed myself. Spending time with them and trying to help them negotiate the police, the medical, judicial, and social service bureaucracies is going to occupy a large chunk of my time for the next several weeks, time that was to be devoted completely to my chapter for you.'

Therefore this volume cannot do justice to this valuable kind of research and to many other approaches that are carried out even without being known. They are all part of the qualitative research movement and contribute to the advancement of learning in the scientific community of education but rarely get the chance to reach the traditional channels of academic discussions, of which this volume is merely one. Nevertheless, the approaches collected in this volume give a rare insight into the fundamental work of educational researchers across three continents. Bridging the gap between qualitative research done in different parts of the world is one important step toward a more global aim in meeting the challenges of education in the nineties. In fact, there will be more and more need for qualitative methods in educational research that can satisfy the future demands of society.

Notes on Contributors

Herbert Altrichter is currently Associate Professor at the Department of Business Education and Personnel Development, University of Innsbruck, after having built up together with Professor *Peter* Posch the action research emphasis of the Department of Education at Klagenfurt University. He gained his PhD from the University of Vienna and did research as visiting scholar at the Cambridge Institute of Education, (1985) and at Deakin University, (1989). From 1978–1988 he was editor in change of the *Zeitschrift für Hochschuldidaktik (Austrian Journal for Research and Development in Higher Education)*. His main teaching and research interests are in teacher education, school development, action research, theory-of-action and research methodology. His main publications include: *Ist das noch Wissenschaft?* (methodological foundation for action research, Munich, 1990); *Lehrer erforschen ihren Unterricht* (introduction into the strategies and methods of action research, co-authored by P. Posch, Bad Heilbrunn, 1990), *Schule gestalten: Lehrer als Forscher* (a collection of case-studies written by teacher researchers, co-editor, Klagenfurt 1989).

Robert Burgess is Director of CEDAR (Centre for Educational Development, Appraisal and Research) and Professor of Sociology at the University of Warwick. His main teaching and research interests are in social research methodology; especially qualitative methods and the sociology of education; especially the study of schools, classrooms and curricula. He is currently writing an ethnographic restudy of a comprehensive school on which he has already published several papers. His main publications include: *Experiencing Comprehensive Education* (1983), *In the Field: An Introduction to Field Research* (1984), *Education, Schools and Schooling* (1985), *Sociology, Education and Schools* (1986) and *Schools at Work* (1988 with Rosemary Deem), together with fourteen edited volumes on qualitative methods and education. He was the President of the British Sociological Association (1989–91).

Günter L. Huber is Professor of Educational Psychology at the University of Tübingen, Germany. He was a teacher, studied psychology and pedagogics at the University of Munich, where he gained his PhD in pedagogics. His research interests include social organization of learning processes and in-service training of teachers; both areas draw his attention to people's implicit theories and methods to get access to these subjective world views. His publications include *Verbale Daten: Eine Einführung in die Grundlagen und Methoden der Erhebung und Auswertung* (1982, together with Heinz Mandl) and a software package and manual for computer-assisted qualitative analysis *AQUAD: Analyse qualitativer Daten mit Computerunterstützung* (1990).

Dietmar Larcher is Professor of Education (teachers' in-service training) at the University of Klagenfurt. His main research and teaching interests are in minority research and intercultural education. He has conducted several projects on identity formation of bilinguals and has also carried out action research on curriculum development for bilinguals in Austria and Italy. At the same time he is active in applied museology. He is currently writing an interpretation of his Nicaragua research-diary. His publications include studies on identity formation of minorities, teaching strategies for classrooms with minority children and texts on communicative learning in museums.

Carlos Marcelo is Assistant Professor at the University of Seville. He studied pedagogy at the University of Seville, where he obtained his PhD in education. His research interest include pre-service and in-service teacher education anf training. He has done research on teacher thinking. His publications include several books: *El pensamiento del profesor* (1987), *Planificación y enseñanza* (1988) and *Introducción a la formación del profesorado* (1989).

Hugh Mehan is Professor of Sociology and Director of the Teacher Education Program at UCSD, a select and innovative program devoted to multicultural education. Against the background of an interactionist approach to social life, he has conducted research on classroom interaction, studied educational decision-making, compared interaction in real and non-real time message systems and examined closely the use of microcomputers in classrooms. He has contributed to a staff development handbook for teachers on the use of microcomputers in classrooms. Most recently he has been studying the discourse of war and peace.

Jean Rudduck is Director of the QQSE (Qualitative and Quantitative Studies in Education) Research Group and Professor of Education at the University of Sheffield. Her research focusses on different aspects of innovation and change in schools, including teacher research as a basis for professional development; she has also been particularly interested in exploring the students' perspective. Recent publications: *Innovation and Change: Developing Involvement and Understanding* (1990); a series of four volumes for teachers on cooperative group work (1988–1991 with Helen Cowie): *Cooperative Group Work: An Overview; School and Classroom Studies; Cooperative Learning: Traditions and Transitions* and *Cooperative Group Work in the Multiethnic Classroom*. She is currently working on a linked set of research studies of gender, race and discipline in comprehensive schools.

Shulamit Reinharz is a Professor of Sociology and Director of Women's Studies at Brandeis University. She is the author of four books: *On Becoming a Social Scientist* (1979 to 1984); *Psychology and Community Change* (1984, with other authors); *Qualitative Gerontology* (1987 co-edited with Graham Rowles); and *Feminist Methods in Social Research* (1992). She teaches research methods and was the former editor of *Qualitative Sociology*. She has published widely on miscarriage and various forms of qualitative research methods.

Michael Schratz is Associate Professor of Education at the University of Innsbruck. His main interests are in school innovation, further and higher education with a particular focus on qualitative research methodology. He taught in Bristol (1974/75) and did research at the University of California, San Diego (1988/89), and at Deakin University (1992). Amongst his publications are *Bildung für ein unbekanntes Morgen: Auf der Suche nach einer neuen Lernkultur (Education for an Unknown Tomorrow: In Search of a New Learning Culture*, 1991) and *Teenage Classrooms* (1992 with Herbert Puchta). He edited *Gehen Bildung, Ausbildung und Wissenschaft an der Lebenswelt vorbei* (1988), a collection exploring whether everyday knowledge and formal education/scientific knowledge contradict one another, and co-authored *Schulen machen Schule* (1991), a book on school autonomy and development.

George and Louise Spindler have collaborated on most publications during the past two decades, and often before that. George is Professor Emeritus in Anthropology and Education at Stanford University and Visiting Professor in Cross-Cultural Studies at the University of California, Santa Barbara. Louise is Lecturer in Anthropology and Education at Stanford and likewise Visiting Professor at UCSB. Their research has focussed on personal adaptation to culture change and urbanization and on education as cultural transmission and acquisition. They have studied three American Indian communities, two German communities, and several in the United States with those foci in mind. They are editors of the widely used *Case Studies in Cultural Anthropology* and many other volumes in education and anthropology and psychological anthropology.

Rob Walker is Professor of Education at Deakin University. His interests are broadly in applied research, action research and evaluation and currently in distance education, and in evaluating drug education programs. He has been interested in the use of photographs in research for a long time but only gets occasional opportunities to try out the ideas discussed here. Writing the chapter came at a good time because he is just beginning work on a research project (with Richard Bates, Chris Bigum, Lindsay Fitzclarence and Bill Green) called 'Schooling the Future'. One of the things they are trying to do in this research study is to investigate the notion of the emergence of forms of post-modern culture among high school students. This project demands extensions of conventional ethnographic method, of which the use of photographs suggests itself as a promising possibility.

Index

Abrhamson, Mark 158, 159
accountability 2, 9, 52, 53
achievement 9, 93–4
Achleitner, I. 62
action research 1, 3, 57, 181
  quality in 40–54
    contexts and prospects 52–4
    quality criteria 3, 45–52
    theoretical background 41–5
Adelman, C. 60, 81
Alexander, R.J. 60
Alhadeff, J. 163
alienation of photograph 74, 82, 85
Altrichter, Herbert 3, 40–54, 57, 58
analysis, data 4, 180
Anderson, R. 11
Angelo, T.A. 57
anthropology 14, 23, 107
Apple, W.M. 9, 19
application
  of action research 52–4
  areas of 3, 5, 143–6, 179–80
AQUAD 3.0 143–5, 148, 150, 152–4
Argyris, C. 45, 50
Auslander, G. 159

Babbie, Earl 158
Bakhtin, M.M. 63
Ball, David 31, 33–4
Ball, Stephen J. 13, 19, 23, 25
Barlow, Phil 26, 30–1, 36
Barthes, R. 74
Becker, Howard 85
behaviour 63, 65, 95–6, 98, 108–11,
  113–16, 119–21, 174
Berger, John 72, 74, 79–80, 82–3
Berger, P.L. 127

Berger, W. 57
Biklen, S. 147
Blythe, R. 14
Boeckmann, B. et al. 130, 136
Bogdan, R. 147, 160
Borg, S. 163
Brody, N. 63
Bromme, R. 54
Brown, D. 141
Burgess, Robert G. 2, 12, 13, 23–39,
  182

Carinthia, bilinguals in 130–6
Carr, W. 57
case study 1, 8, 11, 13–14, 18–19, 21,
  87, 99–103
Cassidy, A. 57
Cazden, Courtney B. 97, 98
Charlesworth, Max et al. 74
Cicourel, A.V. 94
Clark, Ch.M. 140
Clifford, J. 122
codification of data 144–5, 148–50,
  152–3
cognitive development 141–2, 147
Colby, A. 157, 175
Cole, Michael 98
Coleman, James S. 93–4, 98
collaboration 3, 42, 44–5, 48, 51, 52,
  95–6, 181
collection, data 3–4, 14, 23–5, 37, 79,
  83, 86, 129, 131, 133, 146–7, 157,
  159–61, 175–6
collective self-reflection 3, 56–68, 181
  action to self-reflection 65–7
  educational research as interactive
  process 56–8

reflection on collaboration 62–5
researching into educational affairs
58–62
ten principles of 67–8
towards an ontology of educational
knowledge 67
Collier, J.J. and M. 107
Collier, John 84
communication 10–11, 73, 126, 128,
133, 137, 143, 181
meta- 59, 63, 66
comparison 145, 154, 179
compatability of research and aims 44–5
competency 43–4, 50, 97, 126, 128,
137, 141
computer assisted listening 5, 139–55
example of data 146–8
general orientation 139–43
outlook 153–5
procedure of analysis 148–53
software applications to qualitative
research 143–6
confidentiality 13, 20, 52, 163
context
democratic 42, 44
political 4, 53, 130, 180
social 1, 3, 14, 23, 83, 94, 99, 103,
126–7, 133, 182
social drama 26–38
sociocultural 57–8, 68
Couch, S.R. 159
Cowie, H. 11
criticism 10, 51, 60
Cross, K.P. 57
Cuff, E.C. 57
culture
bi- 130
role of school in 106–7, 111, 113,
120–2
school 2–3, 97–8, 142
socio- 127–31
curriculum, limitations of 112, 116–17,
120

Davies, Gill 26, 30
decentralization 53
development, teacher 11, 141
discontinuity, cultural 98
discourse 4, 94, 96, 98–100, 103, 182
discussion 3, 59, 64–5, 66, 84–5
display, data 85–7, 150–2
documentary data 23–5, 31
Dörner, D. 44
Dunn, D. 163

Earley, P. 39
education of women 163
elitism 53
Elliott, John 40, 46, 47, 50, 51, 53, 54,
57
Elton, Lord 18
enhancement functions of computer
software 143–5
epistemology 3, 52, 57, 67
of practice 43–5
equality 93
Erdheim, M. 57
Erickson, F. 97, 98, 99
ethics 3, 44–5, 48, 51
ethnicity 4, 93–4, 99, 103
ethno-psychoanalytical study 57
ethnography 1, 3–4, 12, 14, 23–4, 79,
87, 108, 121–2
ethnomethodology 90
evaluation 2, 14, 60–2, 73–4, 83–5, 97,
133–4, 145, 176, 181
event analysis 3, 23–39
context of social drama 26–38
studying crises 24–6
expectations 43, 47
experience 81–2, 126, 163
of teachers 139–55, 182

feedback 2, 9, 14–16, 18–20, 51–2, 181
Feiman-Nemser, S. 141
Feyerabend, P.K. 41, 42
fieldwork 3, 8–9, 12–15, 84, 107,
159–60, 162–3, 180–3
film 106–9, 122
Firestone, W.A. 147
Fischer, M. 121, 122
Fischer, W. 62
Fishman, Mark 162
Floden, R. 141
Foley, D. 99
Foster, Michele 19–20
Foster, W. 62
frame experiment 43–4
frame of reference 5, 179
Fujita, M. 107
Fuller, F. 141
functionalism 67–8

García, Carlos Marcelo 5, 139–55, 182
Garfinkel, H. 90, 94
Gillborn, David 9, 10–11, 18
Giroux, H.A. 67
Gleit, C. 159
goals 44, 50, 57, 63–5, 67–8, 112, 117–21

Goddard, Geoff 24, 26–7, 29–34, 39
Goetz, J. 149
Goffman, E. 127
Goldbach, K. 163
Gore, J. 142
Goswami, P. 57
Gould, Stephen Jay 74
Graham, B. 159
Gray, John 18
Greenfield, T.B. 61
Gregory, R. 57
Griffin, Peg 98
Groeben, N. *et al.* 140
group work in schools 17
Grumet, M. 9
Gstettner, P. 56
Guba, E. 142
Gumperz, J.J. 98

Hall, V. 38, 39
Halsey, A.H. 98
Handke, Peter 129
Hargreaves, A. 11
Hargreaves, David 20
Haring, F. 62
Harris, M. 91
Harris, S. *et al.* 18
Harrison, Tony 9
Head Start program 93
headship 2–3, 23–39, 182
Heath, S.B. 98
Herrior, R. 147
Herzog, A.R. 176
Holden, K. 176
Hopkins, D. 19, 87
Horn, K. 56
Hossler, D. 158
Huber, Günter L. 5, 139–55, 182
Huberman, A. 142, 144, 148, 150, 152
Hug, T. 67
Hustler, E. 57
Hyman, Herbert H. 159
hypothesizing 144–5, 152–3, 182

identity 20, 61, 65–6, 99, 103, 127,
    129–31, 182
illustration, photograph in 73, 82
individualism 8, 20–3, 59, 65, 67–8,
    127–8, 131, 137
industrial action in school 25–39
innovation 53
intelligence 94–6
interaction 3, 15, 51, 94–8, 100, 104,
    126, 129, 137, 181–2

between teachers 24–5, 38, 150–2
    self-reflection and 56–68
interpretation 13, 25, 72, 79, 83–5, 90,
    96, 108, 122, 129, 133–7, 140, 144–5,
    148, 180–1
interpretive studies 98–9, 103
interviews 2–3, 5, 12, 16, 19–20, 23–6,
    31, 47, 73, 84–6, 157, 159–60,
    162–4, 175, 181–2
    biographical 9–10, 126–37
    crosscultural, comparative, reflective
        4, 106–21, 181
    diverse reflections 109–20
    interpretation 120–1
    purpose 107–8
    research sites 106–7
Isherwood, Christopher 79
isolation of head 27, 39
iterativity of research 49

Jackson, Philip 81
Jackson, Sally 27–9, 31–2, 34, 36
Jensen, Arthur R. 93, 94, 98
Johnson, Lyndon B. 93
Johnston, J. 140
Jones, G. 159
Jordell, K. 148–9

Karabel, J. 98
Kasworm, C. 159
Katz, Jack 160–1
Kemmis, S. 57, 61
Klemm, K. 56
Klinzing, H.G. 140
Knorr-Cetina, K. 67
Kriz, J. 143
Kroath, F. 60
Kroll-Smith, J.S. 159

Labov, W. 94
Lacey, C. 18, 142
language
    empty explanations of physicians
        164–72
    empty explanations of women 172–5
    as social institution in redundancy
        analysis 5, 126–30
    using 72–4, 84, 89, 98, 100–3, 139,
        154, 182–3
Larcher, Dietmar 5, 126–37, 182
Lasker, Judith 163
Latour, B. 67
Lave, J. 94
Lawb, M. 9

Layne, L. 175
leadership 62, 66
LeCompte, M. 149
Leithäuser, T. 129
Lesko, N. 39
Lewin, Kurt 57
Lewis, Oscar 87, 89
Lightfoot, S.L. 18, 21
Lincoln, Y. 142
Lisch, R. 143
longitudinal studies 175
Lorenzer, A. 129
Luckmann, T. 127
Lykes, M.B. 176

McCutcheon, G. 15
McDermott, Ray P. 97, 99
MacDonald, Barry 13, 14, 83
Mackay, H. 38, 39
McKernan, J. 57
macro-analysis through collective
    self-reflection 4, 59, 61–2, 67, 182
management
    classroom 109–11, 113–15, 117–18,
        120
    of educational change 56, 60–2
    of industrial action 26–38
Marcelo, C. 150
Marcus, G.E. 121–2
Marshall, C. 160
matrix, construction of 152
Mead, Margaret 162
Mehan, Hugh 3, 93–104
memory, photography and 80–3, 90
Messinger, Sheldon L. 162
meta-analysis 157–8
methodology 5, 12, 15, 41–2, 94,
    142–3, 179–83
    computer-assisted listening example
        of data 146–8
    procedure of analysis 148–55
    miscarriage 163–4
    redundancy analysis 133–6
    secondary analysis 164–75
Metz, Mary Haywood 90–1
microanalysis through collective
    self-reflection 4, 59–60, 67, 182
Miles, M.B. 142, 144, 148, 150, 152
Miller, S.I. 158
miscarriage data and analysis 163–75
Mishler, Elliot G. 161–2
model of technical rationality 43
modernist texts 106, 121, 181
Mohatt, G. 98

Mohr, Jean 74, 82, 83
Morgan, C. 38, 39
motivation 48, 65
motives 59, 63, 65–6
Mulkay, M. 67
multi-site qualitative research 147

Nadig, M. 57
negotiation 15, 45, 48
Nias, J. 9
Nixon, Jon 9, 18
noise in classroom 109–11, 116, 119–21

objectivity 1, 14, 73, 79, 84, 90, 122,
    127–31, 137, 142
Objektive Hermeneutik 128–31
observation 2–3, 12, 15, 23–5, 31, 157,
    159–60, 181–2
    participant 85, 137
Oevermann, U. 128
Ogbu, J.U. 99
Oldroyd, T. 57
O'Meara, T. 122
opportunity 93, 104
organization
    lesson 97–8
    school 2–3, 23–4, 28, 38
    social 182
organizations 61
Ottaway, A.K.C. 12
Ottenberg, Simon 162
outlook 136–7, 153–5, 180, 183–4

Paget, Marianne 162
partnership supervision 15, 16
performance 2, 4, 9, 93–4, 98, 103
perspectives, differing 2, 21, 47–8, 50,
    111, 113, 120–1, 140
Phelps, E. 175
Philips, S.U. 94, 98
philosophy of science 41
photographs in research 3, 72–91, 181
    example 87–90
    planning an evaluation 85–7
    practical ideas 84–5
    'public' and 'private' photographs
        74–84, 181
    real schools 90–1
    science as pictures, not words 73–4
Pike, Kenneth 91
placements 99–100, 103
planning 15, 56–7, 62, 85
Popkewitz, T.S. 58
Posch, P. 42–3, 53, 57

Powdermaker, H. 157
power 61, 68, 84, 103
practical theory 47–50, 54, 183
pragmatics 3, 45
pressure 48–9, 53, 65
processes of research, historical 58–9,
    62, 64, 66, 68
professionality 42–4, 50, 52, 53–4, 59
Prosser, Jon 87
psychoanalysis 126, 129, 131
publication 13, 52, 143, 176
puppetry 85

quantative research 1, 126, 137, 142,
    155, 159
questionnaires 73
quotation 19–20, 83

Ragin, C.C. 145
Rathmayr, B. 56
reality
    psychosocial 62–5
    'shock' 141, 145, 150
    social 1, 43, 47–8, 122, 127, 143, 181
recording 12, 16, 19, 30–4, 66, 131,
    133, 164
Redfield, R. 87, 89
redundancy analysis 5, 126–37, 182
    as hard work 133–6
    language as social institution 127–30
    in minority research and other
        applications 130–1
    outlook 136–7
    torn between Nazi Hero and
        KZ-inmate 131–2
referrals 99–100
reflection 53, 108, 110–11, 122, 183
    and action research 48–52
    self- 44, 51, 73, 181
    see also collective self-reflection
reflection-in-action 15, 43–4, 57, 59
Reinharz, Shulamit 5, 157–76, 182–3
reliability 1, 12, 72, 90, 137, 140, 142,
    144, 149
results 43, 57–8, 63
reviews 157–8
Reynolds, D. 11
Ribbins, P.M. *et al.* 2
Rogoff, B. 94
role of researcher 128, 180
Rolff, H.-G. 56
Rosaldo, R. 122
Roseville school, Wisconsin 107–22
Ross, D. 123

Rossman, G. 160
Ruddock, Jean 2, 8–21, 87, 181
rules
    classroom 97–8
    for research 41–2, 45
Ryan, K. 140

Sacks, H. *et al.* 97
Sanger, J. 65
Sanjek, R. 162
Sano, T. 107
Saris, W. 159
Schoenhausen, Germany 106–22
Schön, Donald A. 42, 43–4, 45, 47, 52,
    54, 57, 59–60
school profile studies 1–2, 8–21
    background 8–9
    examples 15–18
    feedback 18–20
    fieldwork 12–15
    individual teacher and self-knowledge
        9–10
    staff and institutional self-knowledge
        10–12
Schratz, Michael 1–5, 56–68, 179–84
Schultz, J. 97
Schutz, A. 94
Searle, J. 127
secondary analysis of qualitative data 5,
    157–76, 183
    miscarriage data 163–4
    secondary analysis 164–75
selection of data 87, 89–90
self-concept 50
self-knowledge 9–12, 20–1
Sellers, Peter 103
Seltzer, M. 176
semi-secondary analysis 159
sensitivity 59–60
Shelly, A. 150, 152
Shuy, Roger 98
Simons, H. 13
Smyth, J. 67
Snyder, K. 11
social breath 180–1
social science 72, 74, 90, 129, 157
socialization
    of bilinguals 5, 127–8, 131, 137
    in school culture 3
    of teachers 9–10, 15, 139–40, 142,
        147–8, 151–4, 182
society 4, 20, 59, 67, 128, 130–1, 184
sociodynamics of educational research
    56–68

software applications to qualitative research 5, 143–6, 182
Soltis, J. 159
Somekh, B. 47
Sontag, Susan 72, 74, 79, 81, 83, 89, 90
Spaulding, A.C. 122
Spindler, George and Louise 4, 106–22
Spradley, J. 147
Sprinthall, N. 141
Stasz, C. 74
Stein, M. 157
Stenhouse, L. 51, 53
Stillman, P.R. 57
Stoeckle, John 161
Strand, Paul 72
subjectivity 72–3, 83–4, 89–90, 127–31, 137, 140, 142, 181
surveys 5, 94, 158–9
Sutcliffe, Frank M. 10

Taylor, S. 160
teachers, computer-assisted listening to experiences of beginning 5, 139–55, 182
teaching strategies 47, 50
team research 133–7
Templin, Pat 85–6
Tesch, R. 143, 144
testing, interaction in 95–6, 99
Thies-Sprinthall, L. 141
Tiller, T. 57
Tillmann, K.-J. 56
time, constraints of 15–16, 45, 60, 62–4, 66, 99–100, 112, 117–20, 133, 137, 142, 182
Tisher, R.P. 139, 140, 154–5
Toedter, Lori J. 163
traditional-empirical research 41, 47–8, 72, 154–5
training
  researchers 5, 52, 137, 157, 176
  teacher 5, 17, 139–41, 147
transcripts 12, 16, 18, 19, 66, 131–5, 140, 148, 150, 153
transfer of data 158–62, 176
triangulation 47, 73
Trueba, H. 122
Tuckman, B.W. 142
Turner, R. 127
Turner, Victor W. 24–5

unconscious 126–9
unions, teaching 26–38

validity 1, 52, 72, 90, 137, 140, 142, 144–5, 150
values 9–10, 21, 34–5, 39, 50
Van Den Putte, B. 159
Van Maanen, J. 157, 159
Veenman, S. 141
videotape in research 3–4, 93–104, 182
  educationally handicapped students 98–103
  intelligence in social interaction 94–6
  socialization of students 97–8
visualization 73–4
Volmerg, B. 129

Wagner, I. 56
Waitzkin, Howard 161–2
Walberg, H. 159
Walker, Rob 3, 8, 13, 14, 42, 52, 72–91, 181
Wallman, H. *et al.* 53
Warner, W. Lloyd 160
Warren, Carol 162
Wax, E. 157
Weade, G. 123
Weber, R.P. 154
Weindling, D. 39
Weingart, P. 41
Weitzman, Lenore J. 160
Wertsch, J.V. 94
whole-school focus 8–11, 20
Whyte, W.F. 157
Wideen, M.F. 139, 154–5
Wiedel, Janine 85
Wieder, D.L. 162
Williams, M. 122
withdrawal from group research 66
Witkin, Robert 74
Wittgenstein, L. 128
Wood, H. 94
Woods, P. 4
Woolgar, S. 67
writing 72, 127
  photographs as stimulus for 84–5

Yinger, R.J. 140

Zeichner, K. 142
Zimring, Frank E. 160–1
Zuehl, James 160–1